JOKER FACE

STEVE BEST

Cameras supplied by

FUJIFILM

www.fujifilm.eu/uk

Huge support from

BIG CHEESE COMEDY

www.bigcheesecomedy.com

www.stevebest.com

unbound

Unbound
6th Floor Mutual House 70 Conduit Street
London W1S 2GF
www.unbound.com

© Steve Best, 2017

While every effort has been made to trace all present copyright
holders of the material in this book, we hereby apologise for any
unintentional omissions. You can either heckle Steve where you
sit or write to him and corrections will be made.

The views and opinions expressed in this publication are solely
those of the original authors and contributors. These views and
opinions do not necessarily represent those of Steve Best
or the publishers.

Photography **Steve Best**
Text page design **Catherine French**

A CIP record for this book is available from the British Library

ISBN 978-1-78352-338-2 (trade ppb)
ISBN 978-1-78352-339-9 (ebook)
ISBN 978-1-78352-340-5 (limited edition)

Printed in Italy by LEGO S.p.A

Dear Reader

The book you are holding came about in a rather different way to most others. It was funded directly by readers through a new website: Unbound. Unbound is the creation of three writers. We started the company because we believed there had to be a better deal for both writers and readers. On the Unbound website, authors share the ideas for the books they want to write directly with readers. If enough of you support the book by pledging for it in advance, we produce a beautifully bound special subscribers' edition and distribute a regular edition and e-book wherever books are sold, in shops and online.

This new way of publishing is actually a very old idea (Samuel Johnson funded his dictionary this way). We're just using the internet to build each writer a network of patrons. Here, at the back of this book, you'll find the names of all the people who made it happen. Publishing in this way means readers are no longer just passive consumers of the books they buy, and authors are free to write the books they really want. They get a much fairer return too – half the profits their books generate, rather than a tiny percentage of the cover price.

If you're not yet a subscriber, we hope that you'll want to join our publishing revolution and have your name listed in one of our books in the future. To get you started, here is a £5 discount on your first pledge. Just visit unbound.com, make your pledge and type **Joker** in the promo code box when you check out.

Thank you for your support,

Dan, Justin and John Founders, Unbound

i

Introduction

Hello, my name is Steve Best and I've been a stand-up comedian for over twenty years. There, I've outed myself at last.

I have performed all over the world including South Africa, Malaysia, Indonesia, Bosnia, Holland, Denmark, The Falkland Islands and Southend on Sea. I plan to go further afield.

I have been on huge nationwide tours with Frank Skinner, Craig Charles and Omid Djalili. I have been on TV (a few times).

I am also a photographer. Some would say a clown photographer (a clowntographer – doesn't quite work!). I have met some very weird and wonderful comedy people over my career and have felt the need, the desire no less, to share these misfits with you. This book is a snapshot of the vast number of these comedians on the UK comedy circuit. All the pictures are taken by me. The insights and jokes come straight from the horses' mouths; over 500 comedians. 527 to be precise, 528 counting me. These funny people have been snapped at different stages of their careers – some old, some young, some just starting out, some established, some on the way to fame and fortune, and some already there. Nearly all the shots were taken backstage before or after a gig. A few photos were taken at social gatherings, coffee meet ups, poker games, various London train stations, and some were taken at places too sordid to mention.

After I had taken the photograph I then asked the comedian a few questions

When and where you started comedy*

A one-liner joke of yours**

Four or five facts about yourself that have nothing to do with your comedy career (unless weird and wonderful)***

There is no order to where the comedians are placed in the book, alphabetically or otherwise, it is more to do with how they looked artistically on the page. I have though placed some of the comedians purposely together, due to a romantic connection. I will leave that up to you to find out which ones they are.

I have hugely enjoyed every aspect of bringing **Joker Face** to life. I hope you have as much fun reading it.

---

* There are certain venues where the comedians started their careers that seem to crop up more than others. Due to the ever changing world and nature of the stand-up comedy circuit, many of these places sadly no longer exist.

** Most of the comedians have given me a joke, but a few, due to the very observational nature of their material, have not.

*** I was after facts that were quirky and strange, and either not readily available or completely undiscoverable on the world wide web.

> **66** *Dyslexia is an anagram of horse.* **99**

Steve Best

I am a twin. My twin brother is ten minutes older than me. Time, I'm told, for my mum to have a cup of tea in between deliveries.

One year at senior school I got an A for effort and an A for attainment in every single subject on my end-of-year school report. I then became obsessed with magic and performing and ended up getting an O level grade for my French A level. *Merde!*

I have had two operations in the last couple of years to combat my snoring. The first was an Uvulopalatoplasty (a surgical procedure in which a laser is used to remove most of the uvula at the rear of the mouth).

I'm not being a baby, but that bloody hurt. It didn't work. The second was a Radio-Frequency Ablation or Somnoplasty (in which the inner tissue is heated to 85°C, which results in the tissue beneath the skin being scarred. This treatment generally requires the patient to undergo several sessions). This operation wasn't as painful. I seriously doubt whether this will work either. I'm not going back.

My dad was mayor of Epson & Ewell 1990/91.

I have never played Candy Crush.

Picture taken Montenegro, June 2016

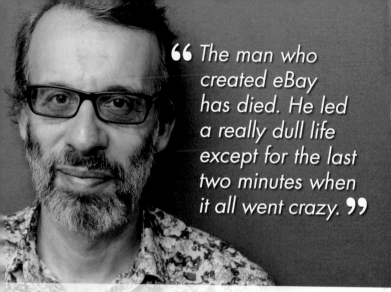

> **" The man who created eBay has died. He led a really dull life except for the last two minutes when it all went crazy. "**

David Schneider

I started comedy in 1983 (blimey!) as part of the Oxford Revue in Edinburgh. I researched a Ph.D. in Yiddish drama and Jewish mysticism at Oxford University. I'm confident that I'm the only stand-up who sings MC Hammer songs in Yiddish.

Career highlight: being in a Woody Allen film. Career lowlight: being cut from the Woody Allen film. I've built up a large following on Twitter, possibly due to the number of people who think I'm actually David Schwimmer from *Friends*.

Picture taken Old Street, London, January 2016

> **Do you reckon the Queen ever pulled her bed covers up to her neck and said, 'Philip, look at me, I'm a stamp'?**

Russell Howard

I started in Bristol at a new act night called Virgin Mirth in 1998. I followed a mad act who ate a banana with a spoon while singing the tune to *The Sweeney*.
I was accused of being a Scientologist.
I scored a Rabona kick at Anfield.
I own four guitars and can't play any of them.
Every T shirt that I've worn on the telly I've given to one of my relatives.
My sister has been nominated for a Bafta.

Picture taken Headliners, Chiswick, February 2016

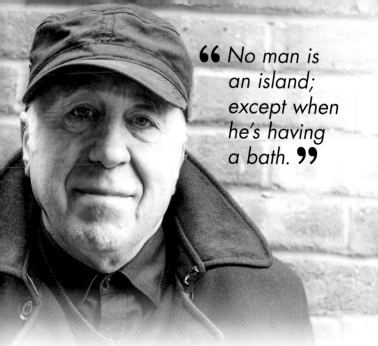

> **66** *No man is an island; except when he's having a bath.* **99**

Norman Lovett

I started supporting punk bands in London in 1979. I'm half Italian.
When you get to sixty you're allowed to support two football clubs. Mine are Ipswich Town and Arsenal.

I have thirty-five pairs of socks in one small drawer. Four people who have died within three months of me meeting them are Bob Crow, Max Wall, Roy Orbison and Harry Worth.

Picture taken Vauxhall, London, February 2016

" *Nobody thought Mel Gibson could play a Scot but look at him now! Alcoholic and a racist!* **"**

Frankie Boyle

I started at The Stand
in Edinburgh, 1995.
I taught myself to swim aged thirty.
I'm a qualified teacher in English.
My parents are native Irish speakers.
I was Scottish schools' speaking
and debating champion.

Picture taken Hammersmith Apollo, January 2016

> **"** What's the difference between a kangaroo and a kangaroot. A kangaroo is an Australian marsupial and a kangaroot is what a Geordie man says when he's stuck in a lift. **"**

Jon Culshaw

I started in the living room at home in front of an edition of *The Sky at Night* and later *The Mike Yarwood Show*. Also I'd copy the voices of the school dinner ladies who were sometimes like Les Dawson's Cissy and Ada. I've seen two total solar eclipses. I was taught to swim by Chris Moyles. I took my first photograph aged five. It was of my two model dinosaurs next to our discarded Christmas tree in the garden. I wanted to make a Cretaceous scene.

I once took over the tannoy of an aeroplane and made the announcements as Ozzy Osbourne, 'This is your captain speaking, rock n' roll. Right, let's turn this flight over there and go to Brazil'.

I'm a fellow of the Royal Astronomical Society.

Picture taken Koko, Camden Town, London, November 2015

> 66 *I asked my son what he wanted for his birthday. He said, 'I wanna watch.' So we let him.* 99

Drew Cameron

I started comedy at primary school in Hove.
It wasn't called comedy then, it was called,
'cheeky little blighter!' I know it happened
because a former school nurse once told me.
I rescue wild animals in my spare time.
I married my first girlfriend. She was my assistant teacher at school.
Me and Jack Wild re-enacted the naked wrestling scene from
DH Lawrence's *Women in Love*, in his back garden.
One Christmas Day, me and the wife, woke up our two children
and we all drove to Gatwick airport. We then flew on Concorde
up to Lapland, where we rode on reindeers and saw Father
Christmas. Then we flew Concord back home and still had
plenty of time to open the presents in the evening.

Picture taken JokeKlub, Great Totham, Essex, March 2014

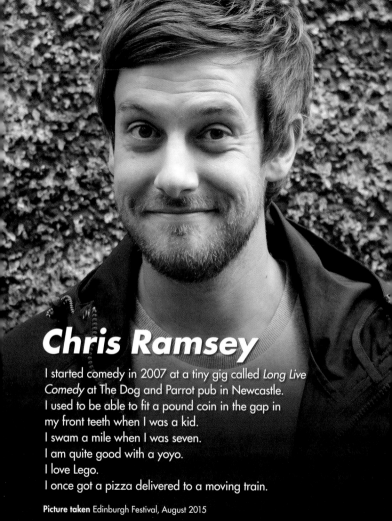

Chris Ramsey

I started comedy in 2007 at a tiny gig called *Long Live Comedy* at The Dog and Parrot pub in Newcastle.
I used to be able to fit a pound coin in the gap in my front teeth when I was a kid.
I swam a mile when I was seven.
I am quite good with a yoyo.
I love Lego.
I once got a pizza delivered to a moving train.

Picture taken Edinburgh Festival, August 2015

> **My grandmother always used to say, 'A stitch in time... may create a wormhole.' She was a physicist.**

Abigail Burdess

I started in 2002 in Edinburgh. My first language was Urdu. The best costume I've ever had to wear was for a post-apocalyptic prostitute. Before writing jokes, I wrote about human rights abuses. Human rights abuses are less fun.

I once did a 'ventriloquism act' in a niqab, with a Bart Simpson puppet, while wheelchair-bound. I regret that.

When I was a child, the actress Susannah York once offered to piss on me, when I was stung by a jellyfish.

Picture taken The Comedy Pub, London, October 2014

10

> **When I started someone told me that if I used the 'C' word I would immediately offend half my audience, which posed the horns of a dilemma; WTF could I do to offend the other half?**

Jeff Lane

My comedy debut was in 2004. When I told my partner I wanted to do stand-up her first response was, 'The biggest problem you will have is you are not at all funny'. My day job is as a psychotherapist. People often suggest that I might be using them for jokes. I have yet to actually tell anyone they are far too tedious for comedy material but I have come bloody close more than once. My former careers have included choir boy, farm worker, psychiatric hospital orderly, market trader, builder and horse riding instructor. I'm a long term member of the George Formby Society. I'm a keen and remarkably unsuccessful gardener and once won second prize in a pig judging contest. I have been mistaken many times for Ben Elton.

Picture taken
Havant Arts Centre,
April 2008

> *"Found my first grey pubic hair yesterday. In a kebab, but they all count."*

Jeff Green

I started at Jackson's Lane Cabaret Workshop in Archway – went there around the end of '87. I was taught by Bob Boyton, John Hegley, Donna McPhail and Bob Mills. First gig: April 6th 1988, a place called Funny Business at Fergies. Headliner was Mike Hayley. Got rebooked and paid some months later – £7 – first money earned from comedy. Green is my third surname (mother married three times). I was born Neilson, then Thomas at thirteen, then Green from sixteen. Kids at school thought I was in a witness protection programme.

I have a 2.1 degree in Mineral Engineering from Birmingham University, where I was also Vice President of the union.

I am an only child in a family of seven; I have two half sisters, two half brothers and two step sisters but no full siblings.

I used to be a campanologist. I'm the same weight as I was when I started comedy: 12 stone 2lb.

Picture taken Hampstead Village, London, July 2014

66 *My parents are exactly the same as yours, average height, and a little bit racist.* **99**

Jo Coffey

I started eight years ago.
Bill Oddie once called me a wanker.
I own seasons 1–8 of *Dallas* on boxset.
I once locked myself in a cupboard during a job interview.

Picture taken RNIB, Camden, London, July 2015

66 *Worst thing about being very tall is every day people stop me in the street to tell me I'm very tall.* 99

Colin Cole

I started in Melbourne Australia 1991.
I am 6' 7".
I've always wanted to be a jockey.
I used to be a hairdresser, bodybuilder and bodyguard.

> **My doctor told me I had a drinking problem. Then I told him vodka is a mixture of alcohol suspended in a solvent of water. So I also have a drinking solution.**

Paul Savage

I've been going six years, since 2007.
I came up with that joke during a heavy drinking session with Ian Cognito.
I've got three knees because my brother hit me with a cricket bat.
I lived in Romania for a while and can speak a bit of Romanian.
I write comic novels.

Picture taken King's Cross, London, June 2016

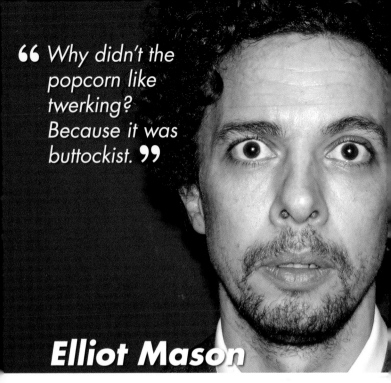

> **"** *Why didn't the popcorn like twerking? Because it was buttockist.* **"**

Elliot Mason

My first gig was at David Goo's open mic night at the Cross Kings pub in King's Cross, London in 2008.
I enjoy paying for things with the exact change.
I was a member of the sixties band The Zombies, for one hour.
I sometimes like to scrunch my eyes up tightly until I can hear a whooshing sound in my ears.
My nan thinks the shop Argos is called Argost.

Picture taken The Hideaway, Streatham, February 2014

> **❝** I had a little dog, but he got run over. Got hit by a speeding car, ironically a Rover. **❞**

Anthony Dewson

Julie Andrews' father taught me to swim.
I share a birthday with Kim Jong-il and Amanda Holden.
My other job is writing junk mail.

Picture taken Sudbury, November 2015

> **It was so cold yesterday my computer froze. My own fault though, I left too many windows open.**

George Egg

I started performing a show on the streets of Greenwich and later Covent Garden when I was seventeen, having been inspired by French anarchic circus, Archaos. When I was nineteen I did my first gig at Up the Creek Comedy Club.

I love cooking, and if I weren't a comedian I'd be a chef. I delivered my third child on Christmas Day. I keep intact all the wishbones from any fowl we eat. You never know when you might need them. I can't play the flute.

Picture taken Edinburgh, August 2015

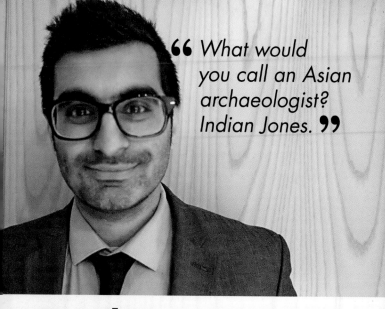

> **"What would you call an Asian archaeologist? Indian Jones."**

Tez Ilyas

I started in June 2010 in London.
I have a bachelor's in Biochemistry and a master's in Management.
I once had a dance-off with *Britain's Got Talent* winner George Sampson.
I have thirty-six first cousins (at least, I lose count).
I once fell off a van.
I got into comedy as a shortcut to fulfil my ambition to play the Doctor in *Doctor Who*.

Picture taken The Harlequin, Redhill, May 2014

Smug Roberts

I started on 27th February, 1995 at the Frog and Bucket comedy club in Manchester when it was in a pub. It was the regular Monday open spot Raw Night.
I never wash my socks. I wear a brand new pair every day (Asda £3 for seven pairs).

I have an in-growing nail on my left foot on my big toe.
I used to run a pub in Newcastle.
I'm scared of mice.
My dentist distracts me by drawing flowers on my nose.

Picture taken Jongleurs, Nottingham, December 2008

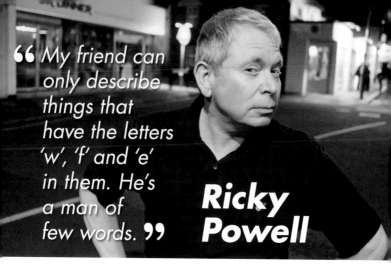

Ricky Powell

I started doing comedy in March 2012 after the missus bought me a comedy course as a Christmas present. I was fortunate as it was either that or a tandem parachute jump. The first 'proper' gig was at The Ark in Caterham, an open spot, where I did what I thought was a hilarious routine on death, blissfully unaware that half the audience had just been to a close relative's funeral and had come to the comedy night to cheer themselves up.

I was born in Peru.

I appeared in *The Fast Show* as one of six Ronnie Corbetts in a Twelve Ronnies sketch.

I was a member of the British Falconers Club and kept birds of prey in the back garden.

I'm 5' 2" tall. I used to be 5' 3" but I've shrunk.

I own a Harley Davidson (don't ride it – can't reach the floor).

Picture taken The George Inn, Walton-on-Thames, May 2014

> **My marriage was a bit like buying a dishwasher – expensive, you get it home, then after a while I realised it wasn't working, then after a few months I thought, 'Fuck it I'll do it by hand'.**

Mike Wilkinson

First gig was at Britons Protection, a fab pub behind the Bridgewater Hall in Manchester. It was about 1998.

I keep chickens.

I'm getting bees this year.

I've supported Dave Spikey.

I organised and helped raise 25K with Jason Manford for the lakes flood fund.

I've got webbed toes.

Picture taken The Rawhide, Liverpool, August 2008

22

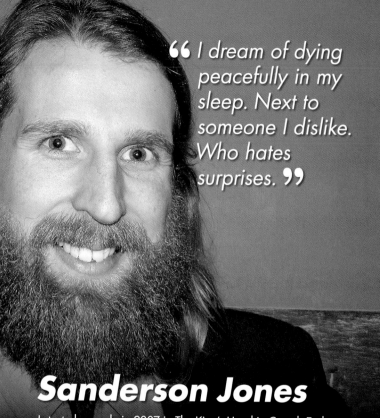

> **❝** I dream of dying peacefully in my sleep. Next to someone I dislike. Who hates surprises. **❞**

Sanderson Jones

I started comedy in 2007 in The King's Head in Crouch End.
I still do comedy, but now I've founded the Sunday Assembly
and am making sure that gets running again.
I am the co-founder and CEO of the Sunday Assembly.
I have twice held the world record for the world's longest hug

> **" I saw my first porn film last week. I couldn't believe how young I looked. "**

Sam Avery

I did my first gig at Unity Theatre
in Liverpool. I did the whole gig
with my flies down.
In a previous life I was in a metal
band and toured with Motörhead.
I used to be in a Subbuteo league...
there were only four of us.
I met my wife at a gong show and she got
me gonged off during my wedding speech.
If you don't like The Smiths I'm not sure we can ever be friends.

Picture taken The Rawhide, Liverpool, April 2008

> **❝ I believe that fellatio killed off all the unicorns. ❞**

Nqoba Ngcobo

I started comedy off and on in 2002, but only took it as my profession in 2008 after my franchise business floundered during the global recession.
I also have Canadian citizenship and can speak French.
I once beat up a police officer who thought I was drunk when I was sober.

My other passion is aeronautics and aviation.
I am allergic to bees.
When my daughter was an infant I accidentally hot boxed her, and blame all her present madness on that mistake.
I have a bullet in my right groin area due to a shooting robbery in 2010.

Picture taken Cape Town, South Africa, August 2009

> **I've got two kids because the first one I didn't pull out and the second one she didn't wanna go back to work.**

Phil Reid

I started on the circuit when
I was twenty-five.
At nineteen years old I was the north west
regional finalist for Bingo Caller of the Year 2005.
Every gig I perform I have to wear matching socks and boxers.
When I was twelve years old I had football trials for
Tranmere Rovers FC.
Got two kids, Liverpool fan, middle name is Reginald.

Picture taken Laughing Pod, Piccadilly, London November 2014

> **What does the musician say in the multi-storey? 'Is this your car?'**

Josie Long

I started comedy when I was a teenager at a stand-up comedy workshop at the Studio Arts Centre in Beckenham, Kent. It's since been closed down but hopefully the two things are unrelated.

I am very quick to get ready in the morning. If necessary I can be up and out within seven minutes.

I like swimming in cold water, in the winter.

I am always the first person on a buffet at a formal event and I think that means I will survive the apocalypse.

5 foot 5, GSOH.

Picture taken Roar with Laughter, Colliers Wood, October 2008

> **Being a dirtbag metalhead from a well-off family, I was a major disappointment to my parents. Until my little sister was born; she's ginger.**

Killian Monson

I started comedy at the Frog and Bucket in Manchester in January 2005 when I was nineteen.
I went to the same school as Tom Stoppard, Adrian Edmondson, Ralph Ineson and William Wilberforce.

I spend my free time creating abstract art videos to post online.
I'm a trained actor.
I grew up in Ireland, England, the USA and Canada.

Picture taken The Rawhide, Liverpool, November 2008

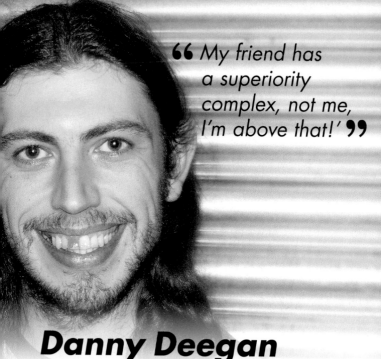

***My friend has a superiority complex, not me, I'm above that!'**

Danny Deegan

I started comedy in 2001 at the Frog and Bucket in Manchester.
I went to the same school as Lisa Riley and the blonde girl
from Hear'Say.
My nephew was the heaviest baby ever born in his hospital.
I have a signed Lennox Lewis glove which I don't know if
he ever used.
I have been spoken to by the police in relation to three
separate murders.

Picture taken York, October 2011

> **Have you ever thought, 'I need to sort my life out,' then put on a load of washing and thought, 'Yeah, that'll do'?** ""

Andrea Hubert

First gig was at a pub in Covent Garden in London, 2010. I can't remember which one.

I once got an ASBO for 'threatening behaviour' on a bus. I think they overreacted. As did I.

The day I got my driving licence, I killed a dog. With my car, I mean – not just in victory at passing on the sixth try.

Chopsticks get the better of me every time. I just can't work them out. I also couldn't pull a ring pull on a can till I was quite old.

When I was a waitress in Leeds, I served Jimmy Saville, and he pinched my arse... even though I was twenty at the time.

Guacamole is my favourite dip. I won't attend a dinner party without it. Sometimes, I bring two pots, one for the guests, and one just for me.

Picture taken Gigglegate, Forest Gate, London, March 2014

" My first name is Goronwy, like an airport runway with a 'g' in front of it, like g-runway, a Welsh name... which then makes people think I am Welsh and instantly compare me to a slightly fat Aled Jones. **"**

Goronwy Thom

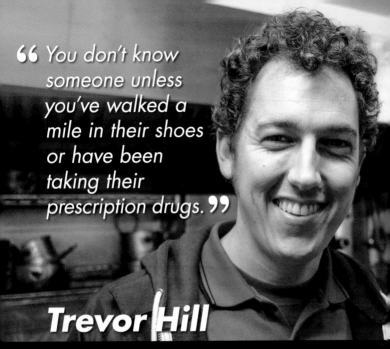

" *You don't know someone unless you've walked a mile in their shoes or have been taking their prescription drugs.* **"**

Trevor Hill

I have the iTunes library of a severely unemployed man.
I only feel emotions after 11:15pm.
I have been pretending to understand what the GDP is for like twelve years. Sorry.
I once got too high and was pretty sure I had potato famine.
Probably the most rewarding period of my life was 2009's *Iron Man 2* trailer.
I don't eat fruit. I have fruit flies in my apartment.
I'm not sure what happens in Vegas.

Picture taken Gigglegate, Forest Gate, London, March 2014

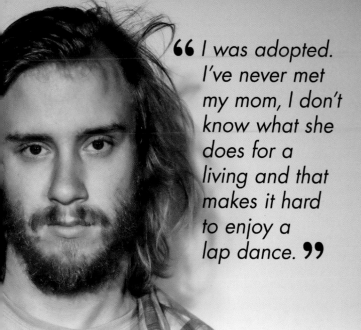

> 66 I was adopted. I've never met my mom, I don't know what she does for a living and that makes it hard to enjoy a lap dance. 99

Bobby Mair

I started comedy in Toronto in September 2005.
My favourite author is John Irving.
My favourite TV show is *Battlestar Galactica*.
As a child I ate a jar of peanut butter a week
and a litre of milk a day.

Picture taken The Comedy Pub, London, October 2014

> **66** Me and my boyfriend play these games to try and annoy each other. The other day he played my morning alarm ringtone for seven minutes, but I think I'm going to win in the long run as I've stopped taking the pill. **99**

Harriet Kemsley

I started in 2011 at a Laughing Horse gig.
I started stand-up upon the advice of my parents.
I'm a vegan who's allergic to raw fruit and vegetables.
I once spent a night in a cell in Brooklyn.
As a child I had a pet chicken called Whiskey.

Picture taken JokeKlub, Great Totham, Essex, March 2014

Fern Brady

I started comedy in 2010 in Edinburgh.
Just before I went full time I looked after fourteen sex
offenders and dangerous ex convicts in a halfway house.
I also worked in a porno shop in Manchester for a bit
selling DVDs. Part of my job was repackaging sticky
second-hand DVDs which I then resold to people.
When I was sixteen my strict Catholic parents put me in
a psychiatric unit for mental teenagers because they
thought I was badly behaved. I had a little skinhead
girlfriend called Rita.
I've had between forty-eight and fifty jobs.

Picture taken The George Inn, Walton-on-Thames, May 2014

> **I still see my ex-boyfriend all the time but I think he's cool with it; I'm all over him.**

Lheila Oberman

I started in comedy in 1985 somewhere in Sussex when I deliberately threw myself off the top bunk onto the floor at JLGB's (Jewish Lads' and Girls' Brigade) summer camp to get a quality laugh from the room after we'd just been told to keep the noise down.

I was named after Leila Khaled, the first female Muslim terrorist to hijack a plane.

I've taught in over 250 London primary schools.

I've been topless on page 3 of the *Daily Star* by accident.

I've slow danced cheek to cheek with Terry Wogan on live TV whilst wearing only a midnight blue corset, fishnets and stilettos.

Picture taken Nancy Victor Gallery, London, April 2014

> **"** *It's great having a Chinese mum. I rang her to get my lottery ticket, I told her my numbers, I went round and there's six Chinese dishes waiting on the table.* **"**

Okse

First gig: 3rd December 2003, 9:45pm, The Bear in Bearwood.
I paint, draw and I also make T shirts.
In the day I work at a dentist, front of house. I'm quite new to it all and I still chuckle when I book people in for 2:30 (tooth hurty).
My mum is Chinese.
I am part of a Bafta-award-winning team who worked on the official Sydney 2000 games. I thought it was rubbish and I think money was exchanged.

Picture taken Jongleurs, Birmingham, September 2009

> **Every man is harbouring communists. Because sperms are communists. Well, technically, they are actually Stalinists – only one of them achieves anything; and millions of them die for nothing.**

Andy Zaltzman

I started comedy when I hosted a stand-up gig at university as a favour to a friend who had organised it, in 1996. I soon retired. And restarted at the open mic night at the Comedy Cafe in 1999.

I was banned from an annual sports quiz after my team had won three years in a row.

I was controversially disqualified from my school under-six sack race for crossing the line out of my sack. I maintain that I had leg-contact with the sack as I touched the finish line.

I delivered our second child in the bathroom at home, before retiring from midwifery with an unblemished one out of one record.

My great uncle was Nelson Mandela's accountant.

Picture taken Nancy Victor Gallery, London, April 2014

> **66** They say it's easy to spot someone wearing a wig. And it's true because I wore one yesterday and saw three people. **99**

Anthony King

My first paid gig (£5) was on the London Comedy Circuit in Dalston. I put the fiver in my sock in case I got mugged. It was 1988.
I like to collect things and own a sixteen inch high statue of Gort (from the 1959 film *The Day The Earth Stood Still*). I also attend vinyl record fairs and love the jazz musician Carla Bley.

Picture taken Barrow Town Football Club, Barrow-Upon-Soar, Loughborough, March 2014

> **66** *My grandmother always said, 'If I don't see you in the week I'll see you in the window'. I never knew what that meant until last week when I was in Amsterdam, and there she was waving at me through a window.* **99**

Neil Masters

My first gig was in 1985 in Culver City, California. As I was about to be introduced, the gig was aborted because a riot had broken out and the police had to be called. I was ushered out the back door to safety.

My second gig was in 1996 at the Comedy Cafe in London.

I am an Italian Citizen as well as an American Citizen.

My mother was from Dundee, Scotland and we are descendants of a Scottish clan.

I have been to the G8 summit where I took Polaroid pictures of John Major and Mikhail Gorbachev.

I was a number one afternoon radio presenter in California from the age of fifteen to twenty-six.

I have a BA in English Literature from UCLA.

Picture taken Nancy Victor Gallery, London, April 2014

66 *I met this beautiful girl the other night but like the star crossed lovers we were it just wasn't meant to be. I'm a scorpio and she's a lesbian.* 99

Christian Elderfield

I started comedy back in August 2010.
I got four yeses on *Britain's Got Talent* in 2013
but it was never broadcast.
I've eaten and fed a kangaroo in the same day.
I once broke my hand whilst playing table tennis (serves me right!).
I managed to get 150,000 signatures on a government
petition to stop the badger cull in 2013 by producing a video
called *Save the Badger Badger Badger* with Mr Weebl,
Brian May and Brian Blessed for YouTube.

Picture taken The Crack, Wimbledon, October 2013

> **" Are we so different?
> Half of your public
> transportation
> is bollocks, half
> of our public
> transportation
> is bullocks. "**

Papa CJ

I started stand-up in 2004.
I have performed at gun point in South Africa.
I have an MBA from the University of Oxford.
I run a charity for underprivileged children in India.
I was on the top 10 of *Last Comic Standing* in 2008 and to
date I have never seen a single episode of any of their shows.
I'm the only stand-up comedian from India to have performed
on four different continents. I did 250 gigs in my first ten months
as a comedian. I introduced English language stand-up comedy
to India and started off the circuit in the country.
I've had an ex Under Secretary General of the United Nations
get on stage at one of my comedy nights in Delhi.

Picture taken Soho Theatre, London, February 2016

> 66 *I had a life changing weekend. For the first time I entered the National Lottery – I've never seen so many otters.* 99

Col Howarth

I started 2 August 2013 at Drones Comedy Club, Cardiff.
I used to be a drummer in a band.
I live in a part of Cardiff that has been regenerated.

> ❝ I'm a recovering alcoholic. Recovering from last night, fucking hammered, again. ❞

Peter Cain

My first gig was in 2001 at one of the London heats of the *So You Think You're Funny* new comedians competition. The gig was unbelievably good (still in my top three ever). I probably should have quit then.

I memorised Pythagorus' theorem to a 100 decimal points to confound the maths teacher who accused me of not paying attention in class.

I worked as a timeshare tout in the Canary Islands for three years in the mid eighties. Aged nineteen, I didn't possess a single pair of shoes for six months.

I earned a living for nearly a year just playing backgammon for money.

My favourite food is roast lamb with all the trimmings. When I was a kid I covered everything in mint sauce to make it taste like roast lamb. Come to think of it, maybe mint sauce is my favourite food.

Picture taken Jongleurs, Oxford, June 2008

44

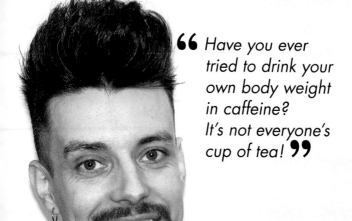

> **❝ Have you ever tried to drink your own body weight in caffeine? It's not everyone's cup of tea! ❞**

Paul Sweeney

I started comedy in London, on the 31st October (Halloween) at a gig in Dirty Dicks, Liverpool Street, organised by a group of actors from the London Dungeons.

I trained in ballet for four years.

I'm a qualified barber.

I started school in Amsterdam.

I am so accident prone that I once broke my arm skating on a pair of Fischer Price 'safety' skates.

I once slapped Dave Grohl around the face.

Picture taken The Crack, Kingston, February 2011

> 66 It's like my psychiatrist always says: 'Mr Thomas, this is a dentists; please stop talking, you're making my job very difficult'. 99

Sy Thomas

I started at Aberystwyth University, Spring 2001.
I once drove through Western Africa and the Sahara Desert in a car that cost £100.
I didn't eat pizza until I was thirty.
I support Wycombe Wanderers Football Club.
I once hi-fived Chico whilst dressed as a horse.

Picture taken Fubbar Radio, London, May 2014

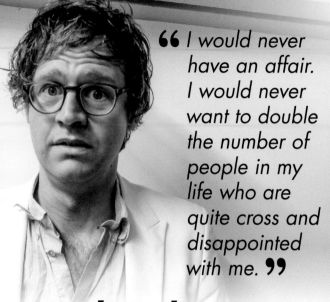

66 *I would never have an affair. I would never want to double the number of people in my life who are quite cross and disappointed with me.* **99**

Mark Dolan

I did my first gig in a bar in Edinburgh called Negotiants in 1996. I was at Edinburgh University at the time. I had no act and wound up talking about the room for ten minutes. In many ways, this has not changed.

I ride a Vespa scooter everywhere, including to gigs bloody miles away.
I have a German wife.
I'm a famous nail biter, and believe it to be nutritious.
I worked for a couple of years at Burger King, where I was on the broiler.

Picture taken Fubbar Radio, London, May 2014

> **❝** *I was in a very quiet country pub one night, wondering how they make a living. A poster said 'Friday night: Dave Wilson'. Thinking there was a band, I went along on Friday. Turned out that Dave Wilson was the bloke drinking in there that night.* **❞**

Dorian Crook

First gig was in a pub in the Elephant and Castle, some acts hadn't turned up so I offered to stand in there and then. With some success. I've been working as an Air Traffic Controller most of the time, but managed to squeeze in an Edinburgh show with Matt Lucas and some live shows with Vic and Bob, thanks to supportive bosses and colleagues.

I fly a light aeroplane in my spare time: once flew to a gig in Stockton-on-Tees. Last year I flew solo to Barcelona and back. This year I am driving in a forty-year-old MGB. I don't believe in food at parties. No-one should wear shorts in a city, unless that city has a beach.

Picture taken London, January 2014

48

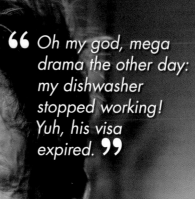

> ❝ *Oh my god, mega drama the other day: my dishwasher stopped working! Yuh, his visa expired.* ❞

Alexander Henry Buchanan-Dunlop

I started comedy in 2012, on Harry Denford's Comedy Course.
I have a marzipan addiction.
I hate sunbathing.
When I was thirteen, I had my appendix removed in Disneyland Paris.
I can speak French.

Picture taken
We Are Funny Project, Dalston, London,
October 2016

> **I am an only child, essentially, 'if at first you don't succeed, quit,' says Mum.** 🙶🙷

Aaron Meszaros

My first time on stage was at the Comics Lounge, North Melbourne, Australia 2004.
I was born on the 1st of April, Good Friday. That's a special kind of fool.
As an Australian comedian, when I started doing comedy in London I had many different jobs.
I was a tour guide for a London tour bus company. I'm not even from this country. I don't know how I managed to get that job.
Currently I actually live in a hostel.
My girlfriend thinks I should be more factual.
I grew up in a small town called Melton, which is located in Victoria, Australia. It is so small that the fact I'm in this book makes me an international star back home.
Queen are my favourite band – of all time.

Picture taken Hampstead Comedy Club, May 2014

Quint Fontana
Andy Davies

I started comedy in 2007 but gave birth to Quint in 2012. I can play the 'William Tell Overture' on my cheeks. I know more about 70s prog rock than someone of my age should.

I get extremely annoyed by people who don't take their hat off when eating in restaurants. I have never watched, and never will watch *Bake Off*.

Picture taken Hampstead Comedy Club, May 2014

> **❝** *I was looking in the paper the other day and I thought 'Hey! That's me!'... It was the Mirror!* **❞**

Alfie Joey

I did my first ever gig at Downstairs at the King's Head in North London, an old established comedy club, under the guidance of the fantastic Huw Thomas.

My first home was a workingmen's club in a County Durham pit village.

I trained to be a priest and then joined a religious order (fifteen years in all in monastic life).

I've loved snooker since I was a lad and enjoy a visit to the Crucible during the World Championships.

I was a bike courier in London Town and my walkie talkie name was Oscar 24.

I've written articles for the Frank Sinatra Appreciation Society and saw him at London Arena in 1990.

Picture taken Jongleurs Battersea, London, 2007

> **❝** *My mum's so pessimistic. If there was an Olympics of pessimism, my mum wouldn't fancy her chances.* **❞**

Nish Kumar

I started comedy at Durham University as part of the Durham Revue Sketch Group.
I am from Croydon, a place routinely voted one of the worst towns in the UK.
I was once forcibly removed from a castle.
My rap name is NK-47.
I know more about Bob Dylan than you do. Regardless of who you are. Unless you're actually Bob Dylan. In which case, 'hello, I am a huge fan!'

Picture taken Hampstead Comedy Club, May 2014

> **❝ I'm profoundly deaf in one ear and thoughtfully deaf in the other. ❞**

Caroline Parker

I started performing stand-up comedy with Abnormally Funny People at Soho Theatre. I think it was 2008. I grew up halfway up a hill, and now live halfway up another hill.
I never turn down offers of chocolate, cocktails or cake.
I have a very firm bum.
I don't know how to be naughty.

Picture taken Middlesex University, July 2015

> **"** I'm not sure if lad culture is moronic as a culture or just oxymoronic as a phrase. **"**

Jacob Hawley

I did my first gig at Downstairs At The King's Head in September 2012.

My dad is a freemason and he refuses to tell me any of the secrets.

At nineteen I spent three months playing Kings of Leon covers in the Greek resort of Faliraki.

I am a godfather and uncle to England's next great footballer.

I frequently lie about my age and plan to do so forever.

Picture taken Middlesex University, July 2015

55

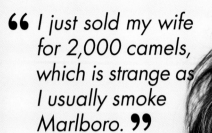

66 *I just sold my wife for 2,000 camels, which is strange as I usually smoke Marlboro.* **99**

Tony Marrese

I started comedy in
January 2010.
My first gig was at
Up The Creek.
I was *Daily Mirror*
Gardener of the Year once.
I can't swim.
I keep chickens.
I'm trying to join
the Illuminati.

Picture taken The George Inn, Walton-on-Thames, May 2014

> ❝ *My underpants rang me then hung up. It was a tester call.* ❞

Chris Gilbert

I recently drank ayahuasca with shaman in Peru.
Ten years ago I drove to Dakar with an old school
friend. The vehicle was a Rover 213. Bad idea.
Brad Pitt and Angelina Jolie have visited our offices.
I have an adopted cat, Humperdinck. Though it's
unclear who adopted whom.

Picture taken RAF Cosford, May 2014

Sara Pascoe

My first gig was at The Bedford in Balham, September 2007. I got drunk on a large glass of wine, talked about *High School Musical* for five minutes. Twelve people smiled at me. I went home euphoric and convinced I had found what I wanted to do with my life. I worked at the Millennium Dome. I am a vegan. I used to be a backing singer for Robbie Williams' dad, Pete Conway. I'm not as tall as you think I am.

Picture taken Bloomsbury Theatre, London, June 2015

> **66** *People who cut corners, don't last long at the Muller yogurt factory.* **99**

Max Dickens

I started comedy in my second year at Leeds University in 2009. My first gig was in a room above the Packhorse Pub in the Hyde Park area of Leeds, and it went oddly well.
I was a radio presenter for two years with Absolute Radio.
I once had a job teaching rich people how to drive speedboats.
My nickname at school was Opal Fruit after some ill advised bright orange and green shirts at back to back school discos.
I once worked at an investment bank and one of my jobs was sanding over the dried bogies the bankers had wiped on the toilet cubicle walls.
My mum told me on the school run once that she went out with Ian Dury from Ian Dury and the Blockheads.

Picture taken The Harlequin, Redhill, May 2014

> **Angelina Jolie likes her men like she likes her coffee. Prepared by another woman.**

Katerina Vrana

I don't think I can stress this enough: I am Greek, born and raised in Greece to Greek parents, grew up and went to school there. I have no idea why I speak English with such a British accent. No one in my family speaks English like this. I had straight hair until I was thirteen. Then I got my period and my hair went curly.

There is a lovely lady who thought 'Katerina Vrana' would be a good name to use to pursue a career in porn. You can see her work in Girl Camp 2004: Lesbian Fleshpots.

Picture taken Walton on Thames, January 2013

> **66** *Don't be too soft or people will wipe their asses with you. Nobody wipes their ass with sandpaper.* **99**

Mark Silcox

I started in 2009 for six months and then again in September 2012. I've been gigging regularly since then.
I own a motorbike.
I have a PhD in Analytical Chemistry from Imperial College.
I am a UK qualified science teacher (PGCE, Brunel University).
I am a proud father of a daughter and son.
I could not convince either of the two to become a doctor.

Picture taken The Harlequin, Redhill, May 2014

> **I love TV.
> I watch
> everything.
> I've watched
> so much on
> Netflix it's
> started
> suggesting I
> go outside.**

David Morgan

I started stand-up while at university in Leicester. I had been doing some improv and it was suggested that I join a free stand-up workshop that was put on by Leicester Comedy Festival in 2007. I have a degree in Interactive Design. And no I won't do your website.

I'm a mega Disney Parks nerd. My signature cupcake is a lemon meringue. Obviously with homemade lemon curd, I'm not an animal. It takes much less time than you'd think to do my hair.

Picture taken The Crack, Wimbledon, November 2011

> **" What's invisible and smells like eggs? Invisible eggs. "**

Liberty Hodes

I started in Newcastle when
I was around eighteen,
open mics and suchlike.
I know the Wetherspoons
Clubs off by heart.
I support Newcastle United.
I have an obsession with
drawing muscle men.
My grandma used to live
near Michael Winner.

Picture taken Up The Creek, Greenwich, February 2015

> **People want hair which is 'full of volume'. My hair is on mute.** "

Damian Clark

I started in March 1996 in
Pockets Nightclub Northbridge, Perth,
Australia. It has since been demolished.
I'm half Canadian and spent a lot of my
childhood on a farm in Welland, Ontario.
When I was nineteen and working nights in a
hotel I was held at gunpoint, blindfolded,
tied and locked up in a cupboard. I escaped.
I was expelled from Perth TAFE College.
They said they'd never had to do that before.
I have been fired from over forty jobs.
Pretty much the only TV shows I watch are cartoons.

Picture taken The Stag Theatre, Sevenoaks, May 2014

> **❝** I've been doing some internet dating and it's gone OK... I met a really thin girl on Match.com. **❞**

Dickie Richards

My first stand-up gig was on 17th September, 2010 at The Star and Garter in Greenwich. I speak fluent Polish. I can wiggle my left ear but not my right one. I went to boarding school in Paris for two years. My middle names are John Thomas.

Picture taken Tooting, London, December 2015

> **'i' before 'e' except after 'c'. But there is an exception, which is weird.**

Jessica Fostekew

I started comedy in London in January 2008.
I am a quarter Austrian.
I got grade 5 piano aged thirteen but now I can't read music any more and can't even remember how to play 'Chopsticks'.

My middle name is Alice.
I have a 2:1 LLB Law degree from LSE (unused).
I've always called my granddad Gordon for no known reason.
His name is Arthur.

Picture taken Downstairs at the King's Head, Crouch End, London, May 2014

> 66 *The worst sport ever is throwing a hand-sized round thing as far as you can. Discus.* 99

Jenny Collier

I started comedy in London. My first gig was in 2011. I once lived in Jeremy Paxman's house. I can't ride a bike although I'm a qualified fitness professional.

Wooden spoons and lollipop sticks make me feel like my arms are going to fall off. I sometimes get frowned at for stroking on-duty guide dogs. I can sing 'Don't Speak' by No Doubt in Welsh.

Picture taken Reeds Weybridge RFC, Whiteley Village, June 2014

> **My girlfriend is Scottish, but she's quite posh. You can tell cause she likes deep-fried Ferrero Rocher.**

Ben Van der Velde

I started comedy in 2007 at the Wheatsheaf Pub in Oxford after being tricked into doing it by a friend.

I once led a conga line down the main street in Jerusalem to Pizza Hut. They rewarded us all with a free slice.

Last year two audience members asked me to re-marry them as an anniversary present. I ended up performing a voodoo ceremony, whilst dressed as Baron Samedi.

My grandad grew up on a South-African ostrich farm and was dentist to the stars in the 1930s.

I can probably beat you at table tennis.

Picture taken Reeds Weybridge RFC, Whiteley Village, June 2014

68

> **I used to make my coeliac girlfriend eat a slice of bread if she annoyed me. She kept doing it. Gluten for punishment.**

Chris Brooker

My first gig was at the Hen & Chickens in Bristol in May of 2001. It was a heat of the BBC New Comedy Awards and I assumed that everyone else was having their first gig too. How wrong I was... I was born in Canada to British parents and moved here with them when I was five. Due to some sort of admin cock-up I was technically an illegal immigrant until 2007. I am an immense fan of professional wrestling since, at the age of fifteen, I saw a WWF show that my best mate from school's brother had recorded off of Sky. I can't stand eggs. Fried, scrambled, boiled. Oddly enough I really wish I liked poached eggs because they look really interesting. In my university days I agreed to do a fire walk for charity. I spent hours being psyched up and put in the correct frame of mind. Got to the edge of the pit. Changed my mind. Did it anyway. Burnt the shit out of my feet. Idiot.

Picture taken Joke Klub, Storrington, September 2010

> **Why do the French only eat only one egg for breakfast? Because in France one egg is un oeuf.**

Philip Pope

My first paid job was with the Oxford Revue Co. (with Angus Deayton, Geoffrey Perkins, Helen Atkinson Wood & Michael Fenton Stevens), but I had already appeared on *Points West* at BBC Bristol when I was a teenager. As a soloist I sang in a new Requiem at St Clement Danes Church in the Strand in London when I was fourteen.

My first television appearance was as part of a report on keep fit for children. I was eight (and doing an exercise – I was not the reporter!) I keep chickens – cleaning out the hutch is worth it for the delicious eggs! I spent a year living in Paris and used to busk on the Métro – I still speak French (which is inconvenient as I live in rural Buckinghamshire).

Picture taken Downstairs at the King's Head, Crouch End, London, July 2014

> **❝** *They say if it ain't broke don't fix it. I say if it is broke put it back, make it look as though it isn't broke. Hopefully the next person to use it will get the blame.* **❞**

Peter Beckley

I did my first gig in August 2003 at The Edinburgh Festival at a venue on the Royal Mile, compered by Logan Murray.

I was once interviewed by Professor Stephen Hawking.

I've run five marathons: Brighton (three times), Edinburgh and London.

I've got a degree in Computer Science.

My first job after graduating was in a travelling carnival in New England (USA).

My nickname at school was Shakin Stevens.

Picture taken Reeds Weybridge RFC, Whiteley Village, June 2014

71

> **"** *I was so proud when my driving instructor described my parking as 'unparalleled'.* **"**

Tom Webb

I had my first gig in London in 2008 under a motorway.
I'm allergic to wool.
I've never heard a song with a glockenspiel I didn't like.
My dad's got an MBE, which means I can get married in St. Paul's Cathedral.
I can juggle. But always prefer not to.

Picture taken The Crack, Kingston, June 2014

72

> 66 *Comedy isn't my full time job, I'm employed by Kodak. I'm the person who draws the red dots in people's eyes.* 99

Richard Risner

I started comedy after finding out about Tony Allen's stand-up workshop at Jacksons Lane in Highgate. Many of us there were also attending Kit Hollerbach's Saturday comedy impro workshops at The Comedy Store. My first open spot was at Bunjies off Leicester Square.

I'm also a clinical hypnotherapist.
I can't eat boiled, poached or fried eggs even though they look really tasty.
I make my own hummus.
I once appeared on *Opportunity Knocks*.

Picture taken Otiz Cannelloni's 60th birthday party, The Railway Tavern, Hornsey, June 2014

> **66** *The military regime in Burma is so repressive that Britain doesn't sell arms to them.* **99**

Mark Thomas

I was a drama student in Yorkshire during the miners strike. Friends and I used to write shows for the Wakefield Labour Club (The Red Shed) and perform them to raise money for the strikers. We would write it in a day and perform it in the evening. But we would not rehearse, which is a bourgeois affectation. My first stand-up gig was in a pub in Putney, 19th November 1985. John Lenahan was compere and Cyril the Turtle was performing. I still keep in touch with them.
I cycled from London to Paris.
I am a United Nations International Association Global Human Rights Defender.
I am an atheist but love church hymns.
The first band I saw live was Queen at Earls Court.
The second was Dr Feelgood at Hammersmith Odeon.
I turned down a chance to meet Joe Strummer three times.
Music is too important to get bogged down with human frailties.

Picture taken Otiz Cannelloni's 60th birthday party, The Railway Tavern, Hornsey, June 2014

> **66** *Beethoven was so deaf, he thought he was a painter!* **99**

Rory McGrath

The first comedy sketch I wrote was a parody of the BBC antiques programme *Gong for a Song* for a school revue when I was fifteen (4th form/year 10). It was the best thing in the revue, apparently, but, I hasten to add, that's not saying much.

I was once traumatised by seeing my accountant fucking a mouse. (This was a genuine, but untrue, posting in my Wikipedia entry.)

I am obsessed with the Periodic Table of the Elements. I was the first person to score a thousand points on *QI* – but only because Stephen gave me a thousand points for knowing that calcium is a metal (see previous).

My first job was as a worm-sexer in a silk-moth breeding institute.

Picture taken Downstairs at the King's Head, Crouch End, London, July 2014

66 *We Jews are supposed to be the chosen people, which I guess is true – God chose us, Hitler chose us.* 99

Wendy Lee

I started stand-up in 1985 and stopped in 1991.
When I was a kid, Barbara Windsor and Ronnie
Knight lived upstairs from my grandmother.
Sometimes they let me walk their dog.
I can type, watch telly and hold a conversation
at the same time.
My arms bend backwards.

Picture taken Otiz Cannelloni's 60th birthday party, The Railway Tavern,
Hornsey, June 2014

66 *Who's a Northerner's favourite RnB star? Our Kelly.* **99**

Candy Gigi

I started comedy in March 2012. My first gig was at a cabaret show in Soho in which I was the only person performing stand-up. I was utterly shit and left wanting to never perform comedy again, a feeling which follows me frequently after gigs even now. I trained to be in musical theatre and to have a career in the West End, but gave up when casting agents kept telling me my face would never blend in with the ensemble.
I think it's something to do with the fact that I have very broad facial features, and I gurn quite a lot, which is an asset to comedy, but to day-to-day life and any other career, it just makes you look terrifying.
My third cousin is Ron Moody, the original Fagin in the film *Oliver.*
I'm Jewish.
I always tell everyone I'm Jewish.

Picture taken The Court Theatre, Tring, June 2014

> ## What do you call a gay dentist? A tooth fairy.

Phil Herbert

I got my first laugh in a nativity play at primary school by saying 'It's A Boy!' I knew then I liked being on stage and getting a laugh. I first performed *Randolph The Remarkable – Fire Eater Extraordinaire* on the street at Covent Garden Piazza after five months of not working and having the fire eating skill. I worked what was an eight minute experiment up into a full forty minute act. I was then invited to try the open mic/gong show at The Comedy Store. I started being booked for three drinks tokens then for £5 then £10 then £20 plus three drinks tokens. About 1982.

I have an NVQ in Health and Social Care and work as a locum for a mental health charity.

I am a classically trained actor. I have been a Life Model for art classes and professional artists for over thirty-five years and have a one-man show called *Naked Splendour – A Life Model Speaks*.

My largest repeat cheque was for £8,008 and my smallest was 48 pence.

Picture taken Otiz Cannelloni's 60th birthday party, The Railway Tavern, Hornsey, June 2014

> **" Home is where your house is. "**

Jonny Drewek

My first gig was at the Cavendish Arms in Stockwell, aged nineteen. I was awarded half a pint of ale.
I grew up on the longest cul-de-sac in Europe.
In 2012 I served George Alagiah a fish pie containing ice. Blunder. It was in an abandoned tower block overlooking the Olympic Park. As a child I was rejected for the title role in Tim Burton's *Charlie and the Chocolate Factory*, on account of not looking 'haunted' enough.
I then focussed on looking haunted throughout my teens. During college I tried to earn a crust selling taxidermied ducklings. I ordered twenty from China and immediately felt awful.
I'm currently helping a Nigerian prince move his father's savings to the UK. I'm getting a large transfer fee and will then quit comedy.

Picture taken The Comedy Pub, London, October 2014

John Hegley

First performance in the name of comedy was at The Comedy Store, hosted by Tony Allen, who was fantastic at bringing the lively crowd to order; then as the acts went on stage, he'd be stood at the side, observing with tall-tittered encouragement.

Sacked fact: I came last in the sack race in the Wolf Cubs Sports Day in Dunstable, in 1963.

Backed fact: in my early stamp collecting days, I would use hinges, not realising that this impinges on value.

Tact fact: in 1971 Mr Smart wrote on my report that I was socially gauche. We did not know what it meant.

Cracked fact: I fell off the slide in Kingsbury Road rec' in the early sixties and fractured my arm... could have had some bearing on fact 1.

Not a one-liner , but a most cracking come-backer: I was at Brabant Road Trade Union Centre on the CAST New Variety night when Mark Kelly was asked why he performed under the name of Mr Nasty.

Audience member: Why are you called Mr Nasty?

Mr Nasty: What's it to you f*** face?

First time I've used asterisks, I think.

Picture taken Otiz Cannelloni's 60th birthday party, The Railway Tavern, Hornsey, June 2014

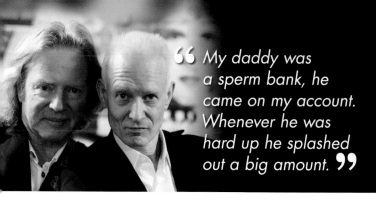

The Panic Brothers

Reg Meuross and Richard Morton

We formed in 1985 and our first gig was at The King's Head in Fulham on 3rd December 1985. We supported Chuck Berry at the Hammersmith Odeon in 1988.

Reg When I was twenty-five I spent two hours drinking expensive cognac and talking to Francois Truffault in Paris and didn't know it.

I met Krishnamurti.

I am double jointed in both my index fingers.

My surname is unique to blood relatives only.

Richard When I was fifteen I had dark shoulder-length hair.

When I left Grammar school with three A levels I didn't go straight to university, instead I decided to form a punky new wave band. I needed serious money to buy a new guitar and amp so I got a job as a labourer on a building site.

I didn't learn to drive until I was forty-two and passed my test the first time.

Picture taken Old Street, London, January 2016

81

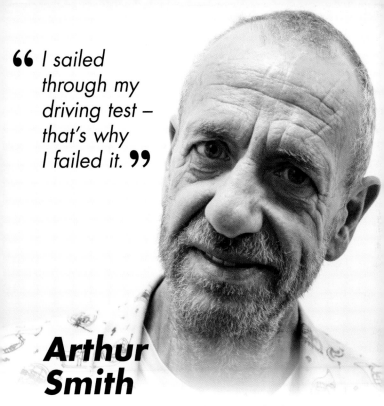

66 *I sailed through my driving test – that's why I failed it.* **99**

Arthur Smith

I started comedy at Southwark Park Primary School in 1961 when my Captain Hook made everyone laugh.
I had a fight with the tallest man in Britain.
I was president of a flower arranging society.
I spent a winter camping in a forest in Norfolk.
I am very interested in cabbages.

Picture taken The Court Theatre, Tring, June 2014

> **Jokes about white sugar are rare but brown sugar – Demerara.**

Olaf Falafel

My partner went into labour when I was on stage at my first ever gig, in Tring in 2011.

By day I'm an illustrator specialising in making things out of plasticine.

I'm the owner of a genuine Blue Peter Badge.

George Lucas owns two copies of my first book.

At the age of twenty-seven I broke my football team's record for drinking ten different pints of alcohol (1 hour 46 minutes).

I was so drunk when I got home, I got confused and pissed in my girlfriend's wardrobe.

I never got to bury my cat when it got run over because a lollipop lady scooped him up with her lollipop and threw him into a passing dustcart just as I was arriving on the scene.

Picture taken
The Court Theatre,
Tring, June 2014

Jacob Cuddihy

> **66** *I saw someone get hit by a TV. Bosch!* **99**

I started my comedy career about twenty-three hours before this photo was taken, at 8pm in the Kings Arms pub in Tring. It may already be over by now.

My first crush was on Ariel from Disney's *The Little Mermaid*.

In a previous life I was Father Kieron Hobbs – the gay priest on *Hollyoaks*. (The now gay dead priest).

I have never fingered a budgie.

If you hurt me, I won't show it immediately; but later on, when I'm on my own, I will probably have a moment of quiet self-reflection wondering why you don't like me and if I've done anything to offend you.

I only do things in fours.

Picture taken
The Court Theatre,
Tring, June 2014

84

Alastair Hogben

I first started comedy doing Logan Murray's crash comedy course for the Tring Comedy Festival in 2014. I'm originally from Manchester and keep trying to persuade my other half that it's better up North. I'm still down South which gives you an indication of how that's going.

I love running. Keeps my head clear. I started doing it when I packed up smoking on 11th August 2007 at 9.30am, and have done three marathons since.

I have been known to have a go on the piano from time to time and my favourite night out is a pub knees up. I'm currently a chartered surveyor.

Picture taken The Court Theatre, Tring, June 2014

> *When I was a child my parents thought I might have OCD because I would sort my toys according to their colour. But it turned out I was just a racist.*

Chin Tee

I started doing comedy in 2013.
My first gig was at the Freedom Fridge at
what was then The Torriano. A friend came to
see me and for some reason decided to bring
his date. They're living together now and I'd
like to think that I helped make that happen
by not being horrifically awful that night.
I was once in a band. I played guitar and sang.
We were played on XFM once.
I am allergic to cats.

Picture taken We Are Funny Project, Putney, London, April 2016

86

> 66 *Andy Murray winning Wimbledon was another example of Scotland punching above its weight. Shame our successes are measured in terms of violence and obesity.* 99

Fred MacAulay

My first gig was in a *So You Think You're Funny* competition at Mayfest, Glasgow on 19th May 1988.

I have two degrees. MA LLD. If I'd done a bachelor's Degree instead of a master's I'd have been BALLD!

I can identify a diseased potato plant, whilst it's growing, by the colour and shape of its leaves.

I have given blood over seventy times. Always voluntarily.

I got Britt Ekland's autograph at a Rod Stewart concert in 1976.

Picture taken The Court Theatre, Tring, July 2014

Tina T'urner
Tea Lady *Tracey Louise Collins*

I was singing in bands and solo projects and wanted to try something different. I had been writing characters for years and in 2012 I decided to bring my character Tina T'urner Tea Lady to life. My mum found a lovely foldaway tea trolley for me in a charity shop. My auntie sent me the tabard and my friend Nick gave me my first gig at Stoke Newington International Airport.
I live on a houseboat.
My grandad sold his car to Des O'Connor.
I love beagles.
I'd like to be a palliative care nurse.
I like to bite my nails and paint them gold.

Picture taken The Court Theatre, Tring, June 2014

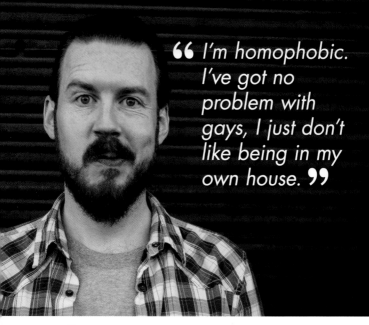

> **I'm homophobic. I've got no problem with gays, I just don't like being in my own house.**

Rhys Morgan

Started my career in February 2016, Angel Comedy, Camden Head, London.
I spent the first few years of my life in Saudi Arabia.
I once had a hernia operation, only to discover that when they opened me up I didn't actually have a hernia;
I'm not sure if I'm using semi-colons correctly;
I'm still not sure which is a courgette and which is an aubergine.

Picture taken We Are Funny Project, Putney, London, April 2016

> **My husband asked me how attractive did I think he was on a scale from 1–10. So I said 'I don't know… six and a half? Maybe a seven?' And he was really upset. He's upset! It's worse for me – I'm the one who's got to look at him!**

Jo Caulfield

I did my first gig at the Comedy Cafe, Old Street, London. I'm still friends with the owner, Noel Faulkner twenty odd years later. I had only been to one stand-up comedy show.

Like lots of comics my first five minute gig went really well. The first time is great because you are so full of ignorance and adrenaline. I then spent five years being terrible!

Although I sound very English I was born in Wales and my parents are both from Northern Ireland.

I left school at seventeen and had no higher or further education.

My brother is a Catholic Priest

I was in a rockabilly band for five years.

Before comedy I had a market stall selling vintage clothing.

I don't like marmalade.

Picture taken The Court Theatre, Tring, July 2014

> **“ Why don't Africans go on cruises? That's exactly how they got us the last time. ”**

Athena Kugblenu

I started performing in London in April 2012, working the open mic circuit.

I met Nancy Cartwright and Issac Hayes on the same day in a village in Ghana when I was eighteen.

I used to teach adults how to ride bikes. It's only easy when you know how.

2015 is my ten year anniversary of trying to learn French. I can now say 'I don't speak French very well' in French.

I have a birth mark in the shape of South America on my stomach. It is also the continent of my mother's birth.

I can crack walnuts using my teeth.

Picture taken David Lloyd Club, Farnham, July 2014

> **66** *I've never been a big follower of fashions or trends; the only 'in' thing I do is 'insecurity'.* **99**

Tom Mayhew

I started performing comedy regularly in 2014, gigging around London in various rooms above/below pubs.

I was born three months premature, when my mum was only twenty-six weeks pregnant.

I have a huge obsession with Winnie the Pooh, and Pooh-related products; there is a four foot, massive Winnie the Pooh toy that lives in my loft.

I am a fan of professional wrestling; one of my all-time favourite wrestlers is Viscera, partly because he wrestled in silk pyjamas.

My hometown is Tring, a town that some people have genuinely thought was a mythical place.

Picture taken We Are Funny Project, Putney, London, April 2016

> **❝** *I would love to have a baby for one reason – I would love to drink a load of Kahlua while breast feeding, just to see if I could squeeze out a White Russian.* **❞**

Robyn Perkins

I started in the UK (London), 21 November 2011.
Before becoming a comedian, I was a potter, a marine biologist and I designed public spaces.
I have worked on designing the 2016 Rio Olympic Park.
I play water polo (in a National League in the UK).
I have always wanted to be a rapper.
I find it very difficult to say no. I once designed and cooked a wedding cake for a friend (at the Savoy) because of this.
I have climbed Kilimanjaro (but somehow lost a bunch of luggage, so did the climb on four pairs of pants – maybe too much information, but it makes my friends crack-up).
I am described as 'Enthusiasm before Organisation'.
I can make anything into a sorbet.

Picture taken The Underbelly (English Comedian of the Year), London, July 2014

> **My girlfriend said she can count the number of people she's slept with on one hand, which is concerning with her being from Chernobyl.**

Peter Phillipson

My first gig was at a pub in Stockport in November 2008.
I'm clinically addicted to Kellogg's Krave.
My mum once won the national lottery jackpot and lost the fucking ticket.
I have served Tom Cruise in a restaurant and kept the fork.
For seven years I constantly moaned to my parents about them not upgrading from an internet dial up connection.
There was an unused wifi box in the drawer next to my feet the whole time.

Picture taken The Underbelly (English Comedian of the Year), London, July 2014.

> 66 *Sometimes when I'm bored, I watch snooker in rewind so it looks like the referee is stealing the balls.* 99

Jack Campbell

My first gig was at
De Montfort University,
Leicester 2010.
I thought I was Scottish.
Turns out I'm Swiss.
I have a tattoo of my
dead dog on my leg.
I had a piece of foam stuck
in my nose for a year
when I was a baby.
I didn't learn how to tie
my laces until I was sixteen.
I still struggle with the idea
of sweet and savoury.

Picture taken The Underbelly (English Comedian of the Year), London, July 2014

95

> **People say that 'forty is the new thirty' but try telling that to a speed camera.**

Tony Cowards

I got into stand-up when I was living in London at a comedy night called The Comedians' Graveyard.
I don't float in water.
I have a mild form of koumpounophobia, which is the fear of buttons. In fact I'm not keen on any really small round objects. I can't go anywhere near a cake if it's decorated with those tiny silver balls. I'm okay with buttons on clothes but loose buttons freak me out a bit and if one pops off a shirt I feel very icky if I have to touch it.
I support Ipswich Town.
I once gave directions to Natalie Portman.
I love Jaffa Cakes.

Picture taken The Underbelly (English Comedian of the Year), London, July 2014

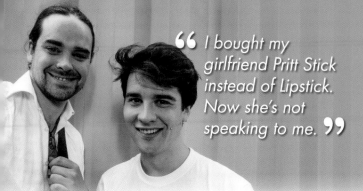

> **❝** I bought my girlfriend Pritt Stick instead of Lipstick. Now she's not speaking to me. **❞**

Jolly Boat
Ed Croft and Tommy Croft

Our first gig for a comedy audience was at the Edinburgh Fringe in 2010, but we've been performing at music and cabaret shows since 2004.

Ed I design board games in my spare time.

I perform a thirty-three hour improvised play, every year.

I once hitch-hiked across Europe, alone.

I have a complete collection of *Fighting Fantasy* books.

I once went crazy and thought I was the son of god, for about three days. A girl dumped me.

Tommy I study Etymology and Dead Languages. I also speak several real languages and an invented one.

I used to be so shy my parents thought I had Asperger's.

I make social media robots and other computer programmes as a hobby.

I can lick my elbow.

And my nose.

Picture taken The Underbelly (English Comedian of the Year), London, July 2014

> **You can't take my dad to a carvery. For him it's not a meal it's a challenge. He has to get as much food on that plate as possible. He's an expert, he's like a Jedi master, he's Toby Wan Kenobi.**

Scott Bennett

My first gig was in Nottingham, late 2009, at the Funhouse Comedy Gong Show.
I have a degree in Industrial Design.
I won Butlins' Beautiful Baby 1980.
I have a kink in one ear.
I can't juggle.

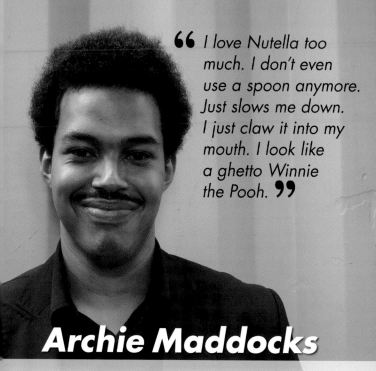

> **66** I love Nutella too much. I don't even use a spoon anymore. Just slows me down. I just claw it into my mouth. I look like a ghetto Winnie the Pooh. **99**

Archie Maddocks

I started comedy in August 2012 after a promoter saw me in a play and praised my comic timing.

I'm a professional playwright.

I work part time in a funeral parlour.

I once uppercutted a camel in Egypt because it scared me.

I was arrested on the first anniversary of 9/11 under suspicion of terrorism (I was thirteen).

Picture taken The Underbelly (English Comedian of the Year), London, July 2014

> **Glasgow's a lot like an orgy with only one woman; it's all right to look at, but there's a lot of wankers.**

Larry Dean

I'm from Glasgow but I started performing stand-up regularly in Southampton in 2010.
I was an (child) Elvis impersonator for a year when I was nine.
I got a 2.2 in a Degree in Comedy.
I am terrified of butterflies.
I used to work as a toilet cleaner for my dad (not a personal one).

Picture taken The Underbelly, London, July 2014

> ❝ My ex girlfriend was like the American Army. She moved in, took over, got rid of a few important people, stayed for a bit, then disappeared leaving me unable to look after myself. ❞

Will Mars

I started comedy at the Piccadilly Comedy Club, London (mid 2009).
I once played the part of Dr Frank-N-Furter, the transvestite lead, in a production of *The Rocky Horror Picture Show* in Spain.
I have lived in Turkey, Tunisia and Spain.
My last job before comedy was looking after 1st class passengers for an airline.
I did very little but go to LA twice a week and spend other people's money.
I survived an earthquake in Turkey in 1999. It was 6.2 on the Richter scale. It was at 3am. I was in bed and drunk. I thought I was a lot drunker until my flatmate burst in and reassured me that 'the room actually is moving!'

Picture taken The Underbelly (English Comedian of the Year), London, July 2014

> **❝** My best friend is a Buddhist Jew, which is someone who believes you should renounce all your material possessions but still keep the receipts. **❞**

David Baddiel

I started comedy in the
Cambridge Footlights, 1983.
My first gig was the King
George IV, Brixton in 1987.
I am OCD about truth.
I can't not tell the truth.
I am left footed but right handed.
I am a fundamental atheist.
I have sugar in tea but not in coffee.
I am surprised to still have my hair.

Picture taken Ealing Comedy
Festival, July 2014

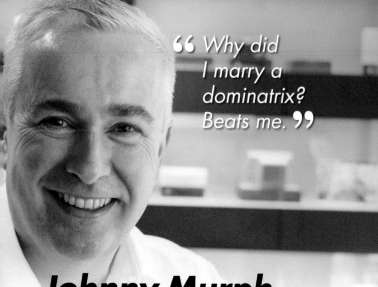

> **66** *Why did I marry a dominatrix? Beats me.* **99**

Johnny Murph

I was meant to go on a public speaking presentation course for work, but ended up at The Comedy School London on a stand-up course. My first gig was on 21st October 2011 in front of 150 people. Everybody laughed. My second gig was in front of three people. Nobody laughed. I preferred the first gig truth be told.

I enjoy rugby and played hooker since eleven years of age and never ever scored a try.

I once gave a man with no legs a leaflet for a dance class. To his credit he did inquire if they ran a hand jive session.

I have never been able to fly without the assistance of an airplane, not even in my mind.

Picture taken Leica shop, Mayfair, London, July 2014

> **We wrote a stoner comedy about two post-Impressionist painters. It's called, Dude, Where Did Vincent's Van Gogh?**

Giants
Will Hislop and Barney Fishwick

We were born two days apart and grew up together. But we started gigging at university and have continued since.

Barney I was in *Dhoom 3* – the highest internationally grossing Bollywood film ever. My first professional gig was a rural Scottish talent competition which I lost to two four-year-old girls sword dancing. At school I was voted 'Second Most Likely to Have an Affair with a Teacher.' I am currently active on Tinder.

Will I served a ginger beer to Kate Middleton. I used to DJ Euro House under the pseudonym Sir Trancelot. I fractured my collarbone celebrating Spurs winning the Carling Cup in 2008. I am also currently active on Tinder.

Picture taken The Cavendish Arms, Stockwell, London, April 2016

Jeremy Hardy

My first gig was downstairs here at the
Balham Banana in 1984.
I can't ride a bike.
I am asthmatic.
I can count to twenty in Dutch.
My grandmother knew Paul Robeson.

Picture taken The Balham Banana, July 2014

> **66** *I love it when people shout, 'What's underneath your kilt?' I always shout back, 'Your future!' They tend not to ask twice!* **99**

Craig Hill

A pal booked a gig for me without telling me at a wee try out room at The Gilded Balloon in 1998. She told me a few days before and I crapped myself but did it anyway.

I was in an amateur production of *Grease* when I had long hair and 'skilfully' (I thought) managed to hide my hair and fashion it into a quiff until someone's granny said she liked the boy with the bun.

I was in South Africa for the last World Cup and celebrated the final in the back of a pick up truck driving through Capetown singing Shakira's 'Waka Waka'.

Twice I've been mistaken for Moby.

I used to be a hairdresser and still have a habit of fixing my fringe on stage that I don't have any more! It's kinda like 'hair mime'.

I always order fish then remember I don't like fish.

Picture taken Ealing Comedy Festival, July 2014

> **If the Catholic Church is against homosexuality how come there are colours in the Sistine Chapel that straight people can't even see?**

Kevin Day

I was dared into doing an open spot in 1985. It was at the old Meccano Club and my opening line was 'sorry I'm late, I came by Tube and fell down the gap. They ought to warn us about that.' Despite that joke, I wasn't scared because I only planned to perform once.

I am a fully qualified Human Resources Manager.
I am severely allergic to lime pickle.
The man who taught Picasso and Elizabeth Taylor to swim failed to teach me to swim.
According to a past life regression I was hanged for kidnapping in 1714.
Tony Blair once sent an aide backstage to ask me to stop doing jokes about Tony Blair at a Labour Party fundraiser.

Picture taken
The Balham Banana,
July 2014

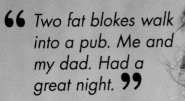

> **"Two fat blokes walk into a pub. Me and my dad. Had a great night. "**

Phil Jupitus

My first stand-up gigs after spending four years as a poet were for Joss Jones upstairs at The Town and Country in Kentish Town. Pure stand-up I always go for 1990. Before then it was a bit of a mishmash of poetry and chat.
Was in the Cubs for two weeks.
Used to watch Barking FC as opposed to West Ham.
Was a qualified scuba diver.
Favourite meal is beans on toast.
First stage role was
King Herod.

Picture taken
The Balham Banana,
July 2014

> **"** I'm from Canada, but most people think I'm American. It doesn't matter, I get it, we all look the same. **"**

Broderick Chow

I started comedy in 2006 in London, but gave up doing regular circuit gigs in 2012 to become a full-time academic. I miss it but I continue to do occasional gigs – the ones I really love.

I trained in professional wrestling for a while but I hated doing the 'promos'. I think comedians are bad at boasting (unless it's backstage) so mine would always come out all self-deprecating. I'm half Chinese and half Filipino, born in Canada, and I've lived in London nine years. Once a guy in Maidenhead didn't believe me when I explained my background and said 'people like that don't exist.'

I make theatre and dance shows.

I'm genuinely the best cook. Like, the best. I don't fuck about.

Picture taken The Tattershall Castle, London Embankment, July 2014

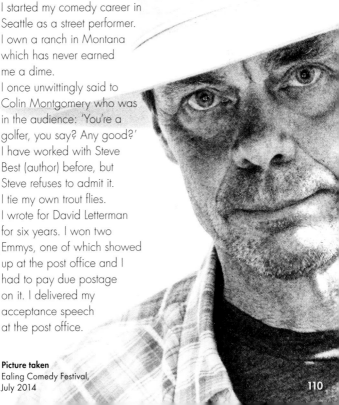

> **I've been licking ashtrays 'cause I hear it's just like kissing a woman who smokes.**

Rich Hall

I started my comedy career in Seattle as a street performer.
I own a ranch in Montana which has never earned me a dime.
I once unwittingly said to Colin Montgomery who was in the audience: 'You're a golfer, you say? Any good?'
I have worked with Steve Best (author) before, but Steve refuses to admit it.
I tie my own trout flies.
I wrote for David Letterman for six years. I won two Emmys, one of which showed up at the post office and I had to pay due postage on it. I delivered my acceptance speech at the post office.

Picture taken
Ealing Comedy Festival,
July 2014

110

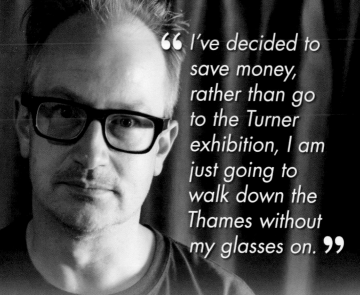

❝ *I've decided to save money, rather than go to the Turner exhibition, I am just going to walk down the Thames without my glasses on.* **❞**

Robin Ince

I began comedy in 1992 at a pub in Belsize Park where I regularly supported a sketch gang called My Big Bottom. The longest gestation period from idea to workable comedy routine is an idea about Eratosthenes who worked out the circumference of the earth via sticks and shadows, begun in 2003, still not workable.
I have supported Chas and Dave.
I have stubby thumbs which means I cannot click my fingers along to jazz.

Picture taken The Tattershall Castle, London Embankment, July 2014

> **Could I be a suicide bomber? No... you have to be there dead on time.**

Joy Carter

I started at the Comedy Café, London, 1998.
I lost £5,000 of a stranger's money gambling in Vegas.
I want to own a cannon.
I was a podium dancer and got sacked for being clumsy and wearing woolly vests.
I eat food in the bath.
I keep all my extracted teeth.

Picture taken
The Tattershall Castle,
London Embankment, July 2014

112

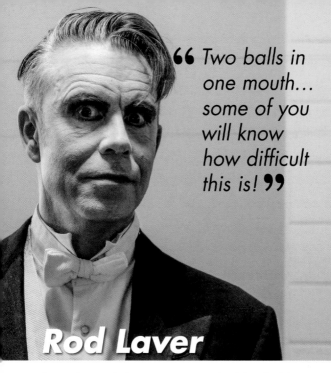

" Two balls in one mouth... some of you will know how difficult this is! "

Rod Laver

I started comedy by running a comedy club called the Goldfish Bowl at the Duke of Wellington pub on Balls Pond Road, Dalston, 1989.
I am a Guinness World Record holder.
I went to the same comprehensive as writer Julie Burchill.
I have a rabbit called Hesquith.
I have twice appeared on *Mastermind* answering questions on electronic bands, Soft Cell and Kraftwerk.

Picture taken Blackfriars, London, November 2014

> **The Swiss must've been pretty confident in their chances of victory if they included a corkscrew in their army knife.**

Rhys James

I started comedy in 2009.
I only have one kidney.
I once spilt Coca Cola on Jude Law at a football match.
The only job I've ever had was as a waiter at a golf club and I was sacked after a week.

Picture taken Downstairs at the King's Head, Crouch End, London, July 2014

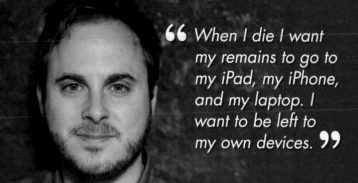

> 66 *When I die I want my remains to go to my iPad, my iPhone, and my laptop. I want to be left to my own devices.* 99

Gareth Richards

My first gig was in October 2004 on the Wibbly-Wobbly Boat for Malcolm Hardy. I mentioned that it was my first gig in my set. Malcolm asked, 'Was that really your first gig?' I said, 'Yes.' He said, 'Yeah, I thought it was.'

At school I was in a band called The Floundering Pidgeon Murders, which never performed or played together as it was purely conceptual.

Before comedy I worked for Barnardo's, Camden Council, Camden and Islington wheelchair service, and the Local Data company, where I had to go to cities and photograph all the shop fronts.

Whenever I read an autobiography I want to be that person for the next couple of weeks.

I once supported Englebert Humperdinck at The Royal Albert Hall. It did not go well.

Picture taken Downstairs at the King's Head, Crouch End, London, September 2014

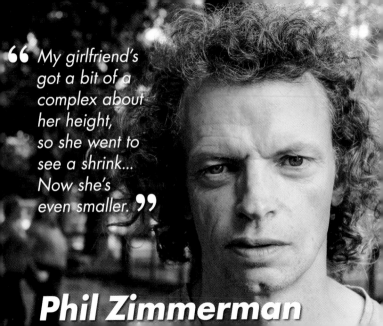

66 My girlfriend's got a bit of a complex about her height, so she went to see a shrink... Now she's even smaller. 99

Phil Zimmerman

❝ I think it's important to do something practical to help the homeless, it's not much but I always read the Big Issue every week. Online. ❞

David Hardcastle

I started in 2007 after doing Logan Murray's course and started up Get Happy Comedy. I designed the official Best Edinburgh Fringe Poster of

> **Before Instagram, I used to waste so much time sitting around having to imagine what my friends' food looked like. 99**

La Voix

Chris Dennis

I started doing comedy down at the word famous Madame Jojo's in 2004. Performing every Saturday to around thirty hen nights certainly cuts your teeth in this industry.

I managed Pamela Anderson for five years.

I have been sued by Liza Minnelli.

I passed grade 6 piano.

I adore cheese and chocolate.

Picture taken The Tattershall Castle, London Embankment, July 2014

Alan Davies

First gig: Whitstable Labour Club, March 1988.
I was still a student. I did a joke about the old suggestive
Flake ads that involved eating a Flake in a condom. I also
had other material. I still like Flakes but almost never buy
them, preferring Minstrels.
I pulled the comedian Keith Dover out of a burning car.
I met my wife at a *QI* recording. She wasn't wearing her glasses
so agreed to give me her number whilst partially sighted.
I sold an ice cream to Geoff Lawson, the Australian fast bowler,
while working at the Wimbledon Tennis Championships in 1989.

Picture taken The Comedy Store, London, January 2015

Keith Dover

I was working at Ford Motor Company and started doing comedy around 1989. That year I won the City Limits New Act of the Year at the Hackney Empire, despite what Wikipedia says! I left Ford in '93 and really enjoyed my time on the circuit, meeting some great people. I now enjoy working on the *Tuesday Club Podcast* with Alan Davies, Tayo Popoola and Ian Stone. And also working with Ian on his BT Sport show, *The Football's On*.

Picture taken
Podcast recording, Holloway, London, November 2014

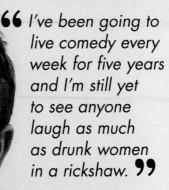

> 66 *I've been going to live comedy every week for five years and I'm still yet to see anyone laugh as much as drunk women in a rickshaw.* 99

James Loveridge

I started stand-up on Tuesday 13th October 2009 at the Lion's Den Comedy Club in King's Cross. I was four pints deep before I went on stage just to stop my hands from shaking. I was a child actor and performed in the West End in *Les Misérables* but gave it all up to play rugby. I still regularly play rugby and like to tell jokes to the opposition whilst playing. I have been punched a lot.

I once sung Robbie Williams' 'Angels' in front of my Maths class in Year 8 and my friends still don't let me forget it.

My brother is now fat and balding. (Hi Chris!)

Picture taken Top Secret Comedy, London, September 2014

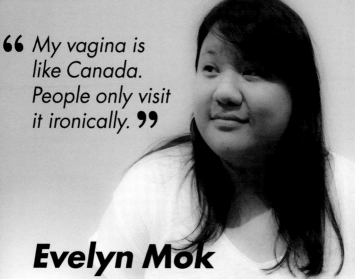

> **66** *My vagina is like Canada. People only visit it ironically.* **99**

Evelyn Mok

I did my very first gig on 15th September 2008 in the first heat of a beginner's competition in Stockholm, Sweden, where I'm from. My mother was born and raised in India, so I had a lot of indian cultural influences growing up. I pretty much thought that I was Indian until the age of ten. I sucked my thumb every night until the age of thirteen.

I became lactose intolerant at the age of twenty-one, but I still have ice cream. Regularly. I am an incredible lightweight. Half of a pint is enough to get me dizzy. I once got so inebriated that I stopped myself from drinking more, went home and in order to come down from the buzz, I went over my tax return. I'm always in the middle of at least one season of *30 Rock*.

Picture taken Top Secret Comedy, London, September 2014

John Hastings

I started in Montreal, Quebec Canada above a boozer bar underneath a roof at a place called The Comedy Works, in 2006… it's gone now and I miss it.
I love wrestling.
I have been written about in medical books because of the nature of my birth.
I have had a gun pulled on me.
I met Malcolm McDowell.
Canadians do not hate Americans.

Picture taken Top Secret Comedy, London, September 2014

> **66** *I think it's very important we protect our kids. That's why I had mine laminated.* **99**

Declan Kennedy

I first performed on my twenty-eighth birthday in the basement of an Italian restaurant near Leicester Square.
Declan Kennedy isn't the name on my birth certificate.
I used to be a lollipop man for Lancashire County Council.
My day job at the time of writing is radio production. The closest I came to getting fired was when I almost took Radio 4 off air by microwaving a potato for too long and setting off the fire alarms. Five fire engines turned up at Broadcasting House. I'm the reason they banned microwaves from Broadcasting House.
My legs are in *Shaun of the Dead*.
I once convinced a future *Thick of It* writer that Richard Briers had fought in the Spanish Civil War.

Picture taken Downstairs at the King's Head, Crouch End, London, September 2014

> **"** The place I come from is predominantly white, quite socially conservative, quite emotionally repressed. It's England. **"**

Alasdair Beckett-King

I started comedy in London 2012, after graduating from film school and realising that stand-up is a cheaper thing to fail at.

I'm a filmmaker and animator by trade, although that makes me sound like I'm a filmmaker and animator in the middle ages.

I love the films of Terry Gilliam, the works of William Blake and the music of Tom Waits, as everyone should.

I was once forcibly ejected from the Shakespeare's Birthplace Museum (via the gift shop).

I know quite a lot about 19th century magicians. Foreign tourists often ask to have their photo taken with me, presumably impressed by this.

Picture taken We Are Funny Project, Dirty Dicks, London, September 2014

> **'Christt! Were you born in a barn?'** Jesus blushed and shut the door. The disciples laughed heartily; it was a joke they never tired of. **"**

Richard Paul Todd

I started comedy in 2011, in a basement, with nineteen other men talking exclusively about masturbation. I talked about biscuit tins and abattoirs.

I can only hear out of one ear due to the over enthusiastic cotton bud applications of Mother Todd.

I can't swim: my leaky ear making swimming lessons a no-no. (I actually can do doggy paddle but for dignity's sake I prefer to drown.)

When bowling in cricket I frequently threw the ball behind me.

I grew up in a triangular shop (aerial view) sharing a yard with the Ebenezer Gospel Hall wherein I attended Uncle Gordon's Smiley Club run by a man in bottle top glasses and a wool hat who was later arrested for what everyone is arrested for these days – tax evasion.

Picture taken We Are Funny Project, Dirty Dicks, London, September 2014

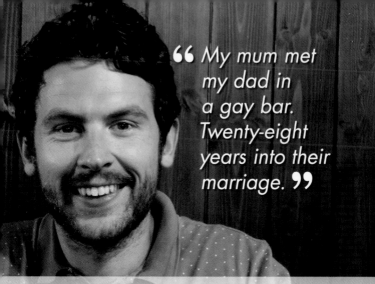

> **66** *My mum met my dad in a gay bar. Twenty-eight years into their marriage.* **99**

George Lewis

I started comedy at the start of 2013 in a room that used to be a set of toilets, below a pub in London. It was almost cancelled due to lack of audience.

I once played the part of a racist school bully in *Hollyoaks*.

I also played the part of a young John Thomson in *Cold Feet*, getting caught wanking.

I also write adverts for a living.

I used to earn money putting plastic screws on plastic cable ties. I got £10 for every one thousand cable ties.

I recently won £500 in Nando's vouchers in the Nando's New Comedian of the Year competition. It's almost all gone.

Picture taken We Are Funny Project, Dirty Dicks, London, September 2014

Trevor Lock

My first ever stand-up gig was at the Bloomsbury Theatre,
UCL in 1995. I got an encore and was then booed off.
My whole career in a nutshell!
Growing up, I rode to school on an imaginary donkey called
Moo. Also, I was captain of an imaginary football team
called Fluff United. I played all the matches alone with a
tennis ball in our back yard.
I once entered the UK from Calais without a passport.
Like many people I'm sometimes deeply moved by smells.
I've probably eaten more caterpillars than the average person.

Picture taken We Are Funny Project, Dirty Dicks, London, September 2014

> ❝ I'm not homophobic. Most of the men I've slept with have been gay. ❞

Andrew Doyle

My first stand-up gig was in 2003. I was in a sketch show and the running time was ten minutes too short, so I filled the gap by attempting stand-up. The audience was very forgiving.
As a child I attended a convent school populated by terrifying nuns.
The only surefire thing that cheers me up is Merchant Ivory adaptations of E. M. Forster.
I have never been to Guernsey.
I am a beast on a badminton court.

Picture taken We Are Funny Project, Dirty Dicks, London, September 2014

> **"** If there's one thing comedy has taught me, it's that talent isn't sexually transmittable. I've slept with so many comics, yet none of them have become any funnier. **"**

Charley Harrison

I started comedy as a result of Spark, which is a true storytelling night in Brixton, in the summer of 2013. It's an open mic where the emphasis is on true and personal rather than LOLS. But people said I was funny so I started doing comedy.

I used to have a pet rat named Wilbur.

I am an experienced London tour guide. When I get dementia all that will be left is cheesy stories about the Tower of London.

I do a fantastic helicopter impression.

I once saw Trudy from *Vets in Practice* buying cheese in a Co-op, in Winscombe, North Somerset.

Picture taken We Are Funny Project, Dirty Dicks, London, September 2014

> **My ex-girlfriend was half-Irish, half-Jewish which basically means she ran around with a pot o' gold but didn't want to share it with anybody.**

Aid Thompsin

My first gig was at The Southwark Rooms. I tried an open spot in 2007 after being encouraged to give it a go by my then girlfriend. I think I was trying to be Chris Rock and rightly died on my arse.

Before comedy I did rap.

I am the reason that school children in Berkshire are no longer allowed to use glass pipettes.

I'm a huge Ingrid Michaelson fan. Regardless of any other success I may attain, nothing will compare to the time she retweeted me.

My dad interviewed Cliff Richard. My dad's not a policeman.

Picture taken We Are Funny Project, Dirty Dicks, London, September 2014

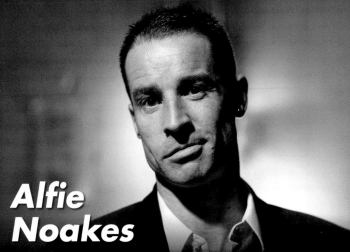

Alfie
Noakes

I did my first stand-up set in 2009 at Dirty Dicks, Liverpool Street, which is where I ran the We Are Funny Project (about twenty gigs a month with a variety of formats). Now we are in Dalston where this picture was taken.

I have been kissed on the lips by Angelina Jolie, Dannii Minogue and Samantha Fox. The latter two on the same night.

I used to have three simultaneous jobs; editor on Channel 4 TV show, reporter on Radio One film show and nightclub reviewer for a magazine.

Having lost my press accreditation at the Cannes Festival I had to climb a tree and film the opening night gala, *Moulin Rouge*, alongside a bunch of French teenagers.

I have motorcycled from Hanoi to Saigon. You have to stop at dusk or the insects that come out simply blind you.

I ran a beach bar in Thailand and named it the Bad Monkey Bar.

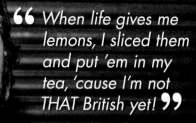

> **"** *When life gives me lemons, I sliced them and put 'em in my tea, 'cause I'm not THAT British yet!* **"**

Alex Martini

My first gig was 18th March 2012, in London.
I'm the only Italian who loves British food.
I'm the only professional comedian on the free/open-mic circuit in London (less than £10k a year, but proudly).
I like to count stairs, but I haven't got OCD.
I've spent less than £100 in four years on clothing, because I don't think how I dress defines who I am.
Everybody thinks I'm nice and jolly but in reality, my sense of humour is really dark.
I think showering is overrated.
I've got one of the weirdest laughs around, so every comedian always points that out when I'm in the audience.

Picture taken We Are Funny Project, Putney, London, April 2016

> **They say even a broken clock is right twice a day, and it's at those times that I try to sell my broken clock.** "

Don Tran

I started in Melbourne, 2008.
I sometimes make decisions by flipping a coin and seeing whether I'm happy with the way it landed.
I read Wikipedia summaries of books to see if they are worth reading. I save a lot of time by avoiding bad books and spoiling the good ones.

Picture taken Downstairs at the King's Head, Crouch End, London, September 2014

134

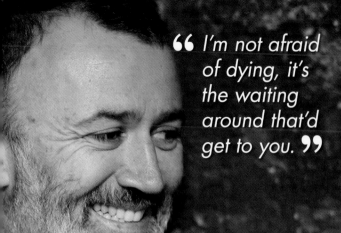

" *I'm not afraid of dying, it's the waiting around that'd get to you.* **"**

Tommy Tiernan

I began in the back room of a restaurant in 1995.
My first gig was forty-five minutes long. I'm sure it was awful
but I came offstage only remembering the good bits.
I'm colour blind.
I'm tone deaf.
I have flat feet.
I once won £10k playing poker.
I have scored for Liverpool.

Picture taken Downstairs at the King's Head, Crouch End, London, September 2014

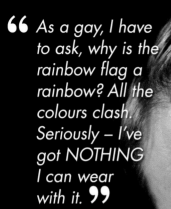

> **"** As a gay, I have to ask, why is the rainbow flag a rainbow? All the colours clash. Seriously – I've got NOTHING I can wear with it. **"**

Harry U Eldrich

My dad is a vicar.
I am a type 1 diabetic.
I am gay and also homophobic.

Picture taken We Are Funny Project,
Dirty Dicks, London, September 2014

66 *Apple have made a Western – i-Noon* **99**

Richard Sandling

My first ever gig was at a Pear Shaped Midnight Show at the Holyrood Tavern, Edinburgh 2005. I was up there in a play and had no intention of being a comedian, but was harangued by a friend of mine into doing a five minute set with no prep time whatsoever so I pretty much made up my first five minute set on the spot.

I have every Rex Stout Nero Wolfe book.

I have watched every single Jason Statham film.

I taught Brian Belo his Media Studies BND.

I used to work security in a women's prison.

I am a massive fan of giant squid and octopuses.

Picture taken We Are Funny Project, Dirty Dicks, London, September 2014

" I'm a vegan. In case you don't know what that is, a vegan is someone who doesn't get invited anywhere twice. "

Oliver Noakes

I started doing comedy in 2011,
in London, in the basement of a jazz
club, to angry folk musicians.
I grew up in Folkestone, Kent.
I'm of Romani, Scottish and Lithuanian descent.
My first ever drink was a warm Baileys
on New Year's Eve 1999. I was twelve.
It was not good.
Before doing comedy I worked on the London
Underground and on the ferries between
Dover and Calais. I also worked for two
summers on rowing boats, on a canal,
but I did not fall in once.

Picture taken We Are Funny Project, Dirty Dicks, London, September 2014

Josephine Lacey

I started comedy in October 2008. I attended a comedy course that ran for three hours on a Sunday for seven weeks. The last week ended with a showcase.

I'm forty-six years old, a mother of three and nana to one.

I worked for many years with entrenched rough sleepers for a charitable organisation. I have set up and managed Rolling Shelters and my last position with the organisation was running the services in the Borough of Brent for vulnerable adults. I officially left in 2010.

I do as much charity work/ campaigning as possible to raise awareness of Autism and Asperger's Syndrome. The matter is very close to my heart as my youngest child has Autism.

I'm of Jamaican-Irish heritage. My father is Jamaican (from Clarendon) and my mum is from Southern Ireland (Cork). I was born and raised in South-West London. I hate physical exercise. I do it but do not enjoy it at all (apart from swimming, I love the water).

Picture taken Top Secret Comedy, London, September 2014

> **❝** My girlfriend worries that I might cheat on her when I'm on a night out. I reassure her and say why would I go out and have a burger when I've got steak at home. The only problem is when you're pissed burgers are well nice. **❞**

Rob Beckett

I can peel a banana with my feet.
I saved a drowning man's life in the sea on Brighton beach.
I've got a cat called Alan.
My dad once punched a goat in the face.
I don't trust anyone that doesn't admit to shitting themselves at some point as an adult.

Picture taken Top Secret Comedy, London, September 2014

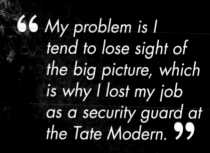

> **❝** *My problem is I tend to lose sight of the big picture, which is why I lost my job as a security guard at the Tate Modern.* **❞**

Mike Shephard

I began stand-up in 2011 after it became apparent that I was not the natural successor to Nobel Prize winning dramatist Harold Pinter. My first gigs were part of the Laughing Horse New Act Competition where I reached the semi-finals, beginning a tradition of semi-success.

I am technically the man who introduced Strongbow to Namibia.

I once appeared in a fringe production of *Macbeth* where I played both Duncan and Macduff, meaning that I had to discover my own murdered corpse. Acting doesn't get tougher than that.

I grew my hair long after appearing on television in a bad wig and finding out that girls seemed to like it.

My favourite death in history is the legendary demise of the Ancient Greek playwright Aeschylus, who was killed when an eagle dropped a tortoise on his head.

Picture taken The Backyard, Bethnal Green, London, September 2014

> **" I once fell into a bag of onions. Got myself in a right pickle. "**

Suzy Wilde

I started in 2010 in a shoddy pub.
I'm the only one in my family who can do impressions.
When I was seventeen I gave a speech at Buckingham
Palace about being poor and stole a napkin (wait
maybe I shouldn't admit that).
I dropped out of my Law degree and did comedy instead.
Who needs fame and power anyway *sobs*.
My mum and dad met working in McDonald's which
makes me a Mcbaby.
I have a phobia of Arnold Schwarzenegger.

Picture taken The Backyard, Bethnal Green, London, September 2014

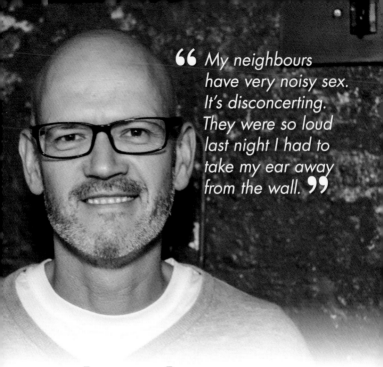

> **My neighbours have very noisy sex. It's disconcerting. They were so loud last night I had to take my ear away from the wall.**

Toby Adams

I started in 1999, at the King's Head. I did three minutes before the recognition of the sound of my own frantic breathing coming back to me through the speakers led me off.

I was a nurse.

I've caught a seven pound chub.

I enjoy ironing.

Picture taken Downstairs at the King's Head, Crouch End, London, September 2014

> **66** *No conversation about someone who smokes weed ends in '...and he got the promotion.'* **99**

Rory O'Hanlon

My first gig was in a bar called Doyles on College Green in Dublin, November 2005.
For my final year biology exam in school, I was on holidays in Spain.
I haven't been to confession in thirty years.
I have three sisters and no brothers.
I used to be a professional contract cleaner.
I get sick if I smoke weed.

Picture taken Top Secret Comedy, London, September 2014

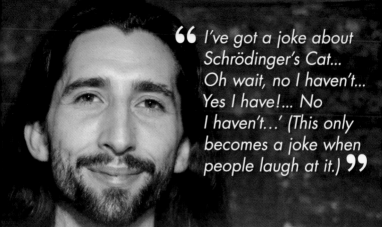

> **66** *I've got a joke about Schrödinger's Cat... Oh wait, no I haven't... Yes I have!... No I haven't...' (This only becomes a joke when people laugh at it.)* **99**

Jay Handley

I did my first gig in November 2010 at the graduation show at
The Midlands Art Centre Comedy Course run by James Cook.
It was a beautiful eighty-seater theatre with raked seating.
I didn't do a nicer gig until performing at The Stand in
Glasgow a year and a half later.
I was a furniture designer/maker for seven years.
I like to make electronic music.
I have a degree in Psychology.
I was an avid tree climber between the ages of eighteen
and twenty-two.
I never learned to tie my shoelaces properly.

Picture taken Downstairs at the King's Head, Crouch End, London, September 2014

> **"** *Of course I'm arrogant… If I wasn't arrogant I would be perfect… and then NOBODY would like me.* **"**

Jonathan The Jester

I started my career on the streets of a small town in Wiltshire, dressed as a jester, messing around with the public at a carnival event.

As a young child I set fire to a forestry commission plantation, completely burning it down, and covered in soot, with singed hair, tried to deny my guilt whilst hiding the matches in my hand behind my back.

I run a community circus.

I was the first clown to appear in a crown court on a contempt of court charge dressed in full motley since Archie Armstrong.

I hold the world record for holding an audience for a street show, which lasted twenty-six hours on the streets of Salisbury in 2005.

I act as an advocate for young people and sometimes get to represent them in court as a Mackenzie Friend.

Picture taken Russell Square, London, September 2014

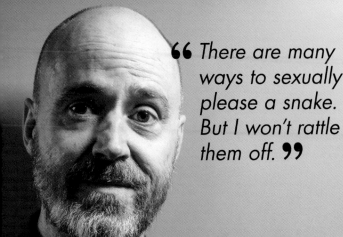

> **There are many ways to sexually please a snake. But I won't rattle them off.**

Nick Elleray

My first stand-up gig was at The Cavendish Arms, London, 5th December 2011.
I once told the complete truth in a job interview. Once.
I have a problem with Catford and will never believe anyone who says it's 'actually pretty nice now'.

I used to work in the busiest ice-cream store in the Southern Hemisphere.
I knew I had to stop living alone once I started treating the mouse in the kitchen as a confidant.
I once attempted to woo a woman by taking her to a Jerry Sadowitz gig. Once.

Picture taken The Crack, Southbank, London, October 2014

> **"** When the Americans killed Osama Bin Laden in his compound they found his stash of porn magazines. I wonder what sort of porn mags he was looking at. I reckon he had a Taliban version of the porn magazine Barely Legal. It just contained a picture of a woman fully-clothed driving... to a polling station. **"**

Alex Perry

I did my first gig in 2008 above an Aussie theme pub in Camden with a sticky floor and sparse crowd.
As a child I was on a special one-off northern edition of the TV show *Rolf's Cartoon Club*.
I'm a Manchester United season ticket holder.
I was in the same year at high school as Jason Manford.
When the IRA bombed Manchester in 1996 it woke me up and ruined my lie-in. (In many ways this was the real tragedy.)

Picture taken The Backyard, Bethnal Green, London, September 2014

148

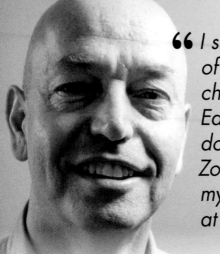

> **66** *I share a lot of DNA with chimpanzees. Each week I go down to London Zoo and throw my spunk at them.* **99**

Geoff Alderman

I took a comedy course about eight years ago. I did one gig, died, and it took about four years before I got the nerve to have another go.

I've worked in some very good advertising agencies as a copywriter.

I used to be a runner and got an AAA bronze medal for the 1500m when I was seventeen.

I nearly got sent to borstal when I was fourteen because me and some friends lit a fire on a building site that got out of control.

My dad used to wash my hair in Fairy Liquid. Never did me any harm.

Picture taken The Crack, Southbank, London, October 2014

> *If looks could kill, I'd make more eye contact.*

Joshua Ross

I started stand-up in August 2011 in Farringdon. It was the Monday of the London riots. I was last on a bill of over twenty comics and played to about twelve people; the nine acts who stayed and three of my friends. It was ace. The second gig was terrible. I spent six weeks in 2005 working on a cotton farm in New South Wales. I worked 108 hours in my first week and witnessed a series of industrialised farming accidents. Before graduating I organised a Pulp Tour around Sheffield which was me walking around the Wicker Bridge shouting at six or so friends and acquaintances.

I got drunk at my own house party when I was sixteen and passed out before the house was trashed.

My great uncle wasn't Ronnie Corbett.

Picture taken Downstairs at the King's Head, Crouch End, London, September 2014

> *I can't bear political correctness. I have a handicapped son, but nowadays you can't say, 'handicapped son', you have to say, 'I have a daughter.'* **"**

Nathaniel Tapley

Back in 2003, one of my friends ran a comedy night. One month he hadn't booked enough acts and asked me if I'd step in. I did, and found the audience's mixture of indifference and outright hostility to be highly addictive. I met my wife when we were performing together in *News Revue*.

My review of Dapper Laughs' Christmas album sent him into the weekend-long breakdown that ended with him on *Newsnight*, in a black polo-neck pretending to be the character Daniel O'Reilly. I've had short stories published in horror magazines and anthologies. I helped build a house in Bangladesh with my actual hands once.

I'm a dual UK–US citizen, and one of my ancestors (Stephen Hopkins) was on the *Mayflower*.

Picture taken The Harlequin Theatre, Redhill, April 2016

> **"** *Caught a glimpse of myself in the mirror the other day and thought 'Damn, you're a handsome man.' It's not that I'm arrogant, I just have really bad taste in men.* **"**

Ben Clover

I started at York University, 2002
(then stopped for ten years).
I work as a journalist.
I have swum between continents.
I modelled for the Swedish Mothercare
catalogue as a child.
I touched Boris Johnson's hair at City Hall once.
It was consensual but I'm not proud of it.

Picture taken Downstairs at the King's Head, Crouch End, London, September 2014.

> 66 I told my girlfriend
> I had a fetish for
> amoeba sex...
> so she split up
> with me. 99

Spen Cockerell

I started doing Comedy in December 2014... I did a course, mainly so I would not have an excuse to back down from my first gig... 'I've spent all this money so...' It was a good launch pad though.

I once made a snarky comment at someone for trying too hard to look like Johnny Depp who turned out to be Johnny Depp.

I've never eaten sushi.

I'm worryingly good at dull administration jobs.

I was once voted into the Top 10 Transvestites in the UK in an online poll (Number 8).

Picture taken We Are Funny Project, Dalston, London, October 2016

> **When I took drugs, I'd do anything to get money. I sold myself. I learnt to take it on the chin. But I do have standards, there's one thing I won't do for money, WORK!**

Andy Zapp

I started comedy in May 2011. First gig was upstairs
in the Queens Head, Denman Street, Piccadilly.
I'm a Cockno-Taff-Pole.
I got chucked out of two art schools.
I have two daughters and two grandkids.
I have an MSc in drug and alcohol policy and practice.

Picture taken Camden Comedy Club, London, October 2016

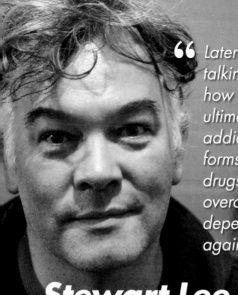

> 66 *Later on I'll be talking you to about how my tragic and ultimately fatal addiction to various forms of lethal illegal drugs has helped me to overcome my previous dependence on born again Christianity.* 99

Stewart Lee

I did a monologue about The Highway Code at sixth form in Solihull in 1984. At school I was leader of a Mountain Walking Club that included 3/4 of the original line-up of Napalm Death. In Canada, in 1975, our tent was attacked by a bear, which was shooed off by my uncle, Roger Davis, who has a non-speaking part as a policeman in the opening scene of Peter Watkins' 1967 film *Privilege*, and once saw the Finnish Mod-punk band The Renegades in a '60s Birmingham beat club. I bought my first flat off the lead singer of The Boo Radleys. I have seen a ghost, but I do not believe in the afterlife.

Picture taken The Hob, Forest Hill, London, October 2014

Bridget Christie

I started in 2004. My first
gig was at the Alexandra
pub in Clapham.
Gene Wilder once
pretended to strangle me,
as a joke, at a book launch.
I have two webbed toes
on my right foot.
I was attacked by a swarm
of jellyfish in Thailand.
One of my legs is
longer than
the other.

Picture taken
Soho Theatre, London,
May 2015

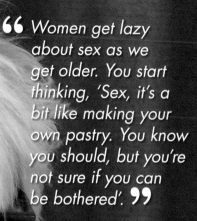

> ❝ Women get lazy about sex as we get older. You start thinking, 'Sex, it's a bit like making your own pastry. You know you should, but you're not sure if you can be bothered'. ❞

Jenny Eclair

I have knitted a dog.
I can't eat anything with tomatoes in, nothing, not baked beans, not spag bol, nothing do you hear?
I used to have anorexia (who would think you could recover this well?)
I have been sacked on numerous occasions.

Picture taken
Foyles Bookshop, London,
October 2014

> **Ron: Doctor, Doctor, I think I'm a pair of curtains. Doctor: No, Ron. You've had a stroke.**

Ronnie Rigsby
Logan Murray

I started in 1984. I got an open spot at the Banana Cabaret, Balham. Ronnie Rigsby started in 1923.
I can swim a length underwater.
I am a silversmith in my spare time.

I have a massive collection of Bonzo Dog postcards from the 1920s and '30s.
I once went Morris Dancing in one of the Bee Gees' homes (think it was Robin Gibbs').
One of my thumbs is double-jointed.

Picture taken The Court Theatre, Tring, June 2014

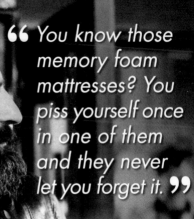

> **66** *You know those memory foam mattresses? You piss yourself once in one of them and they never let you forget it.* **99**

Phil Kay

The comedy started in 1981. I fell over and my stepfather said, 'What are you doing down there?' I said, 'Getting up', and he laughed.

I have been to five births.

I drove 6,993 miles to Vegas and back from New York without a license.

I got a big splinter playing ping pong with Gary from Snow Patrol.

My mum knew Jim Haynes who did the first Happenings at the first Edinburgh Fringe at the first Paperback Bookshop. And Jim was a judge when I won a TapWater award at the Bongo Club. Ah the circle of life!

I once crawled away from the police when they were trying to arrest me.

Picture taken The Comedy Pub, London, October 2014

Breaking up with someone is the second hardest thing in the world, after trying to pick a CD up from a laminate floor.

Josh Widdicombe

Started comedy: January 2008, Laughing Horse, Earls Court.

At primary school there were four people in my year.

I auditioned for the lead role in *The Hobbit*.

I have a pectus excavatum (dent in my chest).

I once supported Jerry Seinfeld by mistake.

Picture taken Downstairs at the King's Head, Crouch End, London, July 2014

Lee Simpson

I guess the first time I knowingly did something that was explicitly comedy was the Comedy Store Players and I guested with them for the fist time in 1987. That was at the Leicester Square Comedy Store.

My uncle Peter was in the Arsenal double winning side of 1971.

My first job after school was as a projectionist.

I really like maps and have an extensive collection of OS Landranger maps.

For a short time I ran a pornography rental business from my school locker.

My superpower is anonymity.

I once sat at a table in a wine bar with Telly Savalas.

I have unusually short hamstrings but an excellent turnout.

I have a tiny head.

Picture taken The Comedy Store, London, October 2014

> *I'm tired today. I put my contact lenses in back to front this morning then accidentally walked seventeen miles 'cause it looked closer.* **"**

Tom Ward

I started in 2011 at the Cavendish Arms in Stockwell. I collect 1980s Walkmans. I have a stash of items in my mum's attic that I nicked from Wimbledon FC's old stadium, Plough Lane before it got pulled down. I ran charity shops for five years and Visage drummer Rusty Egan bought CDs from me. I collect 1980s football shirts. QPR '87/'88 is my second favourite. I gave my favourite to a girl; Liverpool away '88/'89.

Picture taken Downstairs at the King's Head, Crouch End, London, September 2014

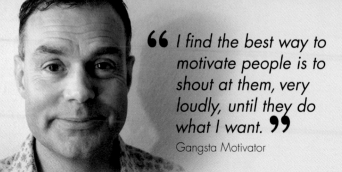

Neil Mullarkey

I started comedy at school, in the school play. I upstaged people horribly with a soda syphon. Then I went to Cambridge because I wanted to be in the Footlights. I failed twenty-two auditions for undergraduate shows but I did get into the Footlights because I wrote my own sketches.

I do very little comedy these days. Really just improv with the Comedy Store Players and occasional gigs as L-Vo (Gangsta Motivator). Nearly all my time is spent running workshops and coaching people, using improv and other theatre skills to help communication, creativity and collaboration. I love it.

I am a qualified table tennis umpire.

My family moved back to the UK from France when I was nearly six. I hadn't learned to read because they leave that till later in the French system.

For part of my gap year I did voluntary work in Handsworth, Birmingham, a city of which I remain very fond.

Picture taken The Comedy Store, London, October 2014

> **66** *I went to the doctors and I said, 'Doctor, Doctor, I'm having trouble hearing people.' And he said, 'Can you tell me the symptoms.' And I said, 'Homer, Marge, Bart...'* **99**

Frank Skinner

My first ever gig was at the Portland Club, Edgbaston, Birmingham on December 9th 1987. It was a charity event and included the Nice People, one of which, Phil Clarke, is head of comedy at Channel Four, and the other, Simon Godley, is my dentist. I'm a former president of the Samuel Johnson Society.

On my first driving test I knocked over someone on a pedestrian crossing. (I failed.) I was the youngest ever member of the Great Britain Vintage Rock and Roll Appreciation Society. I was expelled from school at sixteen for 'embezzling the school meal service'.

Picture taken Greenwich Yacht Club, London, April 2016

164

Josie Lawrence

Being a Kray sister in Denise Black and The Kray Sisters
(a three part harmony group) introduced me to the
wonderful world of the alternative comedy circuit in the
'80s. I improvised with Jim Sweeney and Steve Steen, then
joined the Comedy Store Players at the end of 1985.
I once peacefully dispersed a late night crowd of 300 excited
villagers in Rural China by singing the 'So Long, Farewell'
song from the *Sound of Music*.
I have stood on the very highest point of Blackpool Tower (not
open to the public) wearing silver thigh boots and a basque.
I have a Siamese tooth.

Picture taken The Comedy Store, London, October 2014

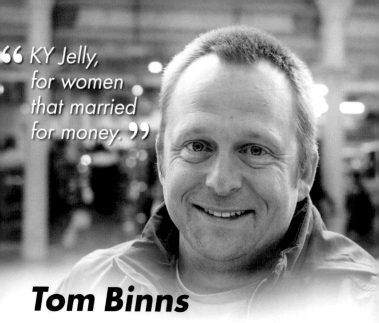

*KY Jelly,
for women
that married
for money.*

Tom Binns

My first gig was at the Zap Club, Brighton, 1992.
I was banned from Wembley from the 1991 FA Cup Final and ended up getting back in and watching it sat on the pitch.
In 2002 I had enough of comedy and decided to run a sail boat charter in Ibiza. I had no sailing experience.

I got the largest fine in radio history (£50k) while working for XFM in 1990 for doing a joke about wanking a pig. I got sacked.
In 2009 on commercial radio I was sacked again for interrupting the Queen's Christmas message on Christmas Day. It made the news around the world.

Picture taken London St Pancras station, April 2016

> **"** *I'm in a long-distance relationship. It's called a restraining order.* **"**

Alex Love

I had my first ever gig at Havant Arts Centre in 2005 in front of 100 people. I was twenty and had no idea what I was doing. It wasn't until I moved to London in 2010 that I started gigging properly.

I used to be a reporter for a local newspaper, which I quit without getting any qualifications, to move to London and pursue comedy. I somehow ended up getting freelance shifts for the *Guardian* for a couple of years.

I am a massive fan of the band The Darkness and have seen them live twelve times.

The first album I bought was the *Smurfs Go Pop*.

Simon Pegg's brothers were neighbours of mine when I grew up. We didn't get on very well and used to have turf wars in an old lady's garden next door.

Until the age of twenty-seven, I had no dental fillings and was really pleased with my teeth. Then I was knocked down by a cyclist who jumped a red light and I chipped six teeth. It's not quite as legendary as the 27 Club, but at least I'm still alive.

Picture taken The Crack, Kingston, October 2014

> **I owe a lot to the safe sex campaign, which is why I no longer do it in the lion enclosure at London Zoo.**

Sarah Mills

I started comedy in 2012 and was really too drunk to be starting anything and it showed. But I think drunkenness pays off in many first time experiences.

I am genuinely 4 ft 11 inches tall which makes me one inch taller than a dwarf.

I'm a classically trained pianist with letters after my name to that effect and everything.

I once filmed a threesome for national television.

I only found out recently that I have an Irish relative called BoBo Delaney. That partially autobiographical sitcom will write itself.

One time I set up a table and chairs in the middle of a mini-roundabout in Stevenage in the dead of night and had a tea party.

Picture taken The Comedy Pub, London, October 2014

66 *In response to Renee Zellweger's face. It's not Botox or surgery. It's a missing person enquiry.* 99

Viv Groskop

I did my first stand-up gig at Lion's Den at The Cross Kings in King's Cross in 2009. A man told me, 'It was just like Victoria Wood', and I burst into tears. He then said, 'Oh, I don't think she's funny. You just look like her.'
My name means 'Lively Bighead'.
I hate avocados.
I speak Russian fluently.
I gave birth to a baby next to a dishwasher.

Picture taken Foyles Bookshop, London, October 2014

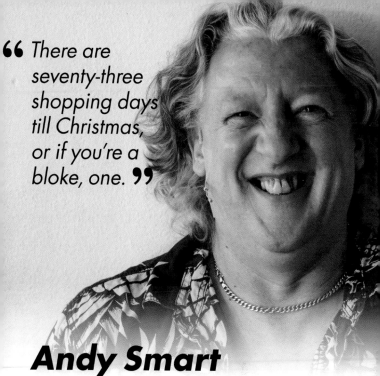

> **"** There are seventy-three shopping days till Christmas, or if you're a bloke, one. **"**

Andy Smart

My first paid gig was 28th December 1981 in the bar of the Everyman Theatre, Liverpool. It was Craig Charles' first gig too.
I've run with the bulls fifty-seven times in Pamplona.
I've performed at every Glastonbury Festival since 1985.
I've performed at thirty-five consecutive Edinburgh Festivals and spent over two years of my life there so far.
I'm a qualified football referee.

Picture taken The Comedy Store, London, October 2014

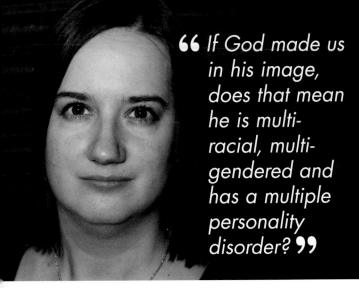

> **If God made us in his image, does that mean he is multi-racial, multi-gendered and has a multiple personality disorder?**

Tori Jo Lau

I've been contemplating dipping my toes in for years, and this picture was taken ten minutes before my first ever set!

I have five guinea pigs and a hamster, but I'm mostly a cat person.

I play a lot of *World Of Warcraft*.

My favourite film character of all time is R2-D2.

Whenever I go out to buy clothes, I end up coming home with blu-rays.

The fastest way to my heart is via pick 'n' mix.

I find people who don't like Disney movies suspicious.

Picture taken We Are Funny Project, Putney, London, April 2016

> **66** *It makes me laugh when people say that comedy is the new Rock and Roll. Yeah, cause I bet Jimi Hendrix would've spent whole weekends liking the Facebook posts of promoters he's not gigged for yet.* **99**

Freddy Quinne

I once got fired from a job at a supermarket for coming into work hungover and being sick in the back of a fridge.

I'm really into chess – I reckon I play about 25 games a week either online or face-to-face against other people.

I owe an ex-girlfriend about £120 from over a year and a half ago and I keep thinking she's forgotten about it, but she fucking hasn't.

When I was a kid I had a hamster called Weetabix.

We went on holiday to France and left it with my granddad. When we got back it was very ill, so we took it to a vet who told us it was suffering from depression.

Picture taken The Rocket Club, Birmingham, October 2014

> **"** I had a phone call from my agent this morning. He said, 'Just want to check you've got October 8th in your diary.' I said, 'Of course I have, it's my diary.' **"**

Dave Gorman

My first gig was a benefit gig in 1990 in Manchester.
One of my hobbies is balancing rocks.
Photos that I took were once used as set dressing on *The Apprentice*.
My dad once got turned away from my show because of my strict no late comers policy. (I no longer have that policy but they are still frowned upon).
I once spoke to someone for twenty minutes without realising that he thought I was Lee Evans.

Picture taken The Soho Theatre, London, March 2016

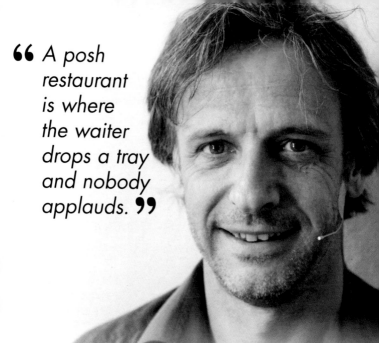

" A posh restaurant is where the waiter drops a tray and nobody applauds. "

Richard Vranch

I first did jokes for money in a double-act in 1981.
I shared a lift in New York with Richard Nixon,
Henry Kissinger, Quincy Jones and Greg Proops.
I've done more shows at the London Comedy Store
than any other comedian.
I do a comedy hulu-hoop act called Dr Hula,
and stand-up in French.

Picture taken The Comedy Store, London, October 2014

Doug Segal

> **" I'm half Russian Jew, quarter German Protestant, quarter Irish Catholic. Which means half of me wants to get drunk on Guinness and schnapps and the other half doesn't want to pay for it. "**

I started adding comedy to what was an already successful 'straight' mind reading act in 2008 in an attempt to create a unique niche for myself. It would have been easier to just buy an outrageous hat.

My legal name is Doug Bruce Wayne Segal.

My first ever TV spot was live on BBC1 at five minutes to midnight on New Year's Eve. I did a totally unrehearsed routine.

I used to heckle Lee Evans at his first regular compere gig.

Marc Almond once tried to chat me up over some Yakult.

I shared a desk with Lord Rothermere (publisher of the *Daily Mail*) for a month.

I used to arrive at the *Daily Telegraph* staff canteen at the same time as Boris Johnson every morning. He puts ketchup on sausage sandwiches.

Picture taken Reigate Grammar School, March 2016

> **" No more Page 3!
> In any
> book. "**

Lolly
Adefope

I started in London in 2013.
I love Ribena.
I'm allergic to apples.
I'm left-handed.
I have a slight-gap between my two front teeth.

Picture taken The Cavendish Arms, Stockwell, London, April 2016

> **I've been having impure thoughts about our babysitter. This worries me because our babysitter is seventy-two years old.**

Rex Boyd

I started in 1986. I took a year out of university and did an open mic night every Tuesday and Wednesday in Kansas City. From 1988 to 1994 I didn't spend more than six weeks in the same city.

I had a moped when I was fourteen, a 450cc street bike when I was fifteen, and when I was sixteen I had a classic muscle car, a Ford Mustang.

I started doing ballet when I was twenty-one at university. I now dance and love Argentinian Tango.

I fell off my bicycle when I was nine. I fractured and separated my left arm to the extent that my arm dangled. Until this day my arm is still crooked.

I gave up doing stand-up in January 2010.

Picture taken Tango Festival, Islington, London, May 2016

> **❝** *What did Big Ben say to the Leaning Tower of Pisa, I've got the time if you've got the inclination.* **❞**

Angelos Epithemiou
Dan Renton Skinner

I did my first gig in a pub in Wandsworth. Weirdly I'd managed to get myself a gig with Arthur Smith, called Arthur Smith and friends, although I'd never met him. I cannot remember how that came about. Anyway. Suffice to say, I died on my you know what.

I have size thirteen feet.

My dad spelt my middle name wrong on my birth certificate (Wrenton instead of Renton).

I'm among only a handful of people I know who will happily watch The Tour De France in its entirety.

I was once unsuccessful in my job application to stack cardboard boxes in a factory.

Picture taken Reigate, February 2010

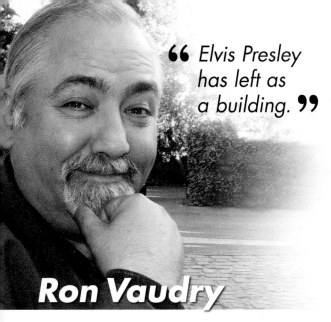

> **Elvis Presley has left as a building. ""**

Ron Vaudry

I did my first set in Montreal Saturday 1st September 1979.
I auditioned for the manager of Stitches Comedy Club on the
Friday and was asked to do the Labour Day Comedy Marathon
for MDA from noon to midnight the next day, with all proceeds
going to the Jerry Lewis telethon. I did twelve sets that day!
I was a published artist in high school.
I was a total pacifist for three years in high school.
Then made adjustments in philosophy.
Always been a white knuckled flier.
Huge John Lennon fan.
Social cynic long before comedy.

Picture taken Screaming Blue Murder, Colnbrook, June 2008

179

> **I don't really do one-liners, especially since you can get the whole gram in a 2ml syringe.**

Chris Dangerfield

I started stand-up proper about seven years ago and my first gig was Downstairs at the King's Head, following Frank Skinner.

I am a world renowned lock-picker and own one of the world's most successful lock pick retail operations.

I am both Bachelor and Master of Arts.

I've had four different guns held to my head by four different gunmen.

I've been approached to be a spy three times.

A band I once formed got a management, publishing and recording deal after our first gig, but lost them all after the second.

Picture taken The Comedy Pub, London, October 2014

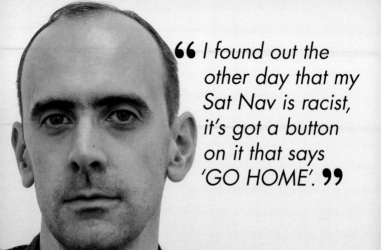

> **❝** I found out the other day that my Sat Nav is racist, it's got a button on it that says 'GO HOME'. **❞**

Dave Bailey

I started in 2003 in a BBC New Comedy Awards Heat (some wine bar in Chertsey). I was a Mascot for Leicester City FC and got to meet David Pleat. You're jealous, I can tell.
I won a silver medal for high jump in the Southern England Athletics Championship in the late '90s.
Every substitute teacher when I was a kid would ask, 'Where's your camera?'
I was born in Truro and consider Cornwall to be heaven on earth.

Picture taken The Crack, Kingston, October 2014

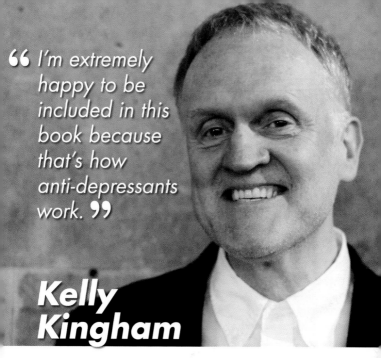

I'm extremely happy to be included in this book because that's how anti-depressants work. 99

Kelly Kingham

I started stand-up in 2010.
I was brought up in an Anglo-Indian family.
I worked as an age-guesser at a rodeo until I was arrested by the Mounties.
I once wrote and produced a musical comedy despite never having been to see one.
I proposed to my wife on the steps on St Paul's Cathedral (by far the best thing I've ever done).
I pray every morning and every night (and often in between).

Picture taken The Comedy Pub, London, October 2014

" *We are the greatest…*
Deal with it. **"**

The Two Johns

Johnny Spalding and Terry Alderton

We started three years ago (2013) at The Fighting Cocks
in Kingston (John's cock won!)
Terry I'm a black belt in judo.
I played football (goal) for Southend United.
I've had a pint with Gerry Adams.
Johnny I was one half of Bell & Spurling, who had hits, with
'Sven Sven Goran Ericsson' and 'Golden Balls (Mr Beckham to You)'.
I was also a part of Babakoto who had an 80's hit with
'Just to Get By'.
On my own I have had dance hits, 'Here I Go Again' and
'People Hold On'.
I am a winner of Michael Barrymore's *My Kind of Music*.

Picture taken The Bloomsbury Theatre, London, January 2015

> **My wife upset me the other night when she put on Facebook, 'I wish I was cuddling up with Brad Pitt tonight!' So I put a comment on, 'Brad Pitt wouldn't shave your back.'**

Dave Spikey

First gig was at the Golcar British Legion in 1987.
I once had a fight with a German bloke over a crab. He was kicking it up the beach to get a better photo. I said something to him that I'd never said before and I dare say I'll never say again. I said, 'Leave the crab alone, mate.'

I am a fellow of the Institute of Biomedical Science.
I can sail a yacht. I have a day skipper certificate to prove it.
I once got caned for mucking about in the school choral service. It wasn't me. I was set up.
I was in *New Faces 1987* in a double act called Spikey and Sykey.

Picture taken Dave's house via Skype (after a haircut), April 2016

184

66 *The other day*
I took a bullet, you
know a Nutri-bullet,
mash up the fruit,
mash up the veg,
drink it up,
breakfast in bed. 99

Steve Whiteley

aka Wisebowm

I began going to improv drop in classes in 2007 and performed in my first live show in London with Hoopla in 2008. I once travelled around the UK working as David Gest's DJ. My parents were going to call me Woody, but decided to give the name to our cat instead.

I'm the voice of Spotify, you know the guy that interrupts your music with lines such as 'working out, want to listen to music uninterrupted by adverts? Then upgrade to Spotify premium'. I'm pleased to say there's been a 77 per cent spike in upgrade sales since I came onboard, which officially makes me the most annoying voice in the entertainment industry.

My ex girlfriend and I once booked a holiday to Salvador, Brazil, but got the wrong flight and ended up in El Salvador.

Picture taken Camden Comedy Club, London, October 2016

This Glorious Monster

Martin Collins, Adam Loxley, Daniel Hoffmann-Gill & Alex Finch *(not in the picture – he doesn't perform, only writes)*

We formed in London in 2012. Daniel and Martin are originally from Nottingham, Adam from Solihull and Alex from Hemel Hampstead.

Martin I was once the lead singer in a rock band but got too fat and bald to do it any more. I went bald at thirty.

Adam I find it hard to find love. I went bald at twenty-seven.

Daniel I have saved two people's life. Separately. I'm holding out with the baldness as best I can.

Picture taken We Are Funny Project, Dalston, London, October 2016

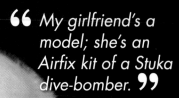

> **"** *My girlfriend's a model; she's an Airfix kit of a Stuka dive-bomber.* **"**

Alexei Sayle

I started at the Comedy Store, 1979.
I'm a professor.
I think I can speak Spanish.
My cat's called Wilf M'Banga.
I don't like kippers.

Picture taken
The Old Queen's Head,
London, October 2014

> **My boyfriend likes role play. He likes to pretend we're married. He waits until I've gone to bed, then he looks at porn and has a wank. 99**

In character as Nervous Woman

Joanna Neary

My first gig was at Clutching At Straws stand-up comedy night in Brighton in the late 1990s.

I collect books on How To Be Charming. i.e: *How To Get Out Of A Car Without Flashing Your Foo.*

I like pickled onions.

I went to art school for seven years. I think everyone should go, like a sort of National Service.

I played* bass with Blood Sausage for a while.

My first gig was supporting Sebadoh. * = can barely play

I wrote sixty-five folk songs and sang them at the Swan Inn Folk Night in Truro when I was twelve or thirteen.

Picture taken The Old Queen's Head, London, October 2014

> **"** Feel more powerful by digging a hole in the ground, burying your head in it and wearing the whole Earth as a giant mask. **"**

Louise Ashcroft

I started comedy in 2013, but I've been a performance artist for a while.

I co-founded the free art master's course AltMFA.

I have taken all the labels of the tin cans in my cupboards to make everyday life feel more unpredictable and wild.

Politically, I believe in Aristocro Marxism – for half the week everyone is a peasant farmer and the other half of the wee everyone is posh.

I don't like spiders but feel guilty killing them, so I transform them into regular insects by cutting two legs of

I like to take lots of ProPlus and Kalms simultaneously, so that they balance out and I feel intensely normal.

I agree with Arnold Schwarzenegger, who says that we should sleep faster in order to save time.

Picture taken
The Old Queen's Head, London,
October 2014

> *Some people wear glasses just for driving. Why don't they get the windscreen made up in their prescription?*

Paul Rogan

I started as part of the double act
The Sean Connery Brotherhood, and did
solo stand-up after that, building my first act
at a workshop in Brixton. My first twenty minute spot
I ended up closing because other acts were doubling up.
It was at the Guilty Pea. I recently played the Guilty Pea
again doing an improv show with my friend and former
Sean Connery Brother Phil Whelans.
I live in Los Angeles now, but really enjoy the 'water cooler'
that is Facebook for keeping in touch with the UK comedy
scene. I miss my London comedy mates.
I'm married with two kids, girls aged eleven and twelve.

Picture taken London, October 2014

Martin Austwick

I started comedy when Josie Long asked me to be in the house band for her comedy night, The Sunday Night Adventure Club, in 2004 or 2005. It was in a little bar in Crystal Palace.

I'm better known for *Answer Me This!*, the podcast my wife and her friend started in 2007, which I was asked to help with because I own some microphones.

I was born with a beard.

I have a PhD in Quantum Physics.

I once played drums with Nigel Kennedy.

I try to write the theme tune for every podcast I'm involved in, even if it's in a peripheral capacity.

I collect guitars. I have too many. My current favourite is a little parlour guitar. I am running out of space.

Picture taken The Old Queen's Head, London, October 2014

> **I didn't go to my Hypochondriacs Anonymous meeting last night. Too ill.**

Paul Lamb

I started comedy a year ago in Southend.
Have now gigged in London.
I was a cop for thirty-one years in Essex.
I was head boy of my school.
I can jiggle my eyes.
Tim Vine bought me a drink.
I once got locked in an electric toilet.

Picture taken Jokers, Westcliff-on-Sea, October 2014

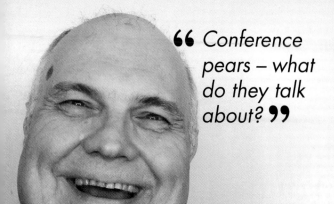

" *Conference pears – what do they talk about?* **"**

Mike McShane

I started in San Francisco.
I am a US Army Veteran 1973–1976.
I am a tree hugger. I actually have a picture of me at five years old, hugging a fucking tree.
I did phone sex for money when I was a young actor.
I used to grow pot in a forest and I slept inside of a tree.

> **66** *The way to a man's heart is through making an incision along the sternum.* **99**

Dalia Malek

I started stand-up in 2012 in London.

I was the first Dalia on Facebook.

I have a PhD in International Human Rights Law.

I cut off RuPaul while making an illegal U-turn in Hollywood and I still feel terrible about it.

I played Jan in my high school's production of *Grease* and got to eat a Twinkie on stage.

I interviewed Mohamed Morsi and then he became President of Egypt. He stopped talking to me and then got overthrown in a coup. Now he's in jail. 'Keep Dalia in your life' is the moral.

Picture taken Downstairs at the King's Head, Crouch End, London, October 2014

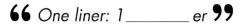

66 *One liner: 1 _____ er* **99**

Sonia Aste

I started comedy in 2012, after going through my
fourth redundancy (I've had four jobs).
I'm an engineer. What kind of an engineer?
After four redundancies, I guess not a very good one.
I can do a double backward somersault ending with a split.
This does not help in job interviews.
I'm the world's worst driver. I do not mention this at job interviews.

Picture taken
Monkey Business, Kentish Town,
London, October 2014

195

> **You know you're watching too much porn when you check your browser history and the pages are stuck together.**

George Zach

I did my first ever gig in Long Live Comedy,
an open mic night at the top of a pub in central
Newcastle, on St Patrick's Day in 2009.
I used to play poker for a living.
When I was twenty-four I spent seven months living on a lazy
boy armchair, successfully betting on football and failing my
year in university. I slept in my bed for the first time when
my long distance relationship visited for two weeks.
I'm barred for life from Morrissons in Byker, Newcastle.
Every time I visit the dentist I faint.
I found out I am circumcised at the age of twenty-eight.

Picture taken Downstairs at the King's Head, Crouch End, London, October 2014

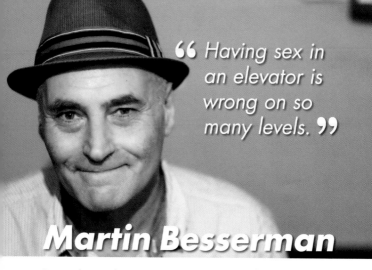

> **Having sex in an elevator is wrong on so many levels.**

Martin Besserman

I started comedy in 2002.
I used to sell net curtains in the market to sexually frustrated middle aged women.
An inspector stopped me from selling vibrators in East Street market saying they were sex aids.
I've spoken at Speakers corner on sex and politics since I was sixteen.
I am a vegetarian.
I worked next door to Jade Goody in East Street market.

I was in a film with Alexei Sayle.
I was the only support act for The Pretenders at Dingwalls in Camden and Depeche Mode as a comedy poet.
I got mugged in a Manchester hotel and was consoled by Alison Moyet.
I snogged Mike Rutherford's of Genesis daughter.
I got off with a girl Russell Brand brought to my club.

Picture taken Monkey Business, Kentish Town, London, October 2014

was a personal trainer for fifteen years and this required a lot of self discipline. I've reflected on all those years of self discipline and I realise… I just want to be fat. And move up North. And just be a fat Northern comic. Like in the '80s. **"**

Sheraz Yousaf

I started stand-up comedy in June 2012 in London. My first gig was on a variety night sandwiched between an act wearing a fake horse head reading a Dulux colour swatch, and a guy who did impressions of household appliances.

For three months last year I had to gig on crutches. I must have heard a funny reference to the fact I couldn't stand up to do stand-up at least four times a week.

Surprisingly enough, in thirty-eight years of being alive I certainly HAVE heard that my name may sound like a wine.

I got a GCSE grade A in Russian.

I played violin for a year at junior school.

At fifteen I went vegetarian for two weeks until I accidentally forgot and ate a burger.

Picture taken Downstairs at the King's Head, Crouch End, London, October 2014

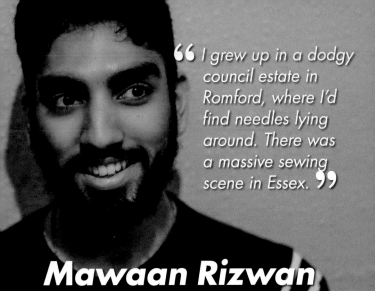

Mawaan Rizwan

I started comedy in 2012 in a sweaty pub in Leicester Square, London.
As a kid I was convinced that my baby brother was Satan.
Tie-dye shirts are my favourite thing to wear, after tie-dye dresses.
My name means 'the one who helps others' in Arabic. I'm actually a very selfish person, but only to be ironic.

Every day I do something stupid in public to experience failure, like asking a stranger for a tenner or requesting to take a pregnant lady's seat on a bus. I do it to build a thicker skin towards rejection. It's not quite working yet.
I got arrested once for twerking on a banker's lap in Canary Wharf.

Picture taken Monkey Business, Kentish Town, London, October 2014

199

> *The problem with trying to write jokes about skeletons is that very little of it is humerus.* "

Paul McGarrity

My first ever stand-up gig was at Ministry of Comedy at UCL in 2006, and it went so well I didn't do another one until 2009.

My day job before comedy was as a professional archaeologist. Hungover, I once fell asleep at the bottom of a grave.

I have broken every one of my fingers whilst playing rugby, despite this and several other injuries, I still play.

I hold a licence to drive a cherry picker for no real reason.

Picture taken Downstairs at the King's Head, Crouch End, London, October 2014

> **"** *The hardest thing about being an atheist cinephile is suspending your disbelief.* **"**

Sam Ely

My first handful of gigs were back in 2010 on nights that no longer run, but I picked it up again in earnest last April at Dirty Dicks. I'm in *The King's Speech* and once refused Cheryl Cole extra nacho cheese.

Picture taken
Monkey Business, Kentish Town, London, October 2014

> *I don't drive fast and that means I get in peoples' ways... Usually I'll just let them go but if they drive up fast, flashing their lights... I'll block their path for as long as I can then make this face as they pass.*

Clive Copeman

I'm an organised emailer so I've checked and I started comedy on the 16th of April 2012.
In 2014, I turned thirty-three.
I have a first class degree in Psychology.
After nearly dying in childbirth my mum always told me I was a miracle.
I've worked in administration now for nearly ten years.
A therapist recently analysed my dreams and identified the recurring theme in my subconscious as disappointment.

Picture taken Monkey Business, Kentish Town, London, October 2014

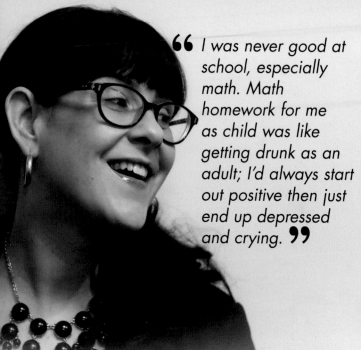

> **66** I was never good at school, especially math. Math homework for me as child was like getting drunk as an adult; I'd always start out positive then just end up depressed and crying. **99**

Allyson June Smith

I started in Calgary Alberta, Canada at Yuk Yuks Comedy Club, September 1st 2000.

I love B-rated horror movies.

My last meal if I was on death row would consist of salt and vinegar crisps and McDonald's french fries.

I used to be a teacher until I found out kids are smarter then me.

Picture taken Barnstormers, Leighton Buzzard, November 2014

> 66 *My girlfriend and I broke up due to creative differences. I thought I was creative, and she thought different.* 99

Phil Wang

I was seventeen. My school put on a comedy night. I signed up for a stand-up spot with a bunch of lifted material (I didn't know how comedy worked, I thought jokes were like songs). It went well enough for me to keep going (and write my own stuff).
I am obsessed with Batman. Just bloody love him. Have been my entire life. Comedy is just my favourite means of affording Batman merchandise.
I have a black belt in Shaolin, because I am a stereotype. And I want to be Batman.
My feet are size 12 (UK).
I have sung for the Bruneian Royal family.
I can tell the difference between Coke and Pepsi.

Picture taken Downstairs at the King's Head, Crouch End, London, October 2014

> **❝** *I used to have this job sticking my finger into these small animals that looked a bit like mice. I didn't get paid for it – it was vole-entry work.* **❞**

Marek Larwood

I started in 2002 at a terrible gig run by a bloke called PJ in Clapham.
I have invented a sport called Volfsball.
I'm a distant relative of famous 1930s English cricketer Harold Larwood.
I grew up on the Isle of Wight.
I was bald when I was born, had hair for a bit but am now bald again.

Picture taken King's Cross station, London, May 2016

> **I'm proud that my Bangladeshi cousins have proven to the Catholic Church that you can literally sink a whole country into the ocean if you don't use contraception.**

Eshaan Akbar

I started comedy in March 2014. My first circuit gig was at Dirty Dicks in Liverpool Street.
I have choreographed over fifty Bollywood dances.
I was a runner-up in the 1997 Young Environmentalist of the Year competition.
My first ever chat up line was aged sixteen and it was 'Will you dance the flamingo with me?' when I meant to say 'Flamenco'. I can't dance the Flamenco anyway.
I speak five languages fluently.
I came third in a five mile steeplechase in school.
Third from last.

Picture taken Rada, London, November 2014

> **"** *The one time I wore skinny jeans, a guy yelled, 'Take those jeans off, you look gay!' I said, 'I'll tell you what's gay, you asking me to take my jeans off.'* **"**

Wilson

I started comedy five years ago at a place called The Hob in Forest Hill, south London, which has closed down now.
I love motocross.
When I was about twenty-two I did a little bit of podium dancing for a nightclub.
I'm deaf in my left ear.
I hate olives.

Picture taken Venue 77, Ipswich, October 2016

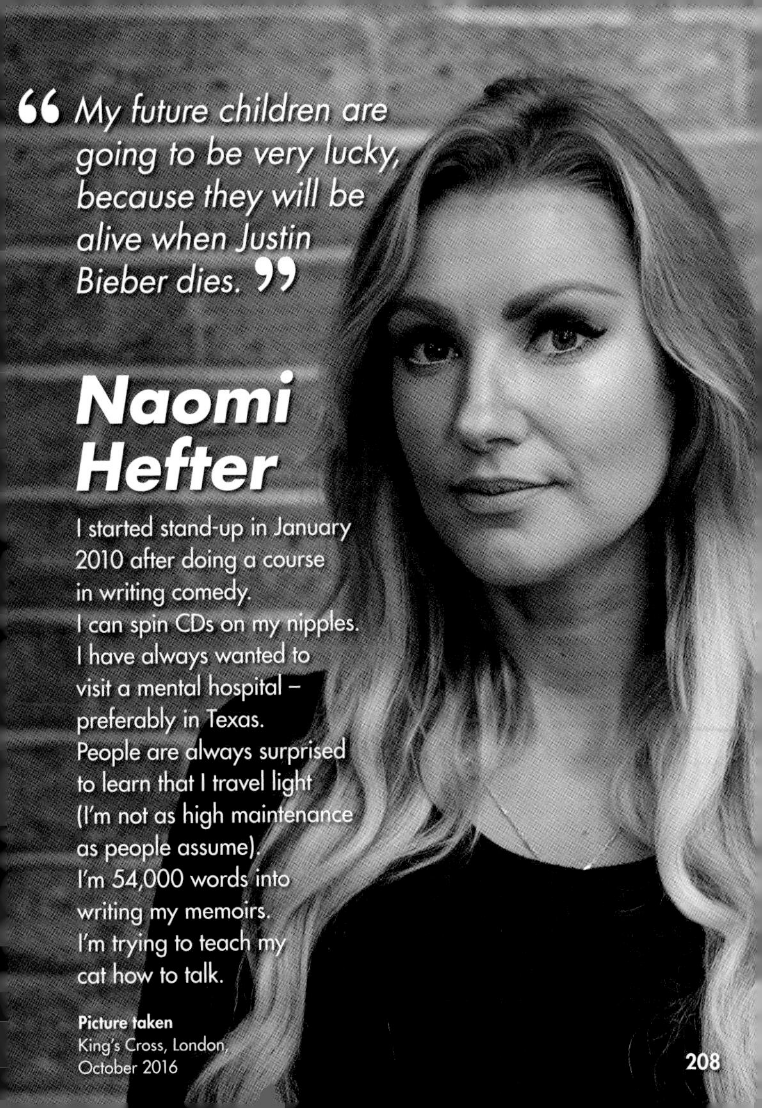

> **My future children are going to be very lucky, because they will be alive when Justin Bieber dies.**

Naomi Hefter

I started stand-up in January 2010 after doing a course in writing comedy.
I can spin CDs on my nipples.
I have always wanted to visit a mental hospital – preferably in Texas.
People are always surprised to learn that I travel light (I'm not as high maintenance as people assume).
I'm 54,000 words into writing my memoirs.
I'm trying to teach my cat how to talk.

Picture taken
King's Cross, London,
October 2016

" I was at a barbecue the other day and I bumped into an old friend of mine. I was just about to put a spoonful of food in my mouth. 'Hey Paul, how you doing, how's Rob?' Rob is a mutual friend. Paul said, 'Haven't you heard, Rob's dead.' Now the question I wanna ask you is what's the appropriate amount of time to wait before I can start eating? **"**

Roger D

I started stand-up in 1990 in London. I was the only comedian to win the infamous talent show the 291 Club. I was born in Ghana, West Africa of mixed parentage, my dad, Scottish, my mum is Ghanaian.
I was the north-west college table tennis champion in 1981.
I have three grandkids.
I'm also a plus size male model.

Picture taken
The Talbot Inn, Ripley,
May 2010

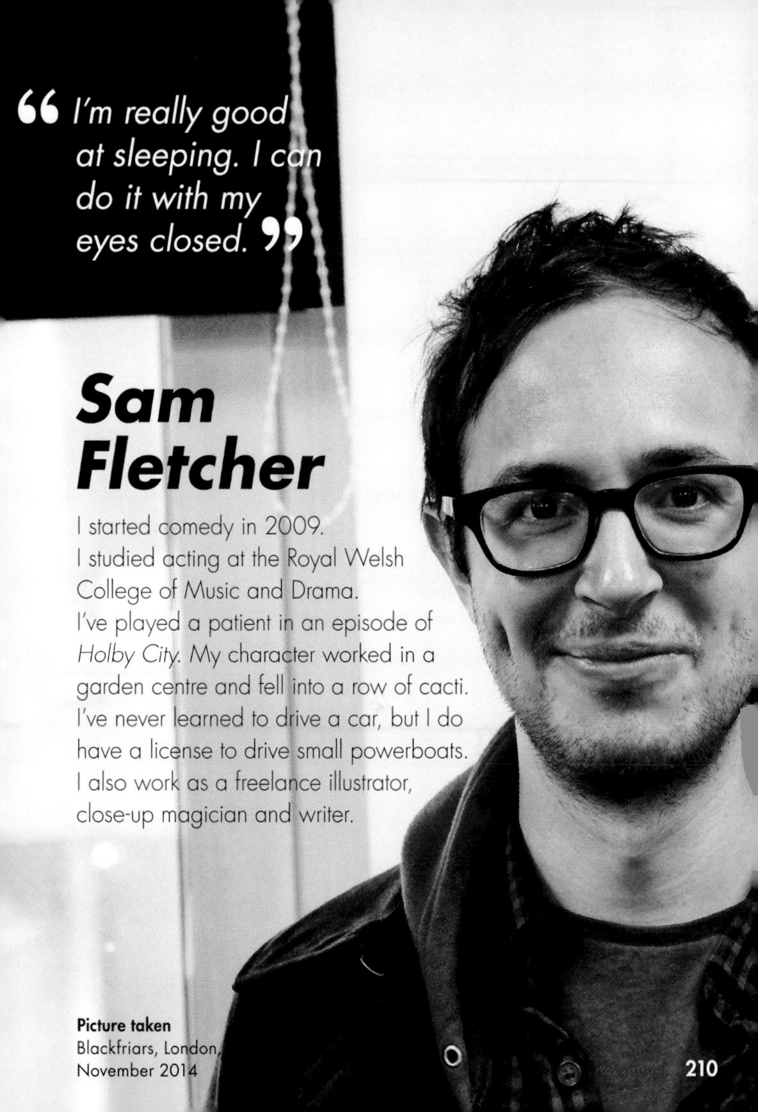

> *I'm really good at sleeping. I can do it with my eyes closed.* "

Sam Fletcher

I started comedy in 2009.
I studied acting at the Royal Welsh College of Music and Drama.
I've played a patient in an episode of *Holby City*. My character worked in a garden centre and fell into a row of cacti.
I've never learned to drive a car, but I do have a license to drive small powerboats.
I also work as a freelance illustrator, close-up magician and writer.

Picture taken
Blackfriars, London,
November 2014

210

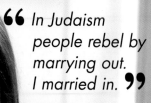

> **"** *In Judaism people rebel by marrying out. I married in.* **"**

Penelope Solomon

I did Jill Edwards' Stand-Up Comedy course at City Lit., then Drill Hall in 1997–1999. Jimmy Carr, Shappi Khorsandi and Jenny Colgan were all on the course with me.
My first acting job was in a play called *Song of Provence*. I got to play the French heroine called Arsule. My mother was delighted, she said, 'Penelope's got the main part, she's playing an arsehole.'

I was Head Girl at my primary school and Deputy Head Girl at my Secondary School.
I auditioned for the *X Factor* with a Yiddish song.
I love Wine Gums.
I used to teach English to refugees and asylum seekers.
I taught English for academic purposes at Queen Mary, University of London.

Picture taken The Gatehouse, Highgate, London, November 2014

211

> *When I'm dead I would simply like the word 'humble' to be written on my statue.*

Julian Deane

I started doing stand-up properly in 2007.
I have loads of kids.
I have an Australian passport.
I am a vegan.
I lie sometimes about being a vegan.

Picture taken RAF Leeming, November 2014

> 66 *Me and my ex-girlfriend were watching some Dutch pornography together one evening when she decided she wanted to re-enact it. So she went to Holland... I haven't seen her since!* 99

Lee Brace

I started performing comedy in 2003 where I attended weekly workshops in Leicester ran by the wonderful Anthony King.
My mother named me 'Lee' after Lee Majors from seventies series, *The Six Million Dollar Man*. It was lucky because my dad was a fan of Dick Van Dyke.
I have based my 'look' on my hero, Buddy Holly (before the crash!)
I have a deviated septum. Jealous?
I'm a massive fan of *Columbo*.

Picture taken Headliners, Chiswick, March 2015

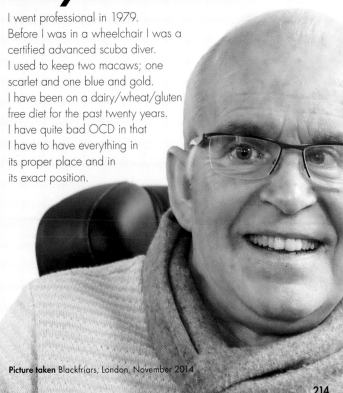

> **A lot of people say if they drink coffee they can't sleep. I'm the opposite, if I'm asleep, I can't drink coffee.**

Wayne Dobson

I went professional in 1979.
Before I was in a wheelchair I was a certified advanced scuba diver.
I used to keep two macaws; one scarlet and one blue and gold.
I have been on a dairy/wheat/gluten free diet for the past twenty years.
I have quite bad OCD in that I have to have everything in its proper place and in its exact position.

Picture taken Blackfriars, London, November 2014

❝ *My obsession with coloured feathers is dying down.* **❞**

Jake Lambert

Started comedy: London, March 2013.
I support Tottenham Hotspur Football Club.
I eat four bowls of cereal a day. Every day.
My favourite colour is green.
I started writing jokes under the Twitter pseudonym @LittleLostLad.

Picture taken Rada, London, November 2014

> **I've always found that when one door closes another door closes as well.**

Chris Neill

I was a radio/light entertainment producer at the BBC. I left in 2000. Linda Smith put me in her sitcom and I was on *Just a Minute*. I did a one-man show in Edinburgh before starting stand-up. First stand-up was in the autumn of 2006.

In Joe Allen's in New York, *Cagney And Lacey* actress Tyne Daly gathered every waiter around our table to hear me say 'blimey' in my London accent.

By the age of twenty I was the proud owner of all the albums Peggy Lee had ever released.

In 1982 I went to the World Cup with my dad. Rather than endure the boredom of watching football, I sat in the stands and read P.G. Wodehouse novels instead. Bizarrely it was still necessary for me to come out to my parents.

Picture taken Muswell Hill, London, March 2014

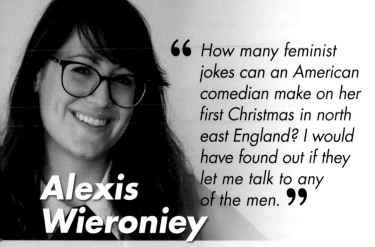

Alexis Wieroniey

> **"** *How many feminist jokes can an American comedian make on her first Christmas in north east England? I would have found out if they let me talk to any of the men.* **"**

My first stand-up gig was on 30th July 2012 in the Red Lion pub in Westminster.

I performed with a sketch group called the Errors of Comedy, in Ealing, for three years before that.

When I was fourteen I had a pet mouse that committed suicide by jumping and hitting its head repeatedly at the top of its cage.

I accidentally moved to the UK when I was twenty-two. I've now been here for ten years and I have citizenship and a passport and everything.

I once slipped on a leaf and fell all the way onto my bum in front of David Cameron.

We're the only family with my surname that we can find in the whole world. We think it's the product of a transcription mistake on a census record when my great grandparents moved to America from Poland.

I gave up wearing matching socks about three years ago. I just don't have time for that.

Picture taken Rada, London, November 2014

> **My father was surprisingly OK with me being gay. Turns out he had no problem with me picking up English guys, just so long as I didn't pick up their accent.**

Kyle Wallace

I started performing comedy just over two years ago, but have worked in the field before when around twenty years ago I worked full time for about eight years as a comedy magician/illusionist.

I have also written a comedy thriller called *Dial M for Mascara*, which got to number nine in Amazon's lesbian and gay fiction (I think they put it in that category because it was about a female impersonator who by accident becomes a serial killer).

Before comedy, for a while I was a scuba diving guide and instructor in Bali and the Maldives.

Picture taken Rada, London, November 2014

> *Men are like buses. Sometimes, when I'm depressed, I wish there was one on top of me.*

Stephanie Laing

I started in 2007 in Aberdeen, and have been gigging on and off since then.
I draw pictures of people's pets and children and dead relatives for money.
I once saw Chris Tarrant at Luton Airport.
I can do a kick-arse headstand.
I have a master's in Community Organising.
When I was twelve I wanted to be a stripper.

Picture taken Rada, London, November 2014

Karen Saich

My first gig was at Up the Creek in Greenwich, where the microphone stopped working half way through my set and I hated myself afterwards. I never meant to continue stand-up, but as a competitive perfectionist I had to carry on. I'm still striving for perfection!

I'm fifty and from south London I was brought up by my nan. All the men in my family died in a nine month period, when I was five, including my dad who committed suicide.

The most important things in life, for me, are the three 'H's'. Health, happiness and humour.

Picture taken Rada, London, November 2014

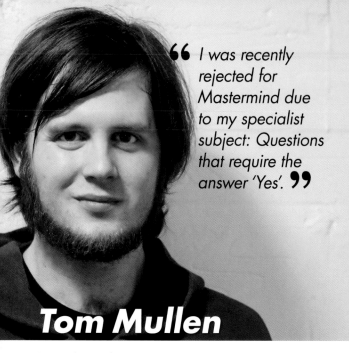

> **❝** I was recently rejected for Mastermind due to my specialist subject: Questions that require the answer 'Yes'. **❞**

Tom Mullen

I started comedy in Essex in 2012.
I work as an analytical chemist in the pharmaceutical industry (not animal testing before anyone asks).
I enjoy baking cakes for friends and family (handy for birthdays!).
I enjoy reading comics, recent favourites have been *Transmetropolitan*, *Chew* and *Battle Pope*.
I play bass in a heavy metal band, Greg(o)rian, and once did a gig while dressed as Abraham Lincoln on my twenty-fifth birthday.

Picture taken Rada, London, November 2014

> **Check you out with your four slice toaster. You live on your own. You need two at the most(er).**

Graham Goddard

My first attempt at being funny on stage was actually in Byron Bay, Australia at a hostel talent show in 2007. I stayed in that hostel for two months and made good use of the free stage. Looking back at that time reminds me of the Edfringe, but with a swimming pool.

I was awarded Cub of the Year in '89.

I have jogged three marathons.

I used to successfully drive unsuccessful bands around for a living.

At school I was told that if I have GCSE Drama on my CV I could get any job.

I have a GCSE in Drama.

Picture taken Rada, London, November 2014

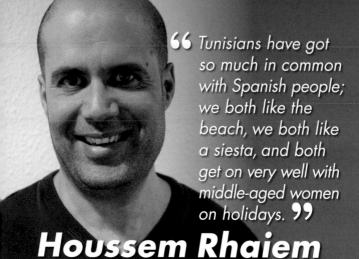

Tunisians have got so much in common with Spanish people; we both like the beach, we both like a siesta, and both get on very well with middle-aged women on holidays.

Houssem Rhaiem

I started comedy in 2009 in London. A critic once called me a slim Omid Djalili.

I'm from Tunisia. I've been in the country for eighteen years. I speak English, Arabic and French.

I pretend to be French at times, just to woo the ladies, and not for immigration purposes.

I'm an atheist. My mum and dad still don't know.

I work in mental health.

I find it difficult to have non comedian friends.

The best thing that ever happened to me is having my son. He's fifteen now and we are good friends. We chill together, play pool and I even help him work on his chat up lines. Last advice I gave him, 'My dad is a comedian,' is not a good chat up line.

Picture taken The Harlequin Theatre, Redhill, April 2016

> **There's not a lot of chance of me being pregnant as my eggs are now so far past the sell by date, I'm in danger of giving myself salmonella.**

Jo Public

My first proper comedy performance was in a school play, aged eleven, in High Wycombe. I started stand-up comedy about four years ago – I took a few 'gap' decades. Aged twelve I rode my boyfriend's racer bike down a hill, the brakes failed and I ended up impaled in the window of someone's front room – luckily they were on holiday!

I've only done one bungee jump ever but it was the highest bungee jump in the UK, 300ft off a crane over a reservoir near Maidenhead. I have no plans to repeat this experience.

I'm a PADI qualified scuba diver although I haven't dived since qualifying in Sharm El Sheik, as my Egyptian teacher was nasty and cruel and scarred me for life.

Picture taken The Laughing Pod, Piccadilly, London, November 2014

> **"** My worst fear about having a daughter is one day being sent a viral video clip of my daughter doing things my wife won't. **"**

Emmanuel Sonubi

I started comedy about a year ago now, just over.
However, I've been performing for ten years. I trained
in musical theatre and dance originally but since the
birth of my son I decided to quit and fell into comedy.
I'm the youngest of six kids and five sisters.
I'm scared to death of pigeons and now most birds
of equal size or bigger.
I gave the lead singer from Nickelback a wedgey
for not doing shots with me.

Picture taken The Laughing Pod, Piccadilly, London, November 2014

> **A person who examines three people says, 'I have three examinees'. A person who tests three people keeps a little quieter.**

Haiste and Lawrence

Marie I have a first class honours degree in dancing.
I fell and broke my nose on stage and carried on performing:
the audience thought the blood was all part of the theatrics.
When I was seven, I volunteered to play piano for the school
assembly as the music teacher was off sick. I neglected to
mention that I didn't in fact know how to play the piano.
It sounded some kind of awesome.
My parents used to tell me that I was from China. I'm not. They're
not. No one in my immediate family has even been to China.

Greg I do not have a first class honours degree in dancing.
I once caught a fish with my bare hands. I have yet to catch
a bear with my fish hands.
I once fell asleep watching *The Exorcist* in a cinema and
got locked in. I woke at 4 o'clock in the morning
and had to break out of the cinema like
some kind of renegade.
I have only broken two bones,
both whilst performing on stage.
NB they were my own bones.
As a student I had a ponytail
which I then chopped off and
still keep in a box somewhere.

Picture taken
Rada, London,
November 2014

> **Being single, sometimes I get lonely and go to the doctor to get a check-up. I just want someone to touch my boobs.**

Katharine Ferns

A comic friend dared me to go on stage to do stand-up for the first time. (When someone double-dares you to do something you have to do it.) I had one week to write five minutes of jokes and did my first open mic in Vancouver, Canada. I was so nervous I don't remember being on stage or what I said but I got booked to come back in two weeks. Then I started doing shows five nights a week when I should have been studying for my final exams at university. I was hooked. So I moved to Toronto to do stand-up and now London, all because of a dare.

I have a bachelor's in Fine Art with a major in Painting.

I was a sailor on a tall ship on the Atlantic ocean.

I used to live with nuns.

I have jumped out of a moving car that had lost its brakes.

I went skydiving to cure my fear of heights. It didn't work.

Picture taken The Laughing Pod, Piccadilly, London, November 2014

227

> **The government blew up my favourite abacus. All in the name of counter terrorism.**

Mike Sheldon

I first started performing in 2014 after joining the incredibly shambolic Monkey Wedding sketch group. About half a year later I branched out into stand-up and started doing torturous things to words. I live on a boat, which is pretty idyllic, but does mean that I basically go to the toilet in a plastic box. I've got a Ph.D. in artificial intelligence and robotics. I'm hoping this will be enough to save me when the machines take over.

One of my side projects caused me to be contacted on two separate occasions by an Amazon executive and a law firm representing Amazon, both asking me to please stop (I didn't). Amazon later tried to recruit me (unsuccessfully). When I was nineteen I got a bemused phone call from the head of the German government's IT department, when some software I was working on mistakenly sent him 3,000 emails in the space of a minute. My GCSE level German had not equipped me for this.

Picture taken We Are Funny Project, Putney, London, April 2016

Billy Miles

I started comedy when I was seventeen in Southend, Essex. When I was born I had some of my bowel removed and now have a pretty odd scar going across my stomach. When in Barcelona I drunkenly fell from a coach and gashed my head up but still managed to get into the club with blood dripping down my face.
I love wrestling (WWE).
I can play the drums.

Picture taken The Laughing Bod, Piccadilly, Leeds – November 2014

> **I used to be really fat... I was so fat that my friends stopped taking the piss out of me and they just got genuinely concerned.**

Darrell Skipper

My first ever gig was about five years ago after I completed a comedy course run by Amused Moose for 'Absolute and Almost Beginners'. My first laugh was after I said two words; 'Custard tarts'. I thought that was quite an impressive words to laughs ratio for a beginner.

I only did about twenty gigs after that then gave it up. I didn't get back into it until March 2014, I've been gigging consistently since.

I did actually used to be really fat, twenty stone at my heaviest. I lost it all over two to three years... Well, not ALL of it. That would be mental. About seven stone of it. I have two cats imprisoned in my second floor flat and I feel guilty every day that they don't have a garden to run around in. One day, my children, one day.

I've been with my girlfriend for ten years. It took me two years prior to that to convince her to go out with me. Who's the loser now, hey, Sarah? I'm in a book! Look!

My dad used to regularly hold me and my brother down and fart on our heads. My dad's farts have smelt the same since 1991.

Picture taken The Laughing Pod, Piccadilly, London, November 2014

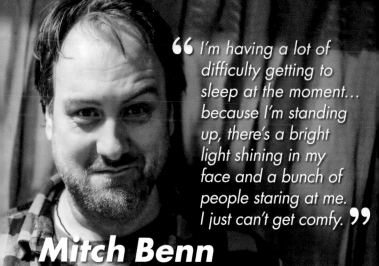

> 66 I'm having a lot of difficulty getting to sleep at the moment... because I'm standing up, there's a bright light shining in my face and a bunch of people staring at me. I just can't get comfy. 99

Mitch Benn

I started in Montréal, Canada, summer of 1991. LONG story.
I went to the same primary school as John Lennon and George Harrison (albeit thirty years later).
My last proper acting job was in BBC's *Merlin*. I played a bandit captain. I got two lines and an 'Aaaaargh'.
I learned double bass at primary school for the sole reason that the school had acquired one from somewhere and I was the only pupil tall enough to play it.
At Edinburgh University I was in a band with Ralph and Joseph Fiennes' cousin and the guy who would go on to invent *Grand Theft Auto*.
I had a couple of body parts permanently surgically removed at the age of fifteen. I leave it to you to guess which ones.

Picture taken The Laughing Pod, Piccadilly, London, November 2014

Sajeela Kershi

I did a course at my local theatre just after 9/11. I got paid £50 for my first gig – then I did a gig at The House of Commons. I died on my hole. I never did comedy again till 2005 when I did the Amused Moose course. I'm multi-lingual – used to speak five languages.

Together with family members I was held hostage by a terrorist group whilst attending a wedding in Karachi. I was three months pregnant at the time.

I gave birth to my son without any pain relief. I wouldn't do that again.

I have hygiene OCD, and other irrational fears and phobias, like having photos of me in the public domain. I believe in the evil eye, so I hope no one who hates me comes across this picture and curses me!

For over two years I've been suffering from severe vertigo, which not only affects my balance but leaves me visually impaired. On stage it just looks like I've had one too many drinks.

I've been kissed by Omar Shariff, Elton John and bitten by a member of The Cure.

Picture taken Edinburgh Festival, August 2016

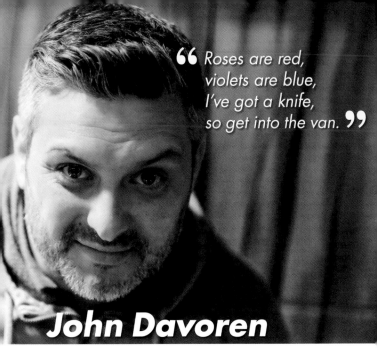

> 66 *Roses are red,*
> *violets are blue,*
> *I've got a knife,*
> *so get into the van.* 99

John Davoren

I started comedy three years ago (2011) at The Comedy School. My first gig was my graduation gig at the Pirate Castle in Camden Town.
I once worked in a bingo hall (that's all I have to say about that).
I'm not vain.

I'm really good looking.
I like spicy food but can't eat it due to IBS.
I was on the ITV show *Man O Man* back in 1998 (hosted by Chris Tarrant).
Somebody told me once that I am related to the guy who invented the typewriter.

Picture taken The Laughing Pod, Piccadilly, London, November 2014

> **"** *Do real ghosts find Halloween patronising?* **"**

Grainne Maguire

I started comedy in 2006.
My first gig was on a barge
called the Wibbly Wobbly Boat.
You knew your time was up when
the MC walked slowly up the central
aisle through the audience making
a T with his hands. I got off stage and
my friend who had came along said,
'Well done. You were so "you" on stage!'
I was horrified. I wanted to be so
Dylan Moran on stage.
I can make balloon animals.
Martin Sheen once said that I sounded
like a cool person.
My sister used to be the mayor
of the town I'm from.
I lie about being able to
play the spoons to impress
people but really I can't.
I was born with six fingers
on my left hand.

Picture taken
The Bloomsbury Theatre, London,
April 2015

234

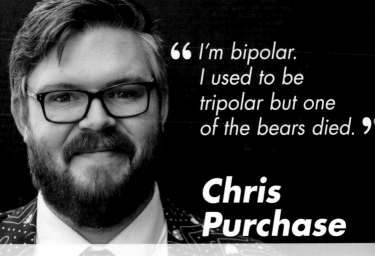

**" I'm bipolar.
I used to be
tripolar but one
of the bears died. "**

Chris
Purchase

I started comedy in August 2009 at the Sno! Bar in Milton
Keynes. I was a radio presenter writing and performing comedy
sketches and another presenter asked me and my co host to do
stand-up in a charity show with two pros. In the end the pros
and host dropped out leaving me and my co host to do forty
minutes each at our first gig.

I used to have a photographic memory until I fell down the
stairs aged nineteen. The only thing I still retain is the theme
track to every TV show I watched before the accident.

I love video games and always have a handheld console on me.

I was a contender on the first series of *Robot Wars* (and met
Phillipa Forrester and Jeremy Clarkson).

I'm manic depressive (bipolar).

I played trombone until I was in a cycling accident
and cut the tendons in my right arm.

Picture taken Brewdog Pub (on his stag do), Soho, London, May 2016

> " A scourge is going round the country of a 'singles table' at weddings, where the couple getting married think that their love will spread to that table and they'll all fall in love with each other. It's bullshit. A singles table at a wedding is a lucky dip of losers! "

Paul Revill

My first gig was in St Albans after completing a six week comedy course in 2010.
I met my girlfriend of three years at my Edinburgh show in 2013. She was in the second row.
I sold the most amount of Hugo Boss fragrance in the UK during Christmas 2009.
I have not drunk alcohol, smoked cigarettes or taken drugs since 2008.
I drive a Ford Fiesta Titanium 1.6TDCI… player!

Picture taken Brewdog Pub (on Chris Purchase's stag do), Soho, London, May 2016

> **66** I used to work on a maternity ward but the matron told me I just wasn't delivering. **99**

Paul Dean-Kelly

Started comedy 2015.
Day job: voice-over artist.
Part time: storyboard artist and photographer.
From: Liverpool.
Degree: fine art.

Picture taken We Are Funny Project, Putney, London, April 2016

> **Other people's children are unbearable aren't they? In retrospect I should never have adopted.**

Tom Hensby

I have been performing sketch and improv for years, but my first proper stand-up gig was at the Up The Creek Comedy Club in Greenwich, July 2014. It was The Blackout on a Thursday night, when the audience can boo off acts they don't like. As an act you have to survive five minutes without the lights going out on you. I beat the 'Blackout' on my first time, which was a huge relief because I am still afraid of the dark.

I'm the son of an East Midlands mushroom farmer.

I once worked in the Stilton cheese factory in Melton Mowbray.

I met my soon-to-be wife in a Brighton Fringe theatre that had a defective fire alarm.

I am a qualified journalist and can still write shorthand at 100 words per minute.

Picture taken The Comedy Pub, Piccadilly, London, November 2014

> **"** *Certain illnesses are made up. They didn't exist hundreds of years ago. Nobody in 12 Years A Slave had Restless Leg Syndrome.* **"**

Gina Yashere

I started comedy in 1995. My first two gigs were at a little arts centre in Camberwell. Can't remember the name, but it's long gone. And Cosmic Comedy Club in Hammersmith, also long gone, where I did a open mic competition, and was beaten into second place by Lee Mack.

I'm a motorbike enthusiast. My last bike was a Triumph Speed Triple.

I am a germaphobe. I bring my own bed sheets, towels, pillow and slippers to hotel rooms.

I'm terrified of spiders. I hope a serial killer doesn't use this to torture me before he kills me. Actually, I LOVE spiders… (for any serial killers reading).

I am a qualified engineer. I worked for British Telecom wiring phone lines, and my last job before comedy was with Otis, building and repairing lifts.

I used to be in a dance group, and was a pretty good body popper when I was a teenager.

Picture taken The Red Imp Comedy Club, Walthamstow, London, December 2014

> 66 Me and my boyfriend broke up after an argument over which pronoun is best. He said 'It's not you, it's me.' 99

Mark Cram

I started 25th February 2010: Northampton University's Got Talent. I was beaten by a juggler, among other things.
I'm deathly afraid of polystyrene.
Mark Cram backwards is pronounced exactly the same.
I'm allergic to chlorine – not allowed to swim in swimming pools.

Picture taken The Railway, Sutton Coldfield, November 2014

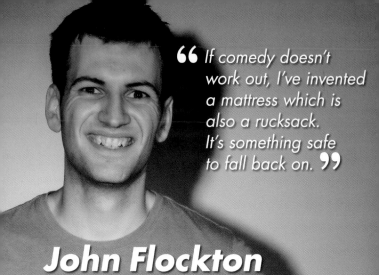

> **"** If comedy doesn't work out, I've invented a mattress which is also a rucksack. It's something safe to fall back on. **"**

John Flockton

I started back in university, writing for the sketch group, WitTank. They graduated way ahead of me though, so for a few years I didn't do any comedy at all. Officially, I'd say I've only picked it back up in the last year (2014).

I did a Theology degree at university, despite being a complete atheist. I think this could be part of the reason I got an overall mark of 66.6.

I once played bass in an eighties hair-metal covers band.

When I was a teenager, I worked as a magician for kids' parties. I went under the stage name Professor Magic.

I've got the hairiest back of any clothes-wearing mammal.

There's no better town than Hull. (That's more of a general fact though.)

Picture taken The Comedy Pub, Piccadilly, London, November 2014

> **When I stay over at my girlfriend's parents', her dad won't let us sleep in the same bed. So I have to sleep with my girlfriend instead.**

Matthew Crosby

My first 'proper gig' was at the Wheatsheaf in Rathbone Place for Ivan the Comedy Ref. He gave me two minutes stage time. I still ran under.

I was an extra in the movie *Shakespeare in Love*. They didn't give me any lines because that would involve paying extra but, when I went to see the film, they'd got someone to dub me saying, 'Hello Will!' in a high-pitched voice.

For most of my twenties the only socks I wore were white sports socks.

I interviewed rugby player Victor Ubogu for the school newspaper when I was sixteen. I don't really watch sport. My opening question was 'Who are you?' He thought that was quite deep; truth was – I just didn't know who he was.

My uncle was the mechanic for Matt and Luke Goss of Bros.

Before I was a comedian I was a teacher. The head of music was a member of the Flying Pickets.

Picture taken The Comedy Pub, Piccadilly, London, November 2014

> *Ann Summers is weird, upstairs is all fluffy handcuffs and chocolate willies. Downstairs; well, someone is gonna get hurt.*

Jason Manford

Jason started at The Buzz Club in Chorlton, 1999.

Jason has a Bronze Duke of Edinburgh Award.

Jason worked at the school library as a kid so he wouldn't be on the playground to get bullied (ironically it got him bullied more!).

Jason has five children so if he looks knackered, just keep it to yourself, yeah?

Jason is a qualified FA referee but hasn't referred a game since 2003.

Jason is an expert in writing in the third person.

Picture taken RADA London, May 2016

243

> **In Australia cricket is probably our second favourite national past time. But our favourite past time happens at every cricket match, which I'm sure you can guess. Racism. Correct. So it's been an interesting time living in the UK as the proud... New Zealander that I am.**

Felicity Ward

I started sketch comedy, at a university I wasn't attending, in 2004. I started stand-up, while I was a tour manager, in 2008.
I'm afraid of Ferris wheels.
The front six teeth in my mouth have false caps on them.
My mother's name is Trevalyn.
I studied Japanese in high school for four years, and I only really remember how to say 'It wasn't warm yesterday.'
My family nickname is 'Spiller', and I have a lot of stained clothing.

Picture taken Leytonstone, London, December 2014

244

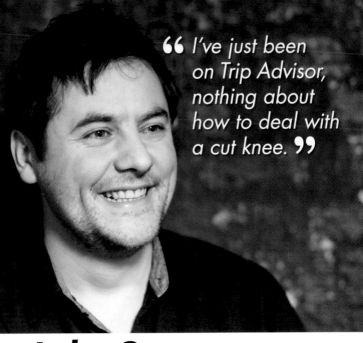

> 66 I've just been on Trip Advisor, nothing about how to deal with a cut knee. 99

Luke Graves

I started in Reading, 2008.
I once worked as a pheasant farmer.
After being dumped by a girl at school, I got revenge
by ringing up a radio station and pretending to be
her new boyfriend.
I have named all the squirrels in my garden.
I managed to get my wallet stolen twice in one night in Vietnam.

Picture taken King's Head, Crouch End, London, December 2014

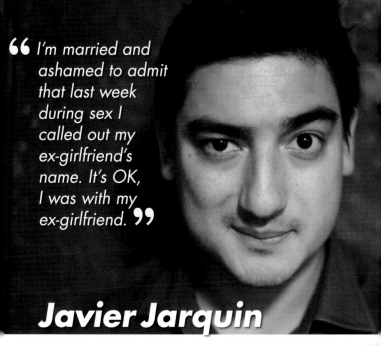

> **I'm married and ashamed to admit that last week during sex I called out my ex-girlfriend's name. It's OK, I was with my ex-girlfriend.**

Javier Jarquin

I did my first gig in Christchurch, New Zealand in 2000. Next one was 2001 – to give you an idea of the size of the scene!

I have a Computer Science degree (which I'm not currently using AT ALL).

I used to have an American accent.

I punched a teacher in the stomach in high school. I was let off because he started it.

I was part of a duo that did acrobatic lip syncing to swing music. We came second in a talent competition to Hayley Westenra.

Picture taken Downstairs at the King's Head, Crouch End, London, September 2014

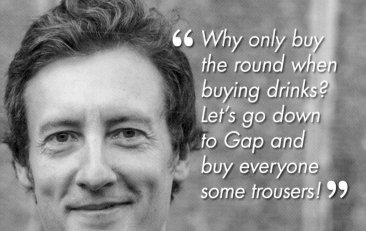

> 66 *Why only buy the round when buying drinks? Let's go down to Gap and buy everyone some trousers!* 99

Stan Stanley

It's a complete cliché how I started in comedy – in the classroom as the class clown running around with the bin on my head to impress Miss Baldwin.
I have been a life-long member of the Airfix Modellers Club and make fibre optic sci-fi models.

I once carried my pet chameleon, Duncan, on the National Express.
I'm actually Andrew Stanley but another comic is called that so I had to change.
I can burp the word 'supercalifragilistic-expialidocious'.

Picture taken The Southbank, London, May 2016

66 *I can't tell my arse from your elbow.* **99**

Nina Conti

My first gig was at the Banana in Balham.
I studied philosophy.
I'm allergic to nuts.
I love bungee jumps.

Picture taken The Hilton, Edgware Road, May 2016

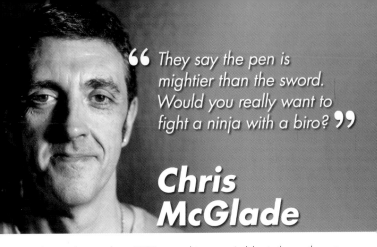

> *They say the pen is mightier than the sword. Would you really want to fight a ninja with a biro?*

Chris McGlade

I started comedy in 1988 in working mens' clubs in the north east. I streaked at Wembley in 1997 to tell a girl I loved her. I ended up winning a national competition and sent a lady in a wheelchair and her family to Disneyland as a result.

I stood as MP in the 2005 general election. I came fourth with 2,379 votes and was seventh highest fourth place in that general election.

In 2010, I got talking to a stranger who sat next to me on a Tube train in London. Unbeknown to me, he was a top West End agent who called in a favour and as a result, I landed a main part in *Billy Elliot the Musical* in the West End, when I had no theatrical training whatsoever.

Halfway through my contract, my dad was murdered at home. He was strangled to death and then set on fire. But despite being devastated, I forgave dad's killer and was back in the show a week later.

Picture taken Camden, London, November 2014

> *My life has been quite sad, from an early age I was diagnosed with the 'BIG C'... dyslexia!*

Nick Clarke

I first got into comedy in 2011. My first gig was at the Mac Theatre in Birmingham. Although I was very nervous I smashed it. I was to soon realise that stand-up was nowhere near as easy as my first gig. I have worked as a bodyguard looking after people such as Jimmy White, and Angie McCartney (Paul McCartney's mom). I once was in Las Vegas at Mike Tyson's fortieth birthday party and I told the security staff that the friend I was with was a premier league football player (he wasn't at all), but ended up getting more coverage than Mike Tyson.

I had to appear in court for driving without insurance (I didn't know I didn't have any. The insurance company canceled without telling me). But I sacked my solicitor because he was adamant I should plead guilty, so I represented myself and the district judge threw the case out of court.

I won the 2014 Sky Poker UK bracelet event.

I have been studying nutrition for twenty years and in 2014 I wrote a diet that anyone can follow to lose one stone in a month.

> **My mum's had four kids, and you can tell that she stopped caring after the first two. She says she was blessed with me, gifted with my sister, then she had my brother, and she'll always remember when she was diagnosed with the other.**

Daniel Sloss

Velvet, moths and frosted glass
freak me the fuck out.
I was on *Robot Wars*,
like three times.
I own a life-size replica of
a Velociraptor.
I have a slight obsession with
The Joker from the *Batman* comics.

Picture taken
The Albert Hall, London,
December 2014

> **"** *I think the worst way to die would be falling down an up escalator until you starved to death.* **"**

Kai Humphries

I started comedy on 22nd October 2008. My first gig was at The Hyena in Newcastle on a new material night that Gavin Webster was running.

When I was nineteen I saved the life of a man who had a heart attack by shocking him with a defibrillator and performing CPR.

I've been trampled by bulls, beaten up by doormen, been through a car window and pulled out of the North Sea after a jet ski accident. But I've never broken a bone.

When I was in secondary school I spent most Friday evenings on after school detention with my teacher that happened to be Ross Noble's mum.

My personal best running 10km is 37m 46s.

I can complete a Rubick's cube whilst telling jokes.

Picture taken The Albert Hall, London, December 2014

252

> **Margaret Thatcher had six strokes and still she wouldn't lean to the left.**

John Scott

I started in 1999 at The Stand in Edinburgh. I did a six week workshop and then a few weeks later I was offered a ten minute slot on a Fringe show.

I've got gypsy heritage on both sides of my family.

This beard is dyed. I'm actually all grey.

I'm going to university at the age of forty-six, studying drama and script writing.

I used to be in a sketch show with Miles Jupp. I was Doctor Watson to his Sherlock Holmes.

I was an extra in the Michael Fassbinder version of *Macbeth*. I played an English soldier invading Scotland and on the day of filming I literally had to climb over Hadrian's wall and invade my own country.

My bedroom, between the ages of thirteen and sixteen, was like a shrine to David Bowie.

Picture taken King's Cross, London, April 2016

> *I used to go to an all girls school where you had to do an IQ test – if it came back negative... you got in.*

Helen Lederer

I started at the Pentameters Comedy Club compered by Arnold Brown in Hampstead.
Then at the Comedy Store (rarely) in 1988.
I like fabric a lot.
I like wine a lot.
I am plump aware. And have not developed a passion for being out of breath.
Double-jointed in thumb.
Like quizzes and charades.

Picture taken Kensington, London, May 2016

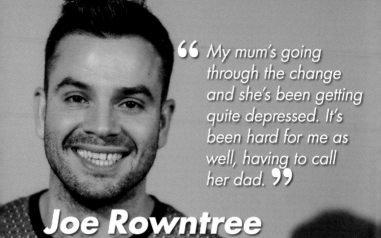

> **❝** My mum's going through the change and she's been getting quite depressed. It's been hard for me as well, having to call her dad. **❞**

Joe Rowntree

I worked behind the bar at Up the Creek in Greenwich when I was a seventeen-year-old student. I plucked up the courage to do a five minute open spot at the infamous Sunday night with the legendary Malcolm Hardy compering. He introduced me as: 'The next guy coming on works behind the bar so he's probably going to be shit, put your hands together for Joe Rowntree.' He was right on both accounts.

I worked in a circus when I was fourteen as a ring boy. I can juggle tennis rackets. I have a class three jaw. Neanderthalic in appearance with a huge overbite. My party trick when drunk is to swallow whole eggs. My record is four. I used to write put downs for Anne Robinson on *The Weakest Link*. I can memorise a pack of cards in under two minutes. I have run three marathons.

Picture taken Leytonstone, London, December 2014

> **People say you are what you eat, so where does Katie Hopkins buy her boxes of arseholes?**

Abi Roberts

I started stand-up comedy in 2011.
I was a finalist in the Costa Light
Comedy Competition at the
Comedy Store.
I speak fluent Russian. I'm the first UK comic
to do stand-up in Russian and English.
I trained as an opera singer.
I share my birthday with Marilyn Monroe.
I'm a massive fan of the TV quiz *Pointless*.

Picture taken King's Head, Crouch End, London, December 2014

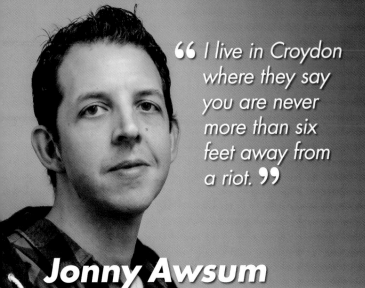

> **❝** *I live in Croydon where they say you are never more than six feet away from a riot.* **❞**

Jonny Awsum

I started comedy in 2011 after working on the bar at The Chuckle Club in London.

I once took Kalms herbal pills to relax me on a driving test; I was so relaxed I drove down a no entry street.

I was taken hostage in an armed robbery. After tying me up and waving a gun in my face one of the gunmen apologised to me for taking a call on his phone.

I grew up in a tiny Derbyshire village called Barrow Upon Trent; if you've never been there it's a bit like the Shire in *Lord of the Rings*.

I used to be able to draw a perfect shamrock on a pint of Guinness, or a cock depending on the customer.

Picture taken The Crown Hotel, Chertsey, December 2014

> **❝** I love running outdoor village festivals, some call it destiny, I call it fete. **❞**

Nick Root

I started comedy two years ago.
I got sacked from Disney for having sex with Mickey Mouse in public.
I work as a film extra and have appeared in over fifty films.
I based my stage name (Nick Root) on an old Tim Vine joke.

Picture taken
The Crown Hotel, Chertsey,
December 2014

258

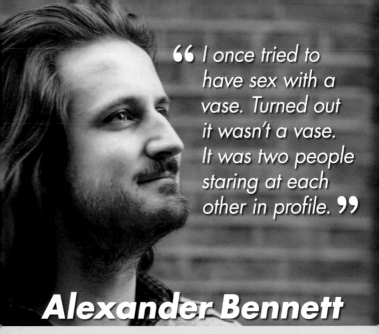

> **"** I once tried to have sex with a vase. Turned out it wasn't a vase. It was two people staring at each other in profile. **"**

Alexander Bennett

I started comedy in the Midlands when I was fifteen (2008).
Unless you're industry reading this, in which case I started
four months ago and am barely trying.
I once woke up in a field with a broken leg. I have no
recollection of how this happened.
I was once threatened with a knife at a gig. Good heckle.
I had a stutter as a child through nervousness.
Now overcompensating through false arrogance.
Me and my friends from my home town hold an
awards ceremony for ourselves every Christmas.

Picture taken Soho Comedy Club, London, May 2016

> 66 *Favourite gag is the one about the Dalmatian puppies... dodgy punchline, but the delivery is spot on.* 99

Chris Ashton

I played in a brass band in my teens.
I had an enormous toy soldier collection as a small child.
I have thrown a 180 at darts, in a pub that is now an Indian restaurant.
I went to Australia in September 2015 with the Great Britain Masters rugby league squad (the over-thirty fives team).

Picture taken Ex-servicemen's club, Slough, December 2014

> **" I know I don't look it, but I'm an immigrant... "**

Radu Isac

I started comedy in Bucharest, Romania in October 2006.
After eleven years I still have my high school graduation suit.
I wear it to every event where it's mandatory to come in a suit.
In my childhood I went to a lot of chess and maths competitions
and won a bunch of prizes. I still remember fondly missing
a lot of school because of them.

In this order I was involved in two car accidents, two motorcycle
accidents and a bicycle one. Most of them were my fault.
I had my first proper beer in a bar when I was ten years old.
I've never brushed my teeth more than once a day. And
last year a girl who'd had a lot of plastic surgeries
complimented me on them.

Picture taken Soho Comedy Club, London, May 2016

> **" I went speed dating the other night, it was really good. I left the house at six and I was home by five past. "**

Mandy Muden

My first gig was at the King's Head.
I once got stopped by the police going through two red lights and stopping at a green light.
I have got a gold medal in Disco Dancing.
When I was twelve I skived school with my friend and Jimmy Savile stopped in his Rolls Royce and offered us a lift.

Picture taken Piccadilly, London, January 2015

> **"** *I grew up just south of London. I got a lot of abuse while I was growing up. Racial abuse, NOT sexual abuse. We weren't that far south!* **"**

Jason Kavan

I first started comedy in November 2003. I was last on in a packed room at Pear Shaped Comedy Club. I did a three minute set and couldn't believe people were laughing at stuff I'd written. I was hooked.

At seven I got to perform with Yul Bryner in *The King and I* at The London Palladium. I hope one day I get to go back and perform there again. It's not going that well so far...

My seven-year-old daughter calls me 'Toucan' because she says I have a big nose. It genuinely upsets me but I laugh it off. I'm being bullied in my own home.

I'm in love with my George Foreman grill. I have tried multiple attempts at cooking an egg on it which have never ended well.

I once bought Beyoncé concert tickets on Gumtree as a gift to my goddaughter but they turned out to be fakes and she was turned away at the door. I did eventually get legit tickets so it ended well for her, not for my wallet.

Picture taken King's Head, Crouch End, London, December 2014

> " I find religion confusing. A couple of weeks ago in Leicester Square I saw a woman in a full burka, sitting, having a portrait done. Not just any portrait, it was a caricature! "

Stephen DiPlacito

My first gig was in December 2011, it was the only gig I did in December 2011. It was at The Cavendish Arms in Stockwell. I had a routine about *The Muppets* that relied on them being known but living off past glory years; their big movie come back in 2012 screwed that up. I now hate *The Muppets*!

I like extreme sports where being overweight isn't a disadvantage. I love skiing and scuba diving because you can get clothes and equipment in XXL.

I saved the family dog when I was fifteen from drowning, my reward was to be bitten and a tetanus jab. I swore at the dog, my mum took the dog's side.

I used to be a maths teacher which I gave up for one simple reason – I wasn't any good at it.

My wife and I have been together for twenty-five years; I have no material about relationships or dating as a result.

Picture taken The Crown Hotel, Chertsey, December 2014

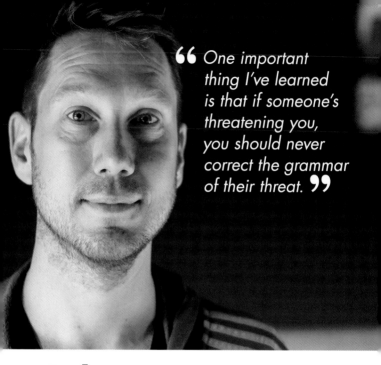

> **One important thing I've learned is that if someone's threatening you, you should never correct the grammar of their threat.**

Toby Brown

I started comedy in 2008 after doing a few best man speeches and enjoying them when everyone assumed I'd hate it.

I've been to Mongolia (underwhelming).

I wish I could sing.

I disgust myself when no one is looking.

I have no sense of shame.

Picture taken Q Ball Snooker Club, Basildon, October 2014

> **"** *I'm half Irish Catholic, half German Jewish. Every time I see Liam Neeson in a film he's leading my people to freedom.* **"**

Meryl O'Rourke

My first gig was at the Downstairs at the King's Head Irish comedy night. In those days they alternated Irish and Jewish comedy on Tuesdays. I'm half Jewish, so my second gig was at the Jewish comedy night the following week.

My husband is a jazz musician who hates comedy. I hate jazz.

I was in a Heinz baby food commercial when I was two months old. Playing a boy.

I was the TV face of Rubella immunisation aged twelve. When I met the patron, Princess Diana, she said, 'See, I'm nothing special.'

My left upper canine has grown sideways.

My daughter is unusually small for her age, my son unusually tall. Me and my husband are average height.

I've lived in Brixton Hill my entire life.

I was due to become a child star spearheading adverts for a new hot chocolate in 1983. At the shoot it was discovered that the chocolate didn't dissolve in water, so the product was scrapped.

I am very sensitive to drugs and have to be prescribed a child's dose of any medication.

Picture taken Piccadilly, London, January 2015

> **❝** When my daughter was born she came out blonde; I didn't work nine months to make a kid everyone thinks I'm the nanny of. **❞**

Ria Lina

1st gig: my second year at St Andrews Uni (1998).
2nd gig: my third year at St Andrews Uni (1999).
3rd gig: my first year at UCL Uni (2000). But UCL is in London, so a comic was born.
I have a Ph.D. in Herpes viruses (but who doesn't these days?).
I used to work for the Serious Fraud Office as an IT Forensic Investigator.
I've made three people with my body (they all got out alive).
I'm married to a man twenty years older than me. I thought he had money. He doesn't.

Picture taken Piccadilly, London, January 2015

> **I've got a tattoo on my chest of Che Guevara. Honestly, the money I've saved on T-shirts.**

James Sherwood

My first gig was at Brunel University in Uxbridge in 2002. But I tend to date things from the car journey home.

I once sang the *University Challenge* theme tune on a BBC2 documentary.

My great-grandfather scored the winning goal in the 1914 Amateur FA Cup Final.

I only like cheese melted.

If the members of Elbow lined up in decreasing order of how much they look like me, Guy Garvey would be at the front, and Pete Turner at the back.

Picture taken Uxbridge, December 2014

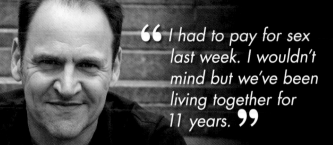

> **❝** I had to pay for sex last week. I wouldn't mind but we've been living together for 11 years. **❞**

Geoff Whiting

I did my first ever gig as part of a national new act competition (The Open Mic Award) on 11th March 1997 at Bath Spa University.

I played in several bands in the 1980s and one of them, called Strange Arrangement, featured on an album called *Chart Attack* which reached number seven in the national album charts in October 1982, selling 140,000 copies.

I was the under-sixteens Surrey District Schools champion at both the 100 and 200 metre sprint and I then ran against Lindford Christie at the under-eighteens Surrey Schools final in Croydon. He beat me.

I took and passed grade 6 Trumpet at the age of thirteen and used to play in a local orchestra.

I acted in a school production of *My Fair Lady* in 1977 alongside James Mates, now the main ITV news anchor. He played professor Henry Higgins and I played Alfred P. Doolittle.

I am a lifelong fan of Chelsea Football Club and have been going to games at Stamford Bridge since 1971.

Picture taken Piccadilly, London, January 2015

269

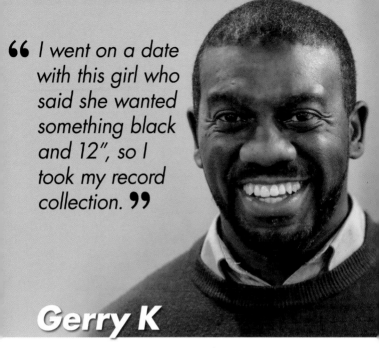

> **66** *I went on a date with this girl who said she wanted something black and 12", so I took my record collection.* **99**

Gerry K

I started in 2002 as a result of a dare. It was the Open Mic Competition that was run by Avalon and the venue was Cambridge Polytechnic.

I design greetings cards, many of which have been published.

I once co wrote a song for Gwen Dickie of Rose Royce fame.

I was once Essex dance champion and invited to join Zoo who were then the regular dance troupe on *TOTP*.

I was on *The Chase* last year.

I was invited to join Mensa.

Picture taken Piccadilly, London, January 2015

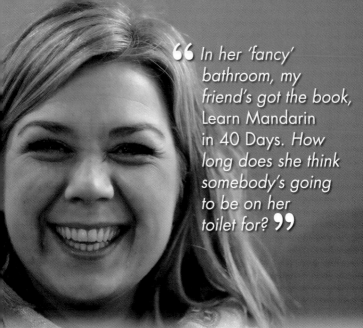

> 66 *In her 'fancy' bathroom, my friend's got the book, Learn Mandarin in 40 Days. How long does she think somebody's going to be on her toilet for?* 99

Nicky Wilkinson

I did my first stand-up gig on 6th December 2011 in Leeds.

I used to play football for Hull City girls.

Aged eight, I nearly killed 200 people; at the top of a hill at a caravan park in Scarborough I accidentally released the handbrake of my dad's Ford Sierra.

Inexplicably I narrated the school nativity play dressed in my dad's cricket gear.

I once dislocated my knee getting out of bed.

Picture taken Piccadilly, London, January 2015

> **66** *My parents keep telling me there is no money in comedy. Their evidence is that after thirty-five years at the top of the business, Lenny Henry sleeps in a Premier Inn.* **99**

Paul Sinha

I started stand-up comedy because I had seen and been inspired by so much stand-up that I decided I would never forgive myself if I didn't at least give it one try. When I used to

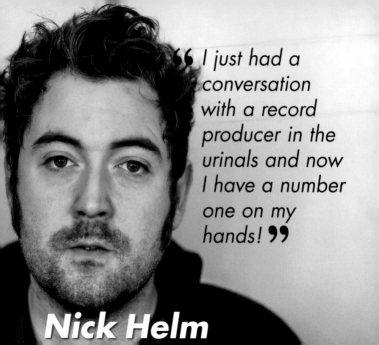

66 I just had a conversation with a record producer in the urinals and now I have a number one on my hands! 99

Nick Helm

> **If at first you don't succeed, you've already been a failure once.**

John Otway

I wasn't supposed to be a comedian, I was supposed to be a mega rockstar. I think people found me trying to be a mega rockstar genuinely funny. My first real performance was in 1969 at a residential music course with the Aylesbury Youth Orchestra. I decided I was going to treat them to an emotional rendition of Peter Sarstedt's 'Where Do You Go To My Lovely'. The audience howled with laughter – an oboe player actually fell off his chair and I had a standing ovation. There was no looking back.

I took four A-Levels: Pure Maths, Applied Maths, Statistics and Physics, and failed all four.

In 1974, I worked out the solution to the Rubik's Cube from first principles with no help whatsoever. It took three months, working on it for approximately five hours a day.

I'm Libra, and have had disastrous relationships with a Sagittarius and an Aries, but have been reliably informed by both girls that the reason they went wrong had absolutely nothing to do with when they were born.

I helped my daughter with her A-Level maths, and she passed.

I have just uploaded the ringtone Crazy Frog onto my iPhone.

Picture taken The Bloomsbury Theatre, London, January 2015

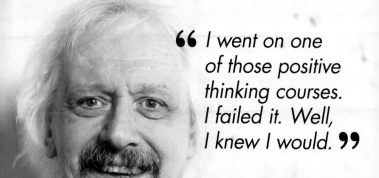

> **❝** *I went on one of those positive thinking courses. I failed it. Well, I knew I would.* **❞**

Peter Buckley Hill

I wanted to be a romantic soulful politically engaged singer/songwriter. My songs were vile, pretentious rubbish. So I started writing comedy songs, which were slightly less bad. It went from there. My first gig was at the Earth Exchange, 1980. Alternative Cabaret, as comedy was then known.

I have Tourette's Syndrome.

I wrote a doctoral thesis on obstreperous students.

For twenty years I collected toilet roll cores, in the belief I would eventually think of a show that I could use them in. Did you know they all have a unique number printed on them?

My father cut me out of his will and I still don't know why.

My lifetime highest score at cricket is twenty-two.

Picture taken The Bloomsbury Theatre, London, January 2015

275

> **My mother said to me Jane Dough you're like a spleen! If we lost you, it would make no difference to our lives whatsoever.'**
>
> Jane Dough, Baker

Anna Morris

I started in comedy in 2010.
I am completely deaf in my left ear.
I worked in TV production for seven years.
My first comedy TV appearance was me dressed as a donkey jumping out of a giant advent calendar on Nickelodeon (a kid didn't turn up who was supposed to do it so they dragged me on).
I once gunged Hermione and Ron from *Harry Potter* while dressed as a sheep (for Nickeodeon while I was working there).
I travelled solo around the world when I was 27 for a year.
I have a phobia of snakes.

Picture taken The Bloomsbury Theatre, London, January 2015

> **❝** I saw a charity advert that said, '19,000 children die needlessly everyday' and that's the wrong way to open that advert cause it sounds like it's going to be followed with 'but two or three of them really had it coming'. Surely it's always needless. **❞**

Katherine Ryan

I started comedy in Toronto 2007 after getting in trouble at the next door Hooters where I worked for writing 'Club Sandwiches Not Seals' on the chalkboard.
I had a shih tzu called Biggie who was 2lbs because he was born a 'little person' but in dog world. He died.
When I was fifteen, I pulled out all my eyelashes.
I met the big man from *Green Mile* at the Playboy Mansion.
I have two little sisters who live on opposite coasts of Canada.
When I was a baby, I had to wear braces on my legs like Forrest Gump.

Picture taken The Comedy Store, London, January 2015

> **Why do they only put flowers on the broken lampposts?** "

Brennan Reece

I started comedy in the Summer of '10 in Manchester.
I have toured with The Who.
I own a black long haired chihuahua called Nelson Mandella.
I used to lie and tell people I was the Milky Bar Kid.
I drive a bright yellow Seat Arosa. That famous car.
I was once offered the chance to be in *Big Brother* and turned it down.

Picture taken The Comedy Store, London, January 2015

> **❝** *You know you're getting old when you're watching a porn film and you're more interested in the plot than the film.* **❞**

Noel Faulkner

I first did comedy in 1978 in San Francisco.

I produced my first show at the age of eleven we did a variety show in our garage me and my mate made six pence each.

The next summer we did the same thing again only this time we just locked the kids in the garage and made off with the money.

I have sailed over 20,000 miles.

I was on the FBI most wanted list and have been deported twice from the USA.

I spent a year in a Ashram in London in the 60s. I was celibate for the whole year, not even a wank at the age of twenty-two.

Picture taken The Comedy Store, London, January 2015

> **I recently visited a safe house for Somali lesbians. Very depressing. Some of them didn't have two clitorises to rub together.**

Jane Bussmann

I started writing comedy when I was nineteen on a weekend course hosted by the greatest sitcom writer of all time, Johnny Speight (*Till Death Us Do Part*).
I have lived all over the world from Mombasa to Pasadena.
I left Africa after four years because I was getting in too many car chases with bent cops. And I hated watching charity workers swigging cocktails.
I can drive Formula 3 racing cars, badly.
I'm a sitcom nut but trying to cook up a reason to work in Bombay.

Picture taken The Phoenix Art's Club, London, January 2015

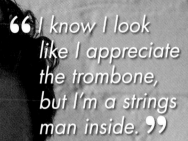

*66 I know I look
like I appreciate
the trombone,
but I'm a strings
man inside. 99*

John
Kearns

I started comedy at
Norwich, University of
East Anglia, 2006.
I can run faster than
you think.

Picture taken
The Bloomsbury Theatre, London,
January 2015

> **How to have more fun in the city: #1 play wink murder on the tube.**

Adam Taffler

I started comedy entertaining hippies at the Lost Horizon sauna at Glastonbury festival in 2001.
I have a moustache.
I'm half Hungarian, half Jewish.
I lift ladies for fun.
I run silent speed dating events.

Picture taken
Up The Creek, Greenwich,
February 2015

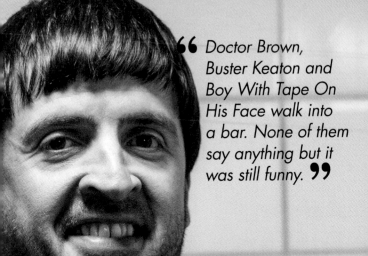

> *Doctor Brown, Buster Keaton and Boy With Tape On His Face walk into a bar. None of them say anything but it was still funny.*

Spencer Jones

I started at Trash Can Cabaret, in Plymouth, 1995.
I used to try and fall asleep while walking along doing a paper round.
I used to be a wedding singer.
I vomit before I go on stage.
I was arrested for stealing two police hats.
I collect shopping lists.

Picture taken Up The Creek, Greenwich, February 2015

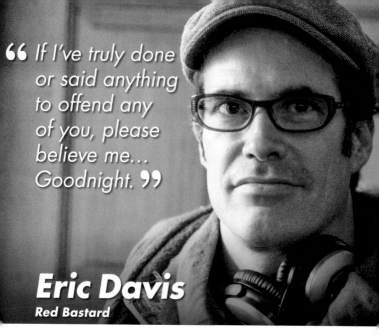

> **If I've truly done or said anything to offend any of you, please believe me... Goodnight.**

Eric Davis
Red Bastard

I started comedy in improvised duet act competitions in high school. We drew slips of paper from a hat, which had a theme written on it. Then we had seven minutes to write a comic sketch which would be performed. There was never enough time to finish it.

I considered myself an only child though I had five siblings from the same father.
My leather pants are one of my few prized possessions.
I am secretly shy.
I used to be a cheater. Now I am in an open relationship.
I hate most clowns.

Picture taken Up The Creek, Greenwich, February 2015

Darren Maskell

I started comedy in 2008 and my first gig was at the Lion's Den Comedy Club in King's Cross, London.

I am an experienced fishmonger.

I had the highest score on *Quackshot* on the Sega Megadrive within the small group of friends I had in the years 1993–1994. A record that I believe to be unchallenged.

I have a tattoo of the National Trust logo.

I am a big fan of Andrew Falkous.

Picture taken Up The Creek, Greenwich, February 2015

> **"** *I love each and every one of you people. If you people were on fire, I'd throw you a stick. If you were drowning, I'd piss on you. I suppose that's meant to be the other way around, but so was I when I came out of my mother and now she walks funny and I get turned on by being strangled.* **"**

John Robertson

I started in 2003, in Perth, western Australia.
I'm a son of a priest and a kindergarten teacher
(can finger-paint and raise the dead, ho, ho).
I have a colossal tattoo on my right shoulderblade taken
from my best friend Mel Tregonning's illustrated story, *Night*.
I invented interactive games on YouTube – 4,000,000 hits,
appearances in *Variety* Magazine and on French TV.
I faked a seizure on *Australian Idol* (it's how I met my wife).
I have owned a ginger cat, a black cat, two fish, an axolotl,
a rabbit, a guinea pig and a dog. They are all dead.

Picture taken Edinburgh Festival, August 2015

> **"** *The major problem with being an artist is the difficulty of creating and developing a decent creative idea that hasn't already been done better by Sting.* **"**

Joz Norris

I started comedy in 2011 in London.
I provide backing vocals on a 1997 Rolf Harris album called *Can You Tell What It Is Yet?*
I have a phobia of metamorphosis.
I once had an asthma attack after falling off a banana boat, and the shock of it I think cured my asthma.
I have given an honorary degree to Arsène Wenger back when I was a deputy headmaster.
I met a ghost in an apartment block in Kensington while delivering census forms.

Picture taken Up The Creek, Greenwich, February 2015

> **"** Do you think cats get pissed off that the only way they can have sex is doggy style? **"**

Dan Lees

My first gig was upstairs
at the White Hart in Stoke
Newington, with Moonfish
Rhumba, an anarchic double act
that liked to rap about beans.
I am a qualified hypnotherapist.
My dad was a
professional wrestler.
The most disappointing show
I ever saw was *Muppets on Ice*.
I have never met
the Queen.

Picture taken
Up The Creek, Greenwich,
February 2015

> **They say you are what you eat, but I do not remember eating a goddess.**

Jayde Adams

I was working as a waitress in a cocktail bar in Cardiff. Which is definitely how the song should go. My boss who is now my best mate asked me what I liked to do – I was a bit directionless, I think at this point I was doing physical theatre and dance – and I said, 'I like making people laugh', and she told me I was a comedian and I should refer to myself as that from now on. My sister also asked me to make my family laugh when she was diagnosed with cancer as they were all sad and it was in the hospital ward I realised I might be good at it.

I was a dancer for twelve years. I've never had a singing lesson. I don't enjoy small talk. I've performed on the main stage at Bestival as a backing dancer for Goldie Looking Chain. I've performed in the O2 (although back then it was called the Millennium Dome). I've been on a stage of some kind since I was eight.

Picture taken Up The Creek, Greenwich, February 2015

> **I'm not a bad person, I'm a good person who does bad things.**

Bob Slayer

I started Comedy in London in 2008 but I had previously been getting on stage with bands in my capacity as tour manager. My first 'gig' was when working with the Bloodhound Gang, the smoking ban had just come in and so they decided to go for a fag break mid gig. Jimmy Pop the lead singer told the audience, 'Our tour manager will entertain you', and pushed me on stage in front of 1,500 bemused fans, he then added, 'Feel free to throw stuff at him'. Which they enjoyed very much.

I toured all around the world nearly non stop for six years as manager of Japanese rock and roll band Electric Eel Shock. I was asked by a then fifteen-year-old Alex Turner to manage his band the Arctic Monkeys and I turned them down.

From the ages of sixteen to twenty-one I was a jockey. I then broke my back and got too fat I also once broke my neck at a gig (at Download Festival I ended my gig by doing a crowd surf in a wheelie bin and got tipped onto my head. Fortunately it was a small crack)

I toured Australia with a goat called Gary.

Picture taken Up The Creek, Greenwich, February 2015

Juliet Cowan

I started when I was pregnant with my first child Conor
and he is now twenty.
I have three children.
I can't grow plants.
I learned to read at school in The Scilly Isles.
I have read every Carlos Castenada book ever written.
I have made a Brazilian bun called Pao de Queijo.

Picture taken London, February 2015

> **In Britain cops have no guns. In America they have guns. And they're fat. Which says: 'I'm not gonna chase you.'**

Russell Hicks

I started stand-up in San Diego, California.

I used to do backyard wrestling when I was a teenager.

I dressed up as a cowboy and jumped off of buildings onto my friends… weird, but we gained a following for a brief time in my home town.

Once, I dressed up as a cowboy, went to a football game (American football) at my high school and stood in the crowd swearing, but cheering on our team so the parents in the crowd were confused as to what to do. They hated the swearing but loved the support. At the end of the game I went up to the announcers booth, and over the loud speaker told the other team they were, 'the suckiest bunch of sucks who ever sucked' (a line à la Homer Simpson, I believe). A small riot (literally) broke out. I was arrested, suspended, and then finally sent home. My mother had twenty-seven messages on her machine from the entire town telling her what an asshole son I was. When I got back to school, I was a hero.

Picture taken George IV, Chiswick, March 2015

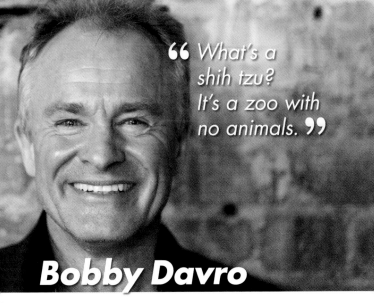

> 66 *What's a shih tzu? It's a zoo with no animals.* 99

Bobby Davro

I started doing impressions of my school teachers when I was about fifteen years old. My headmaster sounded like the PM Harold Wilson. I could do him to a tee.

When I left school I worked for my father in the family business then started doing stag gigs in pubs and clubs. I was nineteen.

My father was British mile champion back in the late forties and ran in two Olympic Games, 1948 and 1952.

I have a bunion on my left foot.

I have a tattoo of a heart with an arrow through it with the initials of my three daughters on it.

I'm psychic and have had many premonitions that have come true.

Picture taken Headliners, George IV, Chiswick, March 2015

> "My mother always gave me great advice, 'Amy you should never buy drugs, you're young and beautiful… you should get them for free'."

Amy Howerska

started comedy in deepest darkest south London in 2009, at a now defunct gig called Why the Long Room.

come from a skydiving family. Three generations of extreme sports idiots. I always feel left out at christmas when everyone discusses their head injuries.

had the highest IQ in my primary school… I still can't tie my shoe laces properly.

once got stuck in a lift with Sir Christopher Lee. It was a very small lift and he kept cracking coffin jokes. Like a legend.

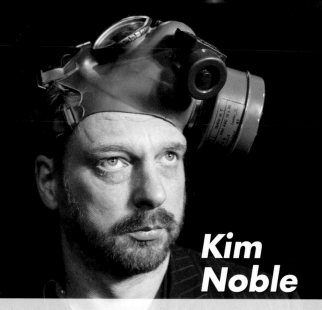

Kim
Noble

Did a try-out at the Purple
Turtle on Essex Road in 1999.
My first actual gig was at the
Hen and Chickens in 1999.
I ended up doing four hours.
I've got Steve Davis's leftover
toast in my freezer. (I saw him
in a cafe and the leftover
toast got shovelled into a bin.
I asked the waiter if I could
go through the bins for it.)
I worked in B&Q for a

year and a half without
anyone knowing.
I once had to take a half a
litre of ejaculate into the US.
I smuggled it in various
small containers.
I beat the bass player of
Wings at table tennis when
I was eight.
When I was a day old I was
stabbed in the throat by a
nurse with some scissors.

Picture taken The Chapel, Islington, London, February 2016

Yuriko Kotani

My first gig was in
London, January 2014
I was born and grew
up in Toyota City.
I like dogs.
My favourite colour
changes every
time I think
about it.

Picture taken
North London Tavern, Kilburn, London,
March 2015

> **❝** *A guy once said to me, in the bedroom: 'I want you to be rough with me'. So I just did a cockney accent.* **❞**

Samantha Baines

I started stand-up comedy at the end of 2013. My first gig was in a pub in Lancaster Gate.

I have met Wills and Kate, Prince Harry, the King and Queen of Sweden and the Princess of Thailand.

When I was at secondary school I lied and said that over the holidays I got my nose pierced and then lasered up again.

I was chucked out of Brownies for teaching the other kids swear words.

I got a tattoo in a bar in Thailand.

I once dated a guy who I didn't hear from for a week because he'd had an accident and was in a coma.

Picture taken North London Tavern, Kilburn, London, March 2015

> *Hi, my name is Sindhu. Rhymes with Hindu... which I am... so it's convenient. Because say I wasn't, say I was Muslim, then it would just be weird.*

Sindhu Vee

My first ever ever gig was for the Funnywomen Comedy Awards heats on Thursday 10th May 2012 at the Green Carnation on Greek Street in Soho. I had not even watched live stand-up till then! (I made it the the semis that year. And I was hooked).

I quit a Ph.D. in Philosophy to get a job instead because it was taking too long. So I know what hermeneutics means.

I used to be an investment banker. Thats the only 'career' I've ever had (before this).

I had a stammer (that I learned to work around) until I was twenty-two.

My actual surname has sixteen letters in it and I have never met anyone else with a longer surname, though I am always looking.

Picture taken Wimbledon Reform Synagogue, March 2016

Edd Hedges

I did my first gig in August 2012 at a small open mic night in Piccadilly Circus that I proceeded to play every week for two months. I'm learning to speak Punjabi.

Before comedy I was training to become a zoologist.
I don't eat beef.
I like Coldplay a bit.
I'm allergic to cats.

Picture taken Downstairs at the King's Head, Crouch End, London, March 2015

" What's red and white? Pink. "

Andrew Pepper

I actually started doing cabaret on the Battersea Barge in 2003, but it wasn't until 2014 that you could legitimately label the work as comedy. Even now I'm mixing the comedic parts with other elements.
I once drove eighteen miles down the M61 with the handbrake on.
Whilst doing a gig in York I shared a dressing room with a ghost who had a thing for the kettle.
When I was a teenager I had epilepsy. The seizures were only ever induced by watching soap operas. True story. I stopped watching soap operas.

I can make very loud noises with my tongue. It's incredibly impressive and serves no useful purpose whatsoever.

Picture taken Edinburgh Fringe Festival, August 2015

300

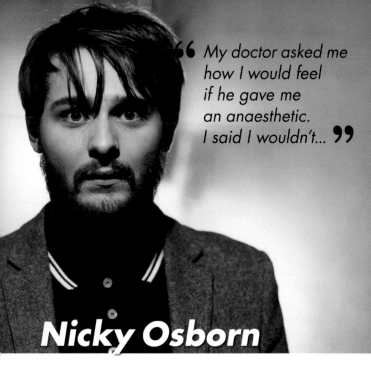

> **"** My doctor asked me
> how I would feel
> if he gave me
> an anaesthetic.
> I said I wouldn't... **"**

Nicky Osborn

I first did stand-up comedy at the age of fifteen at the
Horseshoe Inn in Wellingborough. They did a
monthly gong show.
I have mild cerebral palsy in my right leg.
I once got drunk and stole a hoover.
The first time I was in a plane I jumped out.
I was fired from a bar for disconnecting a keg and flooding it.
I once made a bacon roll for Richard Ashcroft

Picture taken We Are Funny Project, Dalston, London, October 2016

The film Oliver would be a lot less eventful if the cook had just been a bit more generous. 99

Mat Brooks

I started comedy November 2014 on a
Laughing Horse course.
I'm dyslexic.
I work in film and TV.
I have a weird fascination with suits.
I take pictures of things that look like faces.
I lost my sense of smell when I was twenty-one

> **"** When I first heard about the 'thigh gap', I was confused. A gap at the top of your thighs? Did they mean my vagina? **"**

Caitlin Moran

I've just done fourteen stand-up gigs as a dare to myself, really. So my first one was at the King's Head in Crouch End, May 2014.

Unlike every 'powerful' modern woman I have ever seen in a TV drama or a film, I am not compelled to work hard at my job because I had an horrific, traumatising event in my early childhood. I just want to pay my rent.

Picture taken Downstairs at the King's Head, London, April 2015

> **"** Sexists – it's really easy to stop feminism. We just need to stop being surprised when we see women doing things. **"**

Emma Thirkill

I started comedy a year ago, in London at a night called Nice n Spiky.
I can do a very accurate and terrifying impression of the Wicked Witch of the West.
My most prized possession is a nodding pope, not even the current Pope at the time of purchase.
I used to have an imaginary friend who was a pelican called Muncher, he used to steal biscuits (secretly, it was me).
I'm a feminist. And proud.

Picture taken North London Tavern, Kilburn, London, March 2015

> **"We all know men can't do two things at once but they always want to do threesomes! Why?"**

Melanie Gayle

In March 2014 I completed my Comedy Novice Course with a performance at The Washington in Hampstead.
I love chicken wings.
I am double jointed.
I can tap dance and do ballet yah yah!
I had beginner swimming lessons, twice in 2013 and I still can't swim properly.
As a child I was known as Twiggy. Then I put on weight when I got older and was called Fluffy (coz I was fluffy and nice like a dumpling). Now I have lost 4.5 stone I am known as Twiggy again! Twiggy came back like the Mini Skirt!

Picture taken North London Tavern, Kilburn, London, March 2015

> **I've got an obsession with ham, but I try to keep it under wraps!**

Hurt and Anderson

We met at school in Bristol. We first performed in the school talent show. We didn't win it. We took part in our first comedy competition in 2009.

Georgia I once had to help collect a sperm sample from a cheetah.

I am so clumsy that I once knocked myself out six times in a year and ended up in A & E every time.

I once appeared in a KT Tunstall music video and can be seen dancing awkwardly at the back of the crowd, trying to cover my face with my hair.

I am supposedly a distant relative of John Hurt.

Laura I once tried to be on my University's *University Challenge* team and ended up getting a negative final score.

I nearly got run over chasing Charlie Brooker down a road in order to get his photograph.

I can do an uncanny impression of Gordon Brown and an even better one of James Blunt.

Picture taken North London Tavern, Kilburn, London, March 2015

306

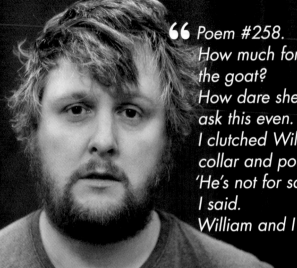

> 66 Poem #258.
> How much for
> the goat?
> How dare she
> ask this even.
> I clutched William's
> collar and pouted.
> 'He's not for sale',
> I said.
> William and I left. 99

Tim Key

I started the poetry in 2005 at my friend Breeno's lounge.
Paul Foot headlined.
My PB marathon time is 4:04:05.
My freezer sealed itself shut three years ago and I
don't remember what's in it.
I've met the Cheeky Girls.

Picture taken The Union Chapel, Islington, London, April 2015

307

> **"** *I just got married, and after thinking a lot about it I decided not to change my name. Obviously, this is not because I don't love my husband. It's because I don't respect him. Or his family.* **"**

Sara Barron

I started stand-up in London in 2014.
I made a 1997 appearance on a Jerry Springer *Too Hot For TV* video.
I've never been very drunk. At most, I've been very tipsy.
I have enormous hands. On two separate occasions, someone has seen my hands and thought to mention the *Seinfeld* 'Man Hands' episode.
My hair is naturally brown. I've been dying it since I was fifteen.

Picture taken North London Tavern, Kilburn, London, March 2015

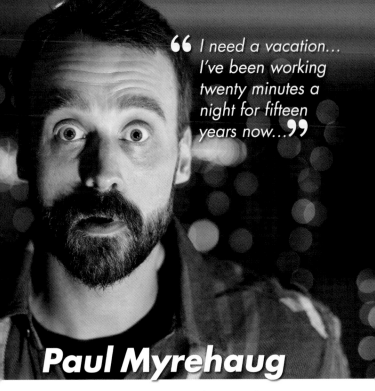

> **66** *I need a vacation...*
> *I've been working*
> *twenty minutes a*
> *night for fifteen*
> *years now...* **99**

Paul Myrehaug

I started comedy May 2000 in Edmonton, Alberta Canada.

I studied Business Marketing.

I worked in a steel mill.

I LOVE playing golf.

I grew up on a farm.

I was circumcised at the age of twenty-four.

Picture taken The Clissold Arms, Muswell Hill, London, March 2015

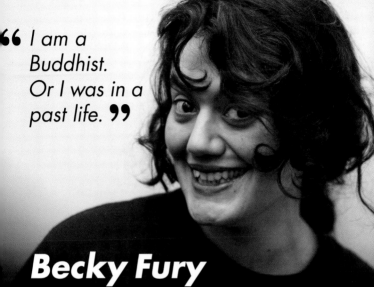

66 *I am a Buddhist. Or I was in a past life.* **99**

Becky Fury

When I was a punk I shaved my face to encourage beard growth because it would look cool and androgynous. Now I'm not a punk and I have to deal with the consequences of my actions. Such is the reality of being an adult.
I am still an anarcho syndicalist. I'm not exactly sure what that means either. I'm going to check it out on Wikipedia too.
My nan worked at West Ham FC and half the World Cup winning '66 squad ate bread pudding she made in her kitchen every Wednesday. I'm not saying that England's poor present performance is due to them not getting my nan's home cooking but it's worth considering.
Becky Fury is my real name.

Picture taken North London Tavern, Kilburn, London, March 2015

Mae Martin

I started doing comedy when I was thirteen, at The Second City in Toronto. All my material was about puberty. I don't have any one-liners. Only longer stories. Which makes taxi drivers, my GP, and all of my parents' friends doubt that I'm a real comedian.
I tell people I'm allergic to coconut but really I just don't like it. It's easier that way.
I once made eye contact with Antonia Banderas.
When I was a kid I used to insist on being naked on Christmas Day for the entire day.
These facts have made me feel sad about my life.

Picture taken
The Union Chapel, Islington, London, April 2015

> **Brixton and Brighton are not that different. In Brighton, they've got the beach… with stones. And in Brixton we've got stoned bitches!**

Arielle Soumahoro

I started comedy in April 2014, at the Keith Palmer comedy school. I did my first gig at Dirty Dicks, two weeks before school graduation.

I was taken from Ivory Coast when I was around three years old; then left Paris for London at eighteen. I spent more of my life in the UK than anywhere else in the world; yet, I still find chips with vinegar an abomination 'de la merde'.

I wish I could talk Djula, my African dialect, but anything related to my African culture was kept hidden from me; the same way that my dad kept himself hidden from his kids

#TheLongestHide&SeekEver. We are a set of three. I have an older sister; the darkest-skinned of us but very 'white' minded. Then me; the lightest-skinned of us but very 'black' minded. Then finally my little brother, who is very much 'balanced'.

Picture taken
North London Tavern, Kilburn, London,
March 2015

> **I want to know what it is like to have an accent that makes people wet their knickers because when I open my mouth people shit their pants.**

Daphna Baram

I started comedy in London in June 2010. My friend Kit said: 'We are getting you a comedy course at the comedy school in Camden for your 40th birthday because Chris Morris saw your speech at my wedding and thought you were doing it for a living. You have no idea who this is, do you? Well you are going anyway'. I know now, but it is too late.

I used to be a human rights lawyer in Israel, representing Palestinians in military courts in the West Bank and Gaza.

I was news editor and deputy editor in chief of a Jerusalem based newspaper called *Kol H'air* (all the city).

I had a heart attack at a Harringay gym in June 2009. I was 39.

My book *Disenchantment: The Guardian and Israel* was published in 2004 and was a result of two Oxford based fellowships.

After thirteen years in the UK I finally got an Indefinite Leave to Remain in February 2015.

Picture taken North London Tavern, Kilburn, London, March 2015

> **The tooth fairy would give me a pound for each of my teeth. I wonder how much I would get for a kidney.**

Murray Shaw

I started stand-up on the comedy module of my Theatre degree at Middlesex University in 2016 (Steve Best was the visiting lecturer). This picture was taken at my first ever gig as part of my final exam.

My great grandfather was too young to fight in the First World War and too old to fight in the Second World War. He also lived till 105.

I was invited to Richard III's funeral at Leicester cathedral.

A dance class I was in came 1st place in an international dance competition in Barcelona. I was dressed as a chicken for it.

I used to have long hair down to my chest.

My favourite animal, currently, is the barn owl.

Picture taken Downstairs at the King's Head, Crouch End, London, May 2016

> **66** *So the universe implodes – no matter.* **99**

Liam Williams

I started comedy at Cambridge University in 2009.
I came second in the Leeds Schools Cross Country Championship in 2000.
I got a C in GCSE Drama.
I'm a pescetarian.
I'm thinking of becoming a vegetarian.

Picture taken
The Union Chapel, Islington, London, April 2015

Sofie Hagen

I started doing comedy in Copenhagen in June 2010.
I have the license to own a sword.
I have a phobia so bad that writing down the word makes me feel sick.
My brother is a magician. I hate magicians. These things are related.
I was almost kicked out of school for setting up a website where students could anonymously complain about the principal or teachers.
My grandfather haunts the house he used to live in. His ghost tells the new owner how to clean.
I worked in a sex shop when I was seventeen. I pretended to be eighteen.
I have a Hemingway novel tattooed on my left foot.

Picture taken The Clissold Arms, Muswell Hill, London, March 2015

> **If we'd been influenced by the computer games from our childhood, we'd have to run round in a darkened room, munching on pills and listening to repetitive music.**

Marcus Brigstocke

I started comedy properly when I was at Bristol University in 1995 as a stand-up and in a sketch group called Club Seals. We made a TV show for the BBC called *We Are History* the year we graduated. I hosted The Comedy Box for two years.

I was a goth – for nearly three years.

I used to be a podium dancer. I used to teach rollerblading to supplement my podium dancing income. I did these two jobs during time off from working on an oil rig.

I was in rehab by the time I was seventeen and have been sober and drug free for twenty-five years.

Pink Floyd are (by some distance) my favourite band. This is because I am posh and angsty.

Picture taken The Comedy Store, London, April 2015

> I grew up in Maidstone. It's no coincidence that an anagram of Maidstone is 'I am stoned'. There's nothing else to do. Just anagrams.

Angela Barnes

I started in 2010 in Brighton. I did a comedy course in 2009, then hit the open mic the following year.
I have ichthyophobia, which is a morbid fear of fish.
I have Grade 9 in figure skating.
My feet are two sizes bigger than my dad's feet.
I never miss an episode of *The Archers*. Never.
I have synaesthesia.

Picture taken The Bloomsbury Theatre, London, April 2015

> **Most famous assassinations are committed by people with three names. Lincoln – John Wilkes Booth, JFK – Lee Harvey Oswald, Martin Luther King – United States government.**

Harry Scott-Montcrieff

I started comedy by accident. Six years ago I used to busk but wasn't very good at making money, mainly because my act was quite threatening and intimidating. My first stand-up gig was in some terrible pub in London in 2011 with some terrible acts, including myself.

I'm a conspiracy theorist. While I was still in the womb my umbilical chord wrapped around my neck. I was pulled out a month early. I was meant to be born on April 1st. I can't ride a bicycle. I violently hate cars.

Picture taken King's Cross, London, October 2016

> **66** I see the Pope drives around in a car with bullet-proof glass in the windows. But Jesus Christ never wore nail-proof gloves, did he? **99**

John Dowie

I started in Birmingham in 1969, amateurish kind of stuff. And for money in 1972 in Edinburgh (I'm still waiting for the cheque). I stopped doing shows for adults in 1995 and switched to doing shows for children. I have cycled pretty much the whole of France and the whole of Holland and Ireland (which was shit because of the state of the roads). I have a fear of heights (why do people always want to meet in tall buildings?). Victor Spinetti directed one of my kids' shows. He said on British TV that there have been two Johns in my life, John Lennon and now John Dowie. I don't like having my picture taken.

Picture taken The Southbank, London, October 2016

> **66** I think Kim Jong Un's hair must be working for the US government, because it's certainly not working for him. **99**

Aisling Bea

I started comedy in 2011 and did my first gig at a poetry and variety night where I thought, 'If I'm awful, then maybe people will think I'm a terrible poet'.
My mother is a retired professional flat race jockey.
My father was a horse vet.
My sister is a costume designer for big Hollywood movies.
I have a degree in French and Philosophy.
I know three people directly connected to Shergar.

Picture taken
The Bloomsbury Theatre, London,
April 2015

> **"** *I was gonna write a poem about not having signal on my phone, it was gonna be called: 'Close but no Wi-Fi.'* **"**

Les Connelly

I started comedy in Leeds in 2014.
I was born in Middlesbrough.
I have a tattoo on the inside of my lip. It says, 'woof'.
I studied Art for six years.
I once had a hamster called The Undertaker;
named after the wrestler.

Picture taken The Rose Inn, Shortly, Ipswich, May 2016

> **What did the jazz singer catch from his guitar? Hepititis A B C D E.**

Isy Suttie

I started stand-up in late 2002 above a pub in Greenwich but started writing comedy songs as a teenager.

If I hadn't been a comedian I would have been a tennis champion.

I have never parked a car on my own without the help of a passer-by.

When I was born I had an extra bit on my forehead which disappeared when I was a toddler.

When I was growing up my mum was an inventor.

Picture taken The Bloomsbury Theatre, London, April 2015

Elis James

I started doing gigs in Cardiff in 2005, and was able to quit my real job and become a full time comedian in 2008. I don't really do jokes, I tell stories. Although I was MCing quite recently and got chatting to an airline pilot. When I asked him what qualifications he had he said 'none,' to which I replied 'do you just wing it?' That is the closest I have come to writing a proper joke and I expect to dine out on it for the next ten to fifteen years.

I have an MA in History and when gigs go badly, I unwind by reading about Lloyd George.

I have a collection of vintage football kits, but I would never wear one because that would be 'sad'.

Welsh is my first language, but I didn't write a Welsh language stand-up show until 2015. When I was previewing the Welsh show, I started forgetting basic English words on stage when I was doing gigs in England. If I had a time machine, I would go back in time, rather than into the future. I once turned down the chance to meet Johnny Marr, because I was so scared of getting it wrong, and the only shirt I would have been happy for him to see me in was in the wash.

Picture taken Borehamwood, January 2016

> **" *Give me a smile!
> I laughed when
> I saw you!* "**

Terry Kilkelly

I started my comedy career at the Unity Theatre in Liverpool. It was when I was studying theatre so it would have been around '89/'90. I played Malvolio in *Twelfth Night* in a theatre in Kuala Lumpur. My family is from Kilkelly in Ireland. I've never been yet and would love to go. I'm terrified of flying. I love comics and got a signed drawing of my Renee character by a Beano artist as a fortieth birthday present. I love Italian food, drink tea by the bucket load and I'm left-handed with cutlery but not pens.

Picture taken The Bloomsbury Theatre, London, May 2015

> **A man on the train said: 'That seat is reserved.' I said: 'Well, it's been very forward with me.' Pulled up my pants and went on my way.**

Lou Sanders

I jumped in the Thames and saved a man who was drowning once.

Someone saved my life once when I was hopping between boats and nearly got caught on a boat engine.

I was one second off winning an eating-dry-crackers competition. I think about it often and how different my life could have been if I'd won that giant fluffy orange duck.

Picture taken
The Bloomsbury Theatre, London,
April 2015

326

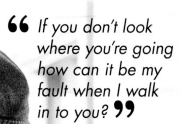

> **"** If you don't look where you're going how can it be my fault when I walk in to you? **"**

Count Arthur Strong

Steve Delaney

I started comedy at the King's Head in Crouch End in 1997.
I used to be a carpenter.
I trained as an actor.
I collect wrist watches.
I've done two solo parachute jumps.
I know Barry Cryer.

Picture taken
The Bloomsbury Theatre, London, May 2015

327

> **I was dating this American girl who was awesome. Awesome – that is American for adequate.**

Stephen Carlin

I started comedy in London in 2003.
I still have one of my baby teeth.
I have no sense of smell.
I have never been to a stag-do.
I wanted to be a firefighter but
I suffer from vertigo.

Picture taken
We Are Funny Project, Putney, London,
April 2016

> ❝ I've got a rare bone condition, Osteogenesis Imperfecta. The only condition in Scotland that still sounds dubious. I have 'Oh aye?' 'Oh aye? Aye right!' ❞

Rhona McKenzie

I did a comedy course in 2008 with Universal Comedy in Glasgow, blagging time off work to do it.

I'm known by five different surnames.

I collected soaps as a kid. I now collect badges.

I've never seen any *Star Wars* films.

I accidentally farted on Nicola Sturgeon's seat in the Scottish Parliament.

I once flew (as a kid, in a cagoule, in a strong wind).

Picture taken King's Cross, London, May 2016

> ❝ *I am not a narcissist.*
> *I mean, look at me!* ❞

Dagfinn Lyngbo

I started doing comedy in 1993 in Bergen, Norway. It was a pub called Nansen, and I did one show every week for almost four years. I started off on Thursdays, but that was the night the scuba-diving club had their pub night, so we had to do Fridays instead. Apparently scuba-divers don't pay much attention to the world above the waterline.

My rock band, Radakis, have only sold 200 records but we did a warm up gig for Black Sabbath. Our audience-number did vary from 13,000 to eleven that week.

In the army I lied about being a computer expert and a photographer – so I got two well paid extra jobs as a teacher. Just a couple of the students were suspicious about my level of knowledge.

I've started gardening school.

I called myself a Christian for a while and led a teenage choir for three years. But then a friend's mother committed suicide and the priest said to him that she burned in hell. So...

Picture taken Civil Service Club, London, April 2015

Me: *My ambition is that after my show people will leave the theatre, and change the world.* Dummy of Brecht: *Well, you're halfway there.*

Ian Saville

I started performing around 1959 (aged six) in a holiday talent show, doing the comic rhyme 'Can't Blow the Candle Out'.
I have a Ph.D. in radical theatre history.
I was booked by the Lisbon Street Magic Festival because they thought I was a different magician called Ian Saville.
I went to the same school as Harold Pinter.
My brother is General Secretary of a Trade Union.

Picture taken
Downstairs at the King's Head, London,
May 2015

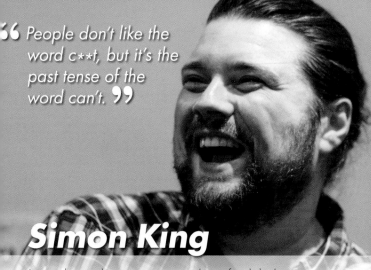

> **People don't like the word c**t, but it's the past tense of the word can't.** 99

Simon King

I started comedy at a run down old comedy club in Vancouver, British Columbia Canada way back on February 8th 2000. I did stand-up for about six months or so then took a long break and restarted again August 2002. Kind of like a born-again comedian.
I can do the splits in both directions.
My eyes sometimes change colour, often linked to my mood or booze consumption. I've been a performer since the age of seven, having started as an actor.
I can do lots of accents, sound effects and impressions although I rarely, if ever, use them in my act any more. Some of the more fun ones include: a saxophone (tenor and alto), a motorbike, a chainsaw and a goose with AIDS.

Picture taken Civil Service Club, London, April 2015

> **I always feel a bit fraudulent when I wear a Wonderbra. Like I need a little disclaimer underneath that says, 'Actual contents may differ from size shown.'**

Sally Holloway

I did my first gig in April 1992 at the Comedy Cafe in London – I was terrible but I loved it. I gave up in 2003 because I got ME. I tried teaching comedy workshops but had to give that up too, so I put all I knew into a book called *The Serious Guide to Joke Writing*. Many people still think ME is a mental illness – I just have to live with that. I'm 5ft 11 1/4. I'm seriously into bean sprouting. When I was young I was a compulsive liar (no really, I was!).

Picture taken
The Southbank, London,
November 2016

*' I never know what to finish on...
but I'm thinking your face. "*

Jake Howie

I did my first gig at a north London open mic night in 2013 and brought fifteen friends along who laughed so loud I thought I was a genius. I soon learned that wasn't the case...
I am from New Zealand and have lived in Denmark, Brazil and now the UK.
I speak Portuguese and I am learning Italian... sooo international!
My parents met in the Church of Scientology (I promise they're normal!).
I once put my finger in a blender to see what would happen... it sliced it open, FYI.
My karaoke safe song is Lindsay Lohan's 'Rumours'.

Picture taken
Gut Rocking Comedy Club, Orpington, October 2016

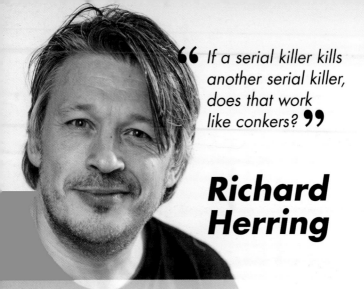

> **If a serial killer kills another serial killer, does that work like conkers?**

Richard Herring

I started doing sketch comedy at school and then at university where I met and worked with Stewart Lee from 1986 onwards. I first went to the Edinburgh Fringe in '87 and started doing stand-up gigs in London in early 1990.

My father was the headmaster at my secondary school.

I once knocked the reigning World Series of Poker champion out of a tournament.

I am the world's only semi-professional self-playing snooker player.

I have the second longest running consecutive daily blog in the world (written an entry every day since 25th November 2002).

I scored thirty-five points on *Celebrity Mastermind*, with a specialist subject of Rasputin, but still lost.

Picture taken The Bloomsbury Theatre, London, May 2015

Mackenzie Crook

I started performing in
Birmingham in a club
called The Retort in
about 1993.
I honestly can't think of
a single actual joke I've
ever written. I've asked
all my friends and they
can't think of one either.
I like sunburn and
air turbulence.
I'd love to find a tarantula
in a bunch of bananas
from the supermarket.
I once got a letter from
Reggie Kray.
I can see four of Jupiter's
moons with the naked eye.

Picture taken
Muswell Hill, London,
April 2015

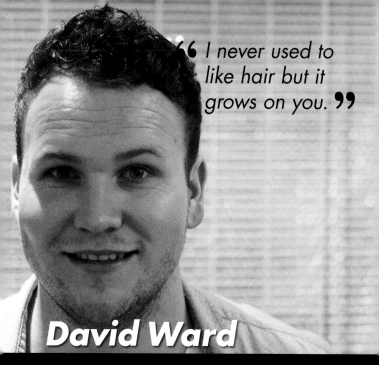

> 66 *I never used to like hair but it grows on you.* 99

David Ward

I started comedy Christmas 2013.
I used to box/play rugby (basically any sport where
I could get hurt).
I am a Tottenham Hotspur season ticket holder.
I'm a crier. Whenever there's a sad film I cry my eyes out.
I've had about a million jobs, from plumber to bar staff.
I love Spiderman and I still haven't completely given up
hope on one day becoming him.

Picture taken Soho Theatre, London, May 2015

> **"** *A good audience is like good cuisine – it takes just one dick in it to ruin it.* **"**

Marcel Lucont

Alexis Dubus

I did my first ever gig in 2001 at the now-defunct Zippy's Bar at the University of Warwick Students' Union for the now-defunct *Daily Telegraph* Open Mic Award. I, however, at time of press, remain funct.

I used to deliver milk to John Craven for cash.

I proposed to my beloved via the medium of Scrabble.

I bloody love hiding.

I once had a hallucinogenic trip on ayahuasca with a shaman called Kevin.

Picture taken
The Bloomsbury Theatre, London, May 2015

338

> **"** *I saw a great piece of graffiti – someone had written on the back of a toilet door, 'DARE TO THINK FOR YOURSELF'. So underneath it, I wrote, 'Okay'.* **"**

Sarah Kendall

My first gig was in 1997. It was at Manning Bar, Sydney University. I entered a student stand-up competition called 5 Minute Noodles. I hated it.

When I was a child I wanted to be Olivia Newton-John.

I can ride a skateboard. Nothing fancy, but I'm competent.

I know the Aviation Alphabet.

I've seen every episode of M*A*S*H*.

I hate it when anything comes to an end. Even if it's something I don't like.

Picture taken Downstairs at the King's Head, London, May 2015

> " *I'd hate to be stuck in the Big Brother house; the people are such jerks. I'd do anything to get kicked out. It'd be like: 'Day 38. Once again, Henry has shat in all the beds.'* "

Henry Naylor

My first stand-up gig was at the Purple Turtle bar in Islington, I think it was Paul Chowdhry's first gig too.

When I was a student backpacking in Brazil, I unwittingly insulted a plain-clothes policeman. He shouted at me and produced his badge, so I shouted back and produced my student railcard. He was baffled enough to let me go.

On the same trip I was taken on a Paraguayan couple's honeymoon. Yes, really. They insisted.

Always a lanky git, I used to be able to jump over my ear-height. I held my Junior School High Jump record for twenty years.

I know lots about sewage. In fact, many punters said my act was full of it. That's because the family trade was sewer pipes.

When I had my wisdom teeth out, the general anaesthetic I was given was strong enough to paralyse me, but not knock me out. I remember being wheeled into the operating theatre, watching the surgeon pulling on his gloves… whilst being unable to cry out or tell them I was still awake.

Picture taken The Southbank, London, April 2016

340

> Being a new dad, I can't believe how much attention babies get. Last time we went out he was surrounded by people cooing and pointing at him in the back of the car... I'd only been gone 45 minutes. **"**

Andy Stedman

My first gig was in December 2014 in London.
I own Dodgeball UK, a dodgeball company!
I was captain of Surrey under-elevens and under-twelves cricket teams.
Uncut Magazine reviewed a CD of mine and said, 'Stedman's voice is sure to melt hearts!' Sadly it isn't.
I'm a massive Elvis fan.
I once beat Steve Best in a poker hand with quad 3s. Very pleasing.

Picture taken
Poker game at Otiz Cannelloni's house, January 2016

> **66** *Dwarf shortage (if you are offended by that then grow up).* **99**

Jimmy Carr

I started at around the turn of the century. My first gig was at the Tutt and Shive on Upper Street, Islington. I share a hairdresser with Benedict Cumberbatch. I'm friends with Stephen Hawking. I've written a song with Robbie Williams. I've beaten Harry Styles at tennis.

Picture taken
O2 Brixton Academy,
June 2015

342

> " I lost my virginity at 16 but I found it again when I got married. "

John Bishop

First open spot: October 2000 at the Frog and Bucket in Manchester.
In 1992 I rode a bicycle from Sydney Australia to Liverpool.
I have a degree in Politics.
I once had a conker that was a 112er.
They are all my own teeth.
I have been a vegetarian for thirty years.

Picture taken
Old Rope, London,
June 2015

343

> **" Smile and the whole world smiles with you. Carve a smiley face in your forehead and it's a different story. "**

Eddie Pepitone

I started comedy in the heart of Manhattan NYC. I was throwing up from anxiety before I went on stage in the early days. The quintessential faux tough guy New Yorker.
I am a vegan.
I love hockey.
I have two dogs.
I am a political activist.

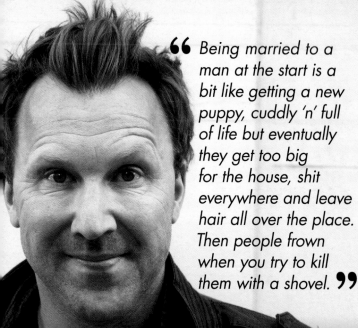

> ❝ Being married to a man at the start is a bit like getting a new puppy, cuddly 'n' full of life but eventually they get too big for the house, shit everywhere and leave hair all over the place. Then people frown when you try to kill them with a shovel. ❞

Jason Byrne

I started in 1995 in Dublin. I MC'd a gig in a venue called The Coach House. I died on my hoop. It was a charity gig for nurses heading to Romania to look after 'AIDS babies'.

I only have one good lung. I can Irish dance. I was a lighting stage designer for seven years. I run a Juijitsu gym in Ireland. I've drunk with Santa in Lapland.

> **66** *My girlfriend has a house on Park Lane. A guy asked her, sarkily, 'Ooo does Daddy drive a Bentley?' To which she replied, 'No! THE CHAUFFEUR drives the Bentley.'* **99**

Darius Davies

My first gig was in June 2007 in the downstairs of a bar called Nevada Smiths. I died. Obviously.

I wanted to be a pro-wrestler and went to school for it. Then I broke my back. I now have steel rods and screws holding me together.

I briefly worked for TFL and in finance. I was rubbish at both jobs.

I had colonic irrigation once, then was independently told that my skin was 'glowing'.

I love salt. Please don't judge me on my sodium intake.

Picture taken Brewery Tap, Peterborough, June 2015

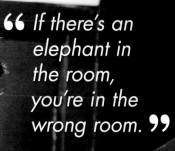

> **"** *If there's an elephant in the room, you're in the wrong room.* **"**

Mike Wozniak

First gig was in Tooting, 1998, in a student revue.
Sporadic bursts of sketch activity from then on until starting stand-up in 2007 at the Comedy Cavern in Bath.
I used to sport a mohawk.
I was glassed on my own stag-do (not related to previous fact).
I am descended from a Polish count who, while hunting bears, was eaten by bears.
I am competent in all three methods of removing the larvae of the Uruguayan bot-fly from human flesh.

Picture taken Old Rope, London, June 2015

6 *My dad's a proper family man, he's got three of them.* **99**

Steve Bugeja

My very first gig was in a staff talent contest while working at a kids camp in America. I won $20 and felt like a superstar. Still to this day one of my best paid gigs.
I've seen the musical *Hairspray* in three different continents.
My second cousin was once the Prime Minister of Malta.
My first TV appearance was on the *Terry and Gabby Show* on Channel 5.
I've never been to a zoo.

Picture taken Old Rope Comedy, London, June 2015

> **"** *I can never remember what a metaphor is, I just remember that it's like a simile.* **"**

David Tsonos

I started comedy in 1999 in Vancouver Canada.
Vegetarian.
Wine enthusiast.
Electric bass player.
Coolest uncle.
Animal rights activist.

Picture taken London, June 2015

> **" I have a rule that I'll never sleep with a woman as skinny as me because I'm just afraid we'll start a fire. "**

Ed Byrne

I was living in Glasgow when I decided I fancied doing stand-up but, at the time, there were no comedy nights that newbies could go on so I started my own club in the basement of a pub called The 13th Note on Glassford Street. It's called Balans now.

That was November 3rd 1993.

I have a cat called Shadwell.

I once nearly drowned when I fell through the ice on a frozen canal in Amsterdam.

My middle name is Cathal. It's Irish for Charles. My wife refuses to ever pronounce it correctly.

At time of writing, I have climbed seventy-seven of Scotland's tallest 282 mountains. My siblings call me Ned for no reason other than it is the derivation of Edward I like least.

Picture taken
Old Rope, London,
June 2015

350

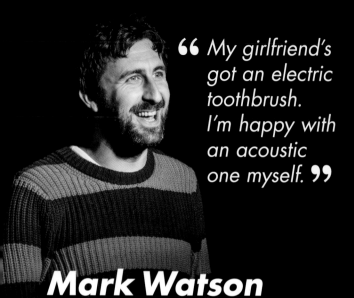

> 66 My girlfriend's got an electric toothbrush. I'm happy with an acoustic one myself. 99

Mark Watson

I started comedy by entering the *Daily Telegraph* Open Mic competition in 2002. I won the competition and they discontinued it after that, so I like to think I'm the reigning champion forever. After that, I did two or three years of barely paid gigs in front of twelve people and gradually worked my way up.

Terrified of thunderstorms, I've had hypnotherapy for it. Won't eat cheese. Am aiming to visit all ninety-two league football grounds in my lifetime. My brother's the youngest ever international football manager. Never been to Alton Towers.

Picture taken Old Rope Comedy, London, June 2015

> **66** *I released an album when I was ten. It was Princess Diana's favourite album... and that won't change.* **99**

Tom Craine

I started comedy in Cardiff. First gig at Chapter Arts Centre.
It went well because I knew everyone there.
I grew up in Bath, it's lovely place. You should visit.
I am 6' 1". I used to be shorter.
Elis James convinced me to try stand-up, and is the reason
I do comedy.
I will never forgive Elis James.

Picture taken Old Rope Comedy, London, June 2015

> **"** Thank you very much! Or as our dyslexic friends would say: 'Thank you very much!' It doesn't affect your speech. **"**

Spencer Brown

I started comedy at six years old when I asked a bishop visiting our school his weight and got a big laugh.
It's been downhill since then.
I cook Chinese food better than most Chinese restaurants*.
I have a black belt in karate.
I play average jazz piano.
I have an unhealthy obsession with modern boardgaming.
The scars on my arms are from pulling a pot of boiling water over myself on the day I learned to crawl.

*Not counting the ones in China

Picture taken Soho, London, May 2016

> **" My local museum has gone bust, not surprising they haven't got any Monet. "**

Mr Andy Andoza

I started comedy two years ago in a little place in Newport Pagnell called The Watershed. I was at their open mic night listening and thought I could do that, so a few weeks later I signed up and went for it, hooked straight away.

I was on Timmy Mallet's *Whack a Day*.

I won a country dancing contest.

I'm not symmetrical; my whole right side is a bit bigger/longer/thicker than my left.

I was once arrested in possession of stolen underpants. In custody the copper wrote 'knicker thief' on the cell door (I bought the pants off a Del Boy in the pub).

I've been chucked out of a fetish party for smoking weed in the garden.

Picture taken Big Grin, Rada, London, June 2015

> **Ode to Wetwipe: I'm clean, but I'm not dry.**

Rousha Browning

I have always loved comedy and wanted to do/write comedy in some form. But when I turned thirty, I said to myself 'OK... you either begin doing comedy in some way this year, or give up the idea of it completely'. This thought scared me, so I signed up to do a stand-up comedy course and haven't looked back since. I have an English Springer Spaniel called Zealand Maximus Black (he's the best dog ever). I have more fancy dress clothing/costumes than my actual everyday wear (I used to dress with a 'theme'). Whenever I'm supposed to be writing, I'll end up finding something in my room that I can balance on my head. I'll then create a character/look and do a mini photoshoot under the guise of 'The Queen of Procrastination'. I find this works perfectly when trying to avoid writing. I was once a Lifeguard. I absolutely LOVE lychees.

Picture taken Big Grin, Rada, London, June 2015

> ❝ *If Robins really were that rockin' they wouldn't be up so fucking early.* ❞

Kit Sullivan

I'm twelve gigs into my stand-up career (hopefully) and the first place I ever performed was the Lion's Den Comedy Club, Soho, London. That was the summer of 2014, so my ratio is currently a gig a month. I guess it's to try and give myself a bit of mystique, like a rare bird or Pokemon.

I met Johnny Depp once on the set of *Sweeney Todd*. He said I looked cool. I replied 'WHAGREDFGHADMMEZISM!'

I pretended to be hypnotised at a Derren Brown show so he would touch my face, and it worked! He's a handsome chap.

I'm an aggressively strong dancer. I've been described as 'MJ with epilepsy'.

I studied performing arts at Southend College.

I once got detention for sneezing too loud.

I was originally meant to be called Thomas like my dad, granddad etc. but my sister Jenny was born first and they thought Tom and Jenny was too close to Tom and Jerry, so my middle name is Thomas.

Picture taken
Big Grin, Rada, London,
June 2015

356

Ardal O'Hanlon

My first ever gig was in the Comedy Cellar, Dublin in 1989.
I have a BA in Communications Studies.
During the World Cup in 1974 I convinced myself and my family that I was paralysed so I could watch every match.
One summer I worked in a pea canning factory in Kings Lynn.
I once managed 340 header 'keepy uppies' with my friend Anthony Tabor in a flat in Battersea.
I play tennis three times a week.

Picture taken Balham Banana, London, July 2015

> **" I am occasionally asked what it's like to kiss a man with a moustache; the simple answer is, I don't know, I'm usually on the supply side of that particular equation. But the best answer I ever heard to that question was from a former lover of mine, a bisexual lady, who described the experience as 'much like going down on a woman with a vagina shaped like a face.' "**

James Ross

I started out in comedy doing improv at university: I wanted to do something on stage and it having no lines to learn meant I could actually fit it in around my course.
A miswired jaw means I can fit my whole fist in my mouth.
I once, while drunk, bit a Tory.
I once, while drunk, sustained a hairline crack up my leg after jumping off a three metre wrought iron gate in gale force winds in order to impress a lady. It didn't work.

Picture taken Big Grin, Rada, London, June 2015

*66 There's nothing
I like more than
a warm hand
upon my
entrance. 99*

Julian
Clary

I started as half of a double
act called Glad and May
in 1978, while a student
at Goldsmiths University
of London.
I am the son of a police
man and a probation officer.
I used to be an altar
boy at the Sacred Heart
Catholic church in
Teddington, Middlesex.
I am a member of the Institute
of Advanced Motorists.
I sometimes drink tap water.

Picture taken
Ealing Comedy Festival,
July 2015

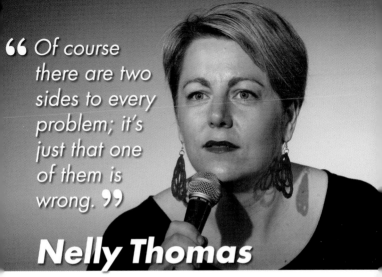

> 66 *Of course there are two sides to every problem; it's just that one of them is wrong.* 99

Nelly Thomas

I started comedy at the Jeez Louise Funny Women's Forum at the Melbourne Fringe Festival in 2002 when I was twenty-eight. I went along thinking it was a writing workshop. It wasn't.

I once wrote a column in a newspaper where I answered questions on – and only on – the Brontë sisters.

I was an under 13s girls BMX Champion.

I worked at a place for five years called Big Rooster. Guess who was the big rooster? (I dressed in a rooster suit and entertained kids at their birthday parties).

I did two years of a Ph.D. in cultural studies at Melbourne University (almost a doctor... maybe a nurse?)

The first time around I was in labour for thirty-six hours. The second time I asked for drugs.

Picture taken Soho Theatre, London, July 2015

> **Last year I did cocaine for the first fourteen times.**

Dylan Gott

I started in stand-up in 2004 in Toronto, Canada.
I've eaten an entire box of corndogs in one sitting.
You want to hang out with me now.
First time I got drunk I tried to do the worm and broke my nose.
I didn't wear jeans until I was fourteen because I found them too itchy.
I'm so sad.

Picture taken Hampstead Comedy Club, Camden, London, June 2015

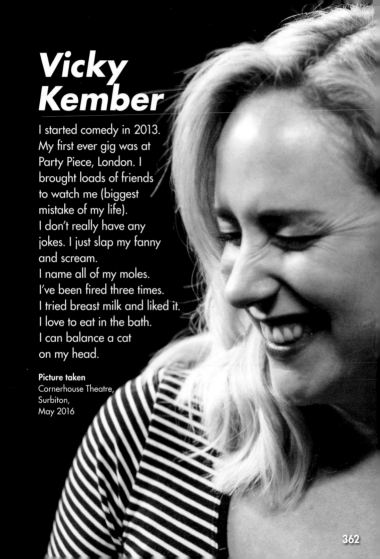

Vicky Kember

I started comedy in 2013. My first ever gig was at Party Piece, London. I brought loads of friends to watch me (biggest mistake of my life).
I don't really have any jokes. I just slap my fanny and scream.
I name all of my moles.
I've been fired three times.
I tried breast milk and liked it.
I love to eat in the bath.
I can balance a cat on my head.

Picture taken
Cornerhouse Theatre,
Surbiton,
May 2016

362

> **They say the First World War was fought because of the assassination of Archduke Ferdinand, but no one is that popular.**

Robert Newman

In 1987 I was writing sketches for *NewsRevue* at the Canal Cafe Theatre. At the end of the run they had a 'smoker' where all the writers could do five minutes. I got away with it and so, I started doing open spots and then half spots on the London comedy circuit, in rooms above pubs. The sort of places I still play. Although nowadays it is more half spots. I am Greek-Cypriot, American, French, English. There's a man called Robert Newman with my date of birth on the USA wanted list. Every time I go to America I am taken into a special room at JFK with cops and National Guardsmen who look at a photo on their screen, look at me, look at the photo, look at me, and then after half an hour say, 'Nah, it's not him,' and let me go. I took a two year break from stand-up to be the primary carer of my first child. I'm the slowest swimmer in London.

Picture taken
Balham Banana, London,
July 2015

> *I'm getting to the level of fatness where I'll soon be joining that legion of men for whom the track suit has nothing to do with keeping fit and everything to do with the elasticated waist band.*

Alan Francis

I started comedy as a student in Manchester. I had to MC the comedy night at the Student Union 'cause there was no one else to do it. I have three nieces and three nephews but no children. I play tennis and chess, not at the same time. I'm a science fiction nerd. I support Hearts FC. I like listening to jazz and going to gigs.

Picture taken Soho, London, May 2016

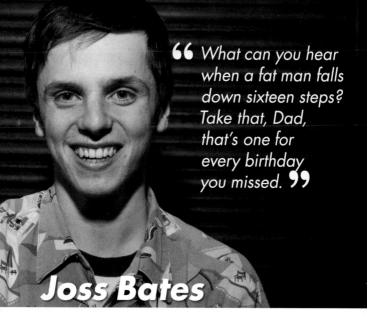

> 66 *What can you hear when a fat man falls down sixteen steps? Take that, Dad, that's one for every birthday you missed.* 99

Joss Bates

I started comedy in September 2015, but my first stand-up gig wasn't until December, before that I was doing sketch stuff. All of it was through my university comedy society (Warwick).
I was an extra in a short film about Elvis.
When I was younger I ate a tub of butter as my school lunch because my mum got the sandwich boxes confused, and I thought it was all I had to eat. I don't like butter any more.
My rap name is Fledging Mammal.
I'm Joss from the infamous Warwick comedy duo, Joss and Lauren. I had a blind dog that my mum named Claude because he was going to be 'Claude' by the cats.

Picture taken We Are Funny Project, Putney, London, April 2016

Jen Brister

My very first gig was when I was twenty-one back in 1996 at the King's Head in Crouch End. I had done a comedy course as part of my drama degree at Middlesex University. I was hilarious. I did my second gig about three months later. I was appalling.

I was a ball girl at Wimbledon tennis in 1990. I handled Boris Becker's balls on more than one occasion. It was also the last time I was seen in a gym skirt.

Whilst travelling in America and Australia I have been fined on three separate occasions for jay walking. I have this crazy British notion of understanding how to cross the road.

I was in the BBC comedy semi finals in 2000 and Spike Milligan was one of the judges. I was later told by a BBC producer that Spike had said I had funny bones and a great pair of Bristols. Needless to say I didn't go through to the final.

I'm gay and half Spanish and have often been referred to as 'The beige lezza'. I now refer to myself in the same way, cause if you can't beat 'em...

Picture taken The Southbank, London, May 2016

366

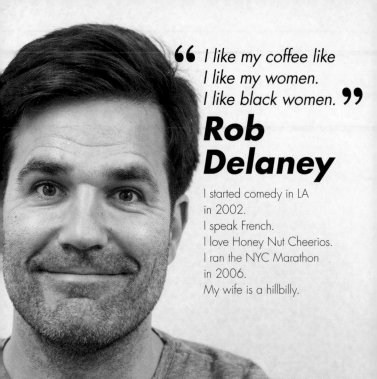

> **" I like my coffee like**
> **I like my women.**
> **I like black women. "**

Rob
Delaney

I started comedy in LA
in 2002.
I speak French.
I love Honey Nut Cheerios.
I ran the NYC Marathon
in 2006.
My wife is a hillbilly.

Picture taken
Ealing Comedy Festival,
July 2015

> **" There's only three things that offend me in society; racism, sexism and foreign women. "**

Lenny Sherman

I started comedy September 2010 in London. My first gig was a showcase at Up The Creek for Harry Denford's London Comedy Course.
I'm a Millwall supporter.
I'm 6' 4".
I've been to prison for fighting at Millwall.
I'm a Catholic.
I am a nice person, honestly ha ha.

Picture taken Southbank, London, April 2016

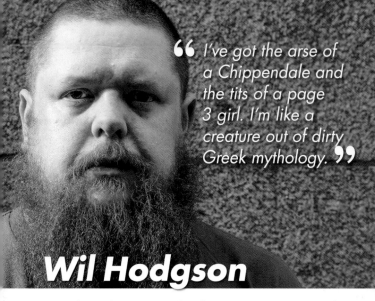

> " I've got the arse of a Chippendale and the tits of a page 3 girl. I'm like a creature out of dirty Greek mythology. "

Wil Hodgson

I started comedy in 2001 and my first gig was at Jesters in Bristol.
My grandfather arrested Ranulph Fiennes in the sixties for trying to dynamite the set of *Dr Doolittle*.

As well as being a comedian I co-run a barbershop/beauty parlour in Chippenham called Hepcats.

I trained to be a wrestler for a while in the early 2000s and participated in thirty-man Battle Royals.

In the early eighties when I was about five I won several *Worzel Gummidge* themed fancy dress competitions that were part of a tabloid campaign to get the series uncancelled.

I wrote an essay at school about a farting competition and got an A plus and a certificate of merit from the head for it.

Picture taken Edinburgh Festival, August 2015

> **The three best things about being a seventh son are that hand-me-downs are back in fashion. When Mum remembered my name she forgot what she was rollicking me for. And when it was my turn the toilet seat was warm.**

Carl Day

I started comedy entering the Laughing Horse Comedy Competition in 2010, making the semi-finals.

I ran the London Marathon in an original medieval suit of armour (35 kgs) in nine hours (BBC coverage still on YouTube).

I was nearly shot at Moscow airport mistaken for a terrorist.

I and my company made the national and international news when my company moved 7,500 tonnes of sand from the UK to Dubai.

I was rescued by the Italian fire brigade from a top floor balcony after locking myself out of my hotel room to take a photo of the Alps in my underpants in sub zero temperature.

Picture taken Ipswich, July 2015

370

> **"** I can't control the muscles in my right hand very much. I can give people the finger, it just takes twenty minutes. **"**

Spring Day

I started doing stand-up comedy at The Tokyo Comedy Store in September of 2001 as I had just been fired from my first job in Japan on my very first day for having cerebral palsy. I learned to speak Japanese fluently at university only to go to Tokyo to find out nobody is saying anything interesting.

I grew up in a home with twenty dogs, five rats, three cats, two birds and a ferret.

I am an occasional voiceover artist in Japan for grammatically erroneous English earthquake warnings, 'In case of an earthquake, buildings may attack you…'

When I was three years old I wanted to grow up to be a mermaid. My plans were squashed when my mother told me I couldn't become a mermaid because, 'There's no money in that.'

I don't want children because I don't need yet another person in my life that loves me less than I love them.

Picture taken Edinburgh Festival, August 2015

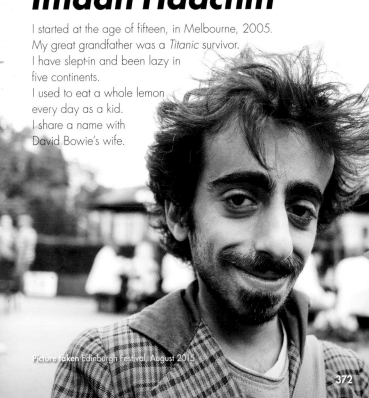

> **66** *If a Philosophy student sits in the woods and figures out the meaning of life... and there is nobody around to hear it... should he have studied Law?* **99**

Imaan Hadchiti

I started at the age of fifteen, in Melbourne, 2005.
My great grandfather was a *Titanic* survivor.
I have slept-in and been lazy in
five continents.
I used to eat a whole lemon
every day as a kid.
I share a name with
David Bowie's wife.

Picture taken Edinburgh Festival, August 2015

372

> **I've always wanted to open a James Bond themed curry restaurant called, The Spy Who Loved Ghee.** 99

Emily McQuade

I did my first comedy gig at the King's Head in Crouch End in 2007. I've taken a few lengthy breaks from comedy, but keep being drawn back in.

I got my first laughs from strangers at aged four by repeatedly yelling, 'Keep the dogs downstairs!' like a mini sergeant major. It was funny in context.

At different times in my life, I created an anti-*Bergerac* comic and a fanzine about indie pop and poetry. Sadly, I no longer have copies of either.

I have unusually bendy fingers, which is useful for both entertaining children and frightening off enemies.

I am a cinema fan with a fondness for the arthouse and the weird. My favourite ever film review was my grandmother's on David Croenborg's *The Fly*: 'He vomits and his hand comes off – Eeee!'

Picture taken We Are Funny Project, Putney, London, April 2016

> ❛ Being deaf, I didn't even realise my husband snored, till my best mate Kath mentioned it... ❜❜

Theresa Farlow

I was diagnosed with ADHD in April 2013 and, as a result, did my first gig on 23rd June 2013. I blame Lee Mack for both. I once gatecrashed Dennis Waterman's party and he complained... that I was wearing a West Ham scarf. Aged nine, I appeared in a Jaffa Cakes TV advert. I've declared myself an Honorary Northerner. I have a Ph.D. in Engineering Geology. I'm apiphobic (Google it) and allergic to cockles.

Picture taken
Edinburgh Festival,
August 2015

374

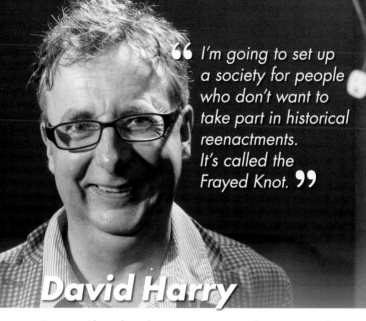

> 66 I'm going to set up a society for people who don't want to take part in historical reenactments. It's called the Frayed Knot. 99

David Harry

First gig: Glastonbury theatre stage 2006 – disaster. I tossed a deck of cards out, the bands broke and the cards scattered over the audience like confetti. I said 'Not like that' and walked off to silence.

I lived on a tea estate in Sri Lanka until I was three.

Travelling solo at sixteen to Paris I jumped onto the outside of a train as it pulled out of Calais station. The guard pulled the cord and threatened prosecution, then took pity on me.

I proposed to my wife (she's in Steve Best's other book) during a storm, at the end of Bognor pier.

I once stood for Hackney Council.

Picture taken Camden Comedy Club, London, October 2016

375

> **66** *Never give up on your dreams.
> When I was seven all I wanted
> was a race car bed. Now
> I sleep in my car.* **99**

Andrew Reza

I did my first gig in December 2014
in the Lions Den Comedy Club.
I had my first grey hair when I was 14.
I used to be able to recite the radio
version of *The Hitchhiker's Guide
to the Galaxy* word for word.
Now I have friends.
Six months ago I tried to do some push
ups and ended up in intensive care.
I used to believe that the slitted covers
on traffic lights were there to stop birds
nesting inside them. I believed this until
I was twenty-three and being taught to
drive by a stranger. I still can't drive.
I have a scar on my right hand from
this one time I tried to open a bottle
of shampoo too quickly.

Picture taken We Are Funny Project, Dalston, London, October 2016

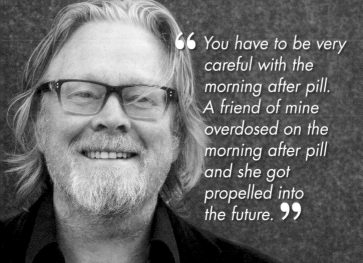

> 66 *You have to be very careful with the morning after pill. A friend of mine overdosed on the morning after pill and she got propelled into the future.* 99

Kevin Gildea

I started comedy in 1988. Myself and the other members of our sketch group Mr Trellis (Barry Murphy and Ardal O'Hanlon) set up The Comedy Cellar with Dermot Carmody and Karl McDermott.
I was Student Union President of Dublin City University.
I love playing football with Rosa and Alex.
I'm an award-winning radio playwright.
I saw a shark on a documentary about sharks.
My left knee is quite sore.

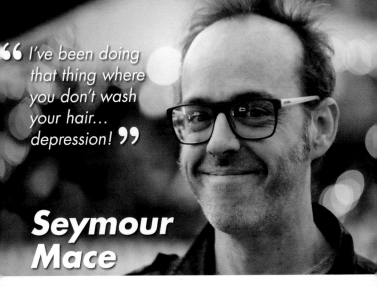

> **" I've been doing that thing where you don't wash your hair... depression! "**

Seymour Mace

I started working in comedy professionally at Gateshead Garden Festival in 1990 when I joined The Natural Theatre Company, a peripatetic, improvisational, street theatre company based in Bath. If it's my first stand-up gig you're after then that was at the Hyena in Newcastle on 6th November 2000.

I've got decks and a mixer and 3,000 7" singles.

I'm in a cake club and I invented the Peanut Butter and Jam Baked Cheesecake.

I've got a tattoo on my right arm of a demon climbing out of hell in the shape of a number 5, my favourite number.

I once got caught in a time loop whilst on magic mushrooms.

Whilst in Japan I auditioned for the part of Big Bird at the Sesame Street Theme Park.

Picture taken Edinburgh Festival, August 2015

> **"** I'm convinced ISIS is going to strike in the UK next. ISIS terrorist jihadis in Syria are fed up with all these Brits going over there stealing their jobs. **"**

David Mills

I had been an actor and a cabaret act for years before seriously getting into stand-up. I did my first open mic gig in London in 2010.
I'm obsessed with KPOP (a musical genre originating in South Korea).

I have three brothers and two sisters.
I speak Spanish.
I was the PR for one of the UK's best-selling fashion/ lifestyle brands.
I saw Stephanie Mills on Broadway in *The Wiz*.

Picture taken Edinburgh Festival, August 2015

379

> **I was on the BNP website last week www-dot-BNP-dot-co-dot-U-K-K-K.**

Bruce Fummey

I hated my job as a financial adviser, saw forty approaching and decided to become a stand-up. I went to a workshop run by Mark Blake in The Comedy Pub in London. The night before the workshop I turned up at Laughing Horse in Richmond and Alex Petty let me on for five minutes. I met my wife when I was sent for treatment for a groin strain and she was the physiotherapist.
In secondary school I was on the school fencing team.

I speak Gaelic badly.
As a teenager I was going to become a church minister. I was told I should get some life experience first, so I studied physics, discovered alcohol and cannabis and never became a minister. Although I live in rural Perthshire I hate the taste and smell of lamb – at least when it's cooked.
My first record was *Calling Occupants of Interplanetary Craft* by The Carpenters.

Picture taken Edinburgh Festival, August 2015

> **66** *My wife and I can't have children – we don't like them.* **99**

Sarah Franken

I started doing open spots in San Francisco in 2002 while living in my car.

I'm a fairly good piano player.

I'm a libertarian.

I've have an eclectic range of fans, from ex members of the Manson family to the late Robin Williams.

I'm a transgender lesbian.

I once chased a heckler off the stage and put him in a choke hold. There was a review of the gig that thought it was an Andy Kaufman bit.

Picture taken Edinburgh Festival, August 2015

> **"** My wife said to me the other day, 'Do you know how everyone in the world has a doppelgänger? I wonder what mine looks like'. **"**

Tony Jameson

I started in Newcastle in September, 2008. My now wife and I were looking for something to do. We spotted open mic comedy above a pub advertised. As we're both comedy fans, we went six weeks in a row. Eventually I plucked up the courage to get on stage, and only regret not doing it sooner. Before comedy I was a film production lecturer at various colleges and universities for eight years.

I've recently started playing American football with the Yorkshire Rams.

When I was sixteen I became a fully qualified football referee. I was Kelly Brooks' driver for a feature film.

Picture taken Edinburgh Festival, August 2015

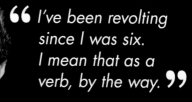

> **❝** *I've been revolting since I was six. I mean that as a verb, by the way.* **❞**

Sameena Zehra

I started performing comedy in 2011. At the end of 2010, I attended a comedy workshop with Tony Allen, did five minutes, fell in love with it and wrote an hour's show for Edinburgh 2011. Because nobody explained to me that you go from five mins, to ten mins, to fifteen mins and so on and I'm crazy!

I'm a story-teller comedian, rather than a stand-up.

I've climbed Machu Picchu.

I had a cat called Chairman Miaow.

I know how to commit the perfect murder (I detailed it in a previous show, *Tea with Terrorists* – some people in the audience took notes – I may have started something there).

I've played the Apollo Theatre in Harlem, New York. (I used to be an actor, and I was part of a production of *Midnight's Children* for the RSC, which toured all over, including New York). Performing in that space was pretty much the highlight of my acting career. I'd love to go back and do the 'world famous open mic night' as a comedian. I will, some day!

Picture taken Edinburgh Festival, August 2015

> **" Abortion jokes...
> they're all in
> the delivery. "**

Bronston
Jones

My first open mic ever was November 1993, Denver Comedy
Works... but I didn't really start taking it seriously until 2008
in Los Angeles.

I was born in Washington D.C. The only way I could be more
American is if I bought a gun... and denied climate change.

I once hit a deer going 60mph on my Harley. I walked away
with a broken thumb. The deer ran off. It owes me a bike.

My favourite song is 'Beautiful Girls' by Van Halen.
It's perfectly ridiculous and makes me happy.

At least once a day someone asks how tall I am.

Picture taken Edinburgh Festival, August 2015

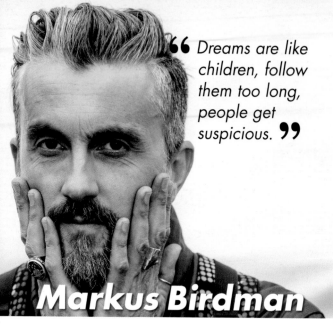

> **"** *Dreams are like children, follow them too long, people get suspicious.* **"**

Markus Birdman

I started comedy after being thrown out of Rabbinical college in 2000. I was a most diligent and devout student, but failed in the parallel parking.

I was in a band that had a hit in Germany.

I once worked for Jimmy Savile.

I delivered a pizza to Eddy the Eagle.

My uncle was the Official Exorcist to the Bishop of Bath and Wells.

I was once chased out of the Gilded Balloon in Edinburgh by security, dressed as a pantomime horse.

Picture taken Edinburgh Festival, August 2015

> *Good evening, my name's Piff the Magic Dragon. You might have heard of my older brother? Steve.*

Piff the Magic Dragon
John van der Put

I started in London in 2008.

I'm 25 per cent Singaporean.

I now live in Las Vegas.

I was in the first ever opera staged at Shakespeare's Globe.

I have a degree in Computer Science from Lancaster University.

For an ill advised six months of my teenage years I was a Christian clown.

Picture taken Edinburgh Festival, August 2015

> 66 *Porridge is made of oats and sadness.* 99

Luca Cupani

I started comedy on the 24th of February 2014 at the King Gong Show of the London Comedy Store (and I won it!).
I'm Italian.
I moved to the UK in 2014.
I have a degree in Classics.
I am a hypochondriac.

Picture taken Edinburgh Festival, August 2015

> **"** *The most important lesson I've learned from social media: if you've just killed a lion, don't take a selfie.* **"**

Ro Campbell

I started comedy at the Edinburgh Stand Red Raw night in February 2005.
I lived in Nepal until I was nine.
I dropped out of law school and moved to the desert to live with Aboriginal people.

I was a professional stagehand for eight years.
I once deliberately almost blinded David Walliams with a pea.
I have performed stand-up comedy professionally in thirty-eight countries.

Picture taken Edinburgh Festival, August 2015.

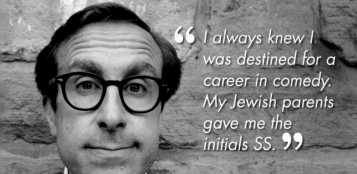

> 66 *I always knew I was destined for a career in comedy. My Jewish parents gave me the initials SS.* 99

Simon Schatzberger

My first gig was in March 2015 at a synagogue in Muswell Hill, booked by the Rabbi for Purim, a Jewish festival.

I was Nottingham chess champion when I was seven years old.

I had a trial to play with Nottingham FC youth team but it coincided with Yom Kippur (a Jewish holiday).

I always dreamed that Brian Clough would have put me in his team. I still believe he would have.

My dad escaped from Nazi-occupied Vienna in 1938.

At sixteen I was picked by Sue Townsend to play Adrian Mole.

Picture taken Edinburgh Festival, August 2015

Paul Currie

I started performing comedy on stilts. As a stilt walker I couldn't stop talking and chatting to people when I was hired. I was an utter motormouth. These gigs were and still are (because I still love stilt walking) between two and three hours long. So in about 2002 it occurred to me while watching some comedians in a club doing five minutes and ten minutes spots that I had hours and hours of material and the confidence to get up and try it... On my own two feet not on my stilts. So I first did a five to ten min routine in Oct/Nov 2003 at the age of twenty-nine in Auntie Annie's Bar in Belfast at a little sweaty cabaret ran by a seriously funny clown called Neal Hall.

I dream of opening a bohemian cafe/bistro in Belfast someday. I'm a Jim Henson Muppeteer and had the honour in 2010 to perform with master *Sesame Street* puppeteer Carroll Spinney aka Oscar the Grouch and Big Bird.

I have performed on many kids' TV puppet shows since 2006.

I teach circus skills to little kids of two to seven years as well as working with adults and teenagers with learning difficulties and mental health issues in the Belfast Circus School.

I am a painter and sculptor, and make my own puppets.

Picture taken
Edinburgh Festival,
August 2015

390

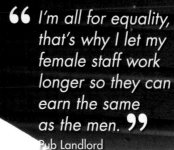

Al Murray

I started comedy at university, doing sketches and then the odd sound effects stand-up thing I used to do. I was lucky to have met Stewart Lee and Richard Herring on my first day at university; they were doing a sketch show and that seemed like it might be a fun thing to do. Then after university I came to London and sort of got started doing gigs.

I'm the great great great grandson of the writer William Thackeray who wrote *Vanity Fair*. It's interesting but in all honesty it doesn't really amount to a thing.

The funniest thing I have ever seen – and I always feel bad about admitting this – is a woman walking along the South Circular in Catford slipping in dog poo. She was like something out of a cartoon.

I've been on telly in Cambodia – I went to the Khmer boxing a few years ago and if you put money into the winner's purse they show you on TV.

I love to BBQ.

Picture taken Edinburgh Festival, August 2015

391

> **I like my women with a bit of meat… failing that, some chips.**

Steve McLean

I started in March 2013 at the Jester Jesters night in Farringdon. I remember the room was so cold that I could see my breath. Those guys are still going and run a lovely night in the Betsy Trotwood. Before that I'd dabbled in performance poetry. As a poet I'd found myself on some pretty decent bills supporting people like John Hegley and John Cooper Clarke.

I once had a pee next to Richard Branson, I said, 'You're Richard Branson'. He said. 'I know'.

I was twice a contestant on the game show *Goldenballs*.

I was born in a town called Dumbarton, which is where David Byrne of Talking Heads and Jimmy McCulloch of Wings were born.

Jana of the Jungle was my first crush. She defended the jungle and the laws of nature in a furry leotard.

Picture taken We Are Funny Project, Putney, London, April 2016

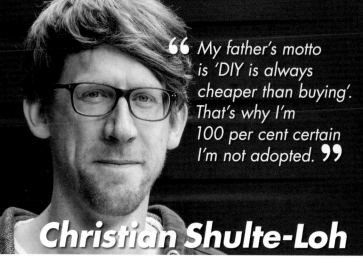

> **My father's motto is 'DIY is always cheaper than buying'. That's why I'm 100 per cent certain I'm not adopted.**

Christian Shulte-Loh

I had written stand-up bits as a teenager but never dared to perform. I felt: what if somebody sees me do it? I wanted to avoid that at all cost. So I waited until I did an Erasmus semester in Belgium in 2002. I thought: it's a different country, so nobody will notice. And it worked out: not many people did notice. That's how I started my stand-up career. My first ever gig was in English – just because I was being a coward. Only years later did I start in German.

I caught the tambourine that Noel Gallagher threw into the crowd at the last ever Oasis concert in Germany. I'm two metres tall. That's why I have a tambourine now.

My full name, Christian Josef Hugo Schulte-Loh, is almost two metres long.

I am allergic to cats and springtime.

Picture taken Edinburgh Festival, August 2015

> **My dad said, 'Always dress for the job you want, not the job you have.' He looked ridiculous picking litter dressed as Batman.**

Jason Simmons

I first performed comedy in July 2011 at Up the Creek and started writing comedy to pretend I was actually working in an office job I hated.

I'm am a 1st dan black-belt in ShinKen-do.

I used to work at the Tower of London.

I auditioned for the *X Factor* in 2004 and made it to the second stage of auditions, but was never on TV.

I once performed as an Elvis tribute act in a care home and had to leave the building dressed as Elvis with the residents shouting 'Elvis has left the building' out of the windows as I loaded up my car.

I'm currently learning hypnosis.

Picture taken Whyteleafe Tavern, Whyteleafe September 2015

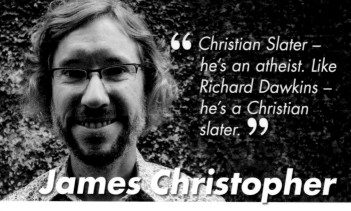

> **" Christian Slater – he's an atheist. Like Richard Dawkins – he's a Christian slater. "**

James Christopher

I did my first gig in 2005 in Newcastle. I'd been keeping a notebook of amusing ideas for around a year, so booked a gig to give them a try.
I didn't realise there was a difference between pro nights and new material nights, so did my first gig to 120 Geordies on a Friday night. I lost them about halfway through my set, but my last line got a big laugh.
My date of birth is 5.6.78
I was born with my umbilical cord wrapped around my neck, which usually means a cesarean section is required. But it wasn't necessary as my umbilical cord was roughly twice the normal length. It is preserved in York Hospital as a medical curiosity.
When I was seventeen, I opened a student bank account and was given a four digit PIN number. I also started working for M&S and was given an ID number to log-in to the tills. It was the same number – 4651 (I don't use either any more!)
My great grandmother was a renowned clairvoyant.

Picture taken Edinburgh Festival, August 2015

> *A male friend of mine once kindly offered to be a sperm donor. But he pulled out at the last minute.*

Maxie Wade

I have wanted to become a comedian since I was nine, after one assembly when I had to tell a joke in front of the whole school and became hooked. It wasn't until I was twenty-three that I plucked up the courage to ask for my first open mic gig, in Leeds. It was run by none other than James Christopher. He gave me a gig for the following month; the week before I messaged him wanting to drop out, he talked me out, mainly because he liked me and wanted to see me again. Four days before my first gig, we went on our first date and fell for one another. By the time I did my first stand-up gig, we were a couple.

I have run three marathons (I even ran the Paris and London Marathons two weeks apart).

I was voted Prom Queen in high school.

I have been diagnosed as bipolar and have since raised over £2,500 for mental health charities.

When I was seventeen I appeared in a short horror film where I had to play a werewolf.

Picture taken Edinburgh Festival, August 2015

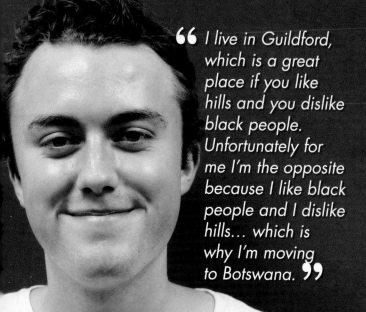

> 66 *I live in Guildford, which is a great place if you like hills and you dislike black people. Unfortunately for me I'm the opposite because I like black people and I dislike hills... which is why I'm moving to Botswana.* 99

Tom Lucy

I started comedy on 4th November 2012 in London when I was sixteen years old.
I once played tennis with Brad Pitt's stunt double.
I was taught history at school by Malcolm Hardee's son.
I know everything about James Brown.

Picture taken Edinburgh Festival, August 2015

397

> **Like most people from Ireland, I was born a Catholic... which actually came as a bit of a shock to my parents who were both Jewish.**

Michael Redmond

I did bits and pieces of comedy in Dublin but my first really proper stand-up gig was in London in January 1987 at the notorious Tunnel Club in South London... and I survived it. I almost died when I was only five years old during what should have been a routine operation to remove my tonsils. I somehow haemorrhaged and was on the critical list for three days.

Upon leaving school, I trained for five very unhappy years to be an accountant. Although my parents were not snobs, I went to quite a posh fee-paying school in Dublin which was steeped in a British rather than an Irish tradition. I have twin sons and when they were about four years old, I decided to shave off my moustache. They genuinely didn't seem to recognise me at first and it took me a few days to regain their confidence.

Picture taken
Comedy Store, London,
September 2015

398

> *"Heckling is like hunting, and you're tracking an angry brown bear with a cotton bud."*

Johnny Vegas

I accidentally started as a drunk student. And determinedly as a drunk ex-student in 1995. I started as a heckler at The Citadel in St Helens and got up at the end and did a rant.
I no longer suffer gout.
Alter egos are real if your dad is nasty enough.
I hear my dad's granddad's voice when I play roulette.
I'm a goat whisperer.

Picture taken Comedy Store, London, September 2015

> **Golden showers in the bedroom? Just think of the mess. I don't even eat toast in bed.**

Jon Udry

I started doing comedy with my juggling when I started street performing in Cornwall in 2004.
I was a member of the Junior Cornish Magical Society.
I hate bats and grapefruit. (Both will ruin any fruit salad).
At the age of ten, my stage name was The Great Alfonse. I even had business cards.
In 2005, I was the first to be awarded the prize of British Young Juggler of the Year.
As a child, I used to lie to the teachers at playgroup about having an elephant and a giraffe as pets.

Picture taken Cabaret Boom Boom, Crookes Social Club, Sheffield, December 2015

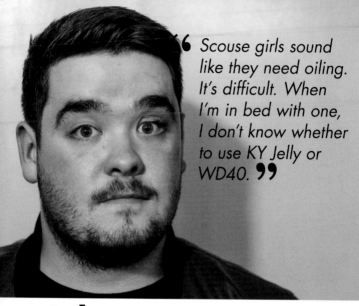

Scouse girls sound like they need oiling. It's difficult. When I'm in bed with one, I don't know whether to use KY Jelly or WD40.

Adam Rowe

I started at the Hot Water Comedy Club, Sunday 27th June 2010.
In year nine, I was the second best mathematician of my age in England.
I dropped out of a Mathematics degree after less than a week.

I have had a muscle removed from my leg and put into my eye lid.
I will drink rum until there is no rum.
I love battle rap, particularly the UK's biggest league; Don't Flop.

Picture taken Comedy Store, London, September 2015

> *...used to think an ocean of orange soda actually existed. But it was just a Fanta-sea.* 🙵🙵

Bec Hill

I started comedy in Adelaide, Australia, 2005.

Growing up, my family were in a medieval society, which involved attending monthly feasts in period costume.

If I've had a few ciders, I'm VERY good at pub games (pool/darts/etc) for the first round. Then my ability rapidly decreases.

As a child, I was terrified of mannequins.

I was forced to overcome my fear when my dad brought a mannequin home one day. It was a lady mannequin Dad saved from being thrown out. My parents put a fake beard on her and called her 'Bob'.

Picture taken
Hen and Chickens, Highbury and Islington, London,
December 2015

> **I think think sex between two people who love each other is a beautiful thing... as long as they don't mind you being there.**

Daniel Audritt

I started comedy in a pub called The Cavendish Arms in Stockwell, London in December 2013.

I talk about relationships a lot on stage, but that's because it's the only thing I'm interested in. Even at school when they asked us to write an essay on the birth of Jesus, I wrote one on how well Joseph dealt with the affair.

I grew up playing ice hockey.

I was born in the hospital car park.

I studied English and Drama at Hull University.

The first band I saw live was Toploader.

I'm from Swindon.

Picture taken West Cliff Theatre, Clacton-on-Sea, September 2015

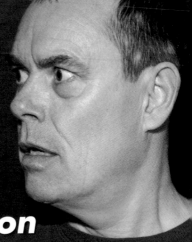

> **❝** *Do I hate it when people ask questions and then answer them themselves? Yes, I do.* **❞**

Kevin Eldon

I started comedy in a school play in 1974, unconsciously. The play was *Maria Marten and the Red Barn*, supposedly a heart-rending tragedy. My character was Jasper Ryan, a bow street runner. My costume was a cloak, a top hat and a huge moustache. I looked ridiculous. As soon as I came on stage there was a laugh and I proceeded to go with that and gurn and mug my way through the whole thing. And I've never stopped mugging and gurning since, for which I can only apologise.

I've been in the same blues band for thirty years.

I've been underground in Switzerland and have seen the Hadron Collider.

I once stood outside John Lennon's old house in Liverpool for an hour crying and later found out it was the wrong house.

I cook quite staggeringly good roast potatoes.

Picture taken Koko, Camden Town, London, November 2015

404

" A bad high jumper walks into a bar. "

Currer Ball

I started in 2013, in a
sad place.
I'm a 31" waist.
I have a Myspace page.
I have an intimate birthmark.
I prefer the caterpillar to the
butterfly. The honour of the
former's sacrifice outshines
the latter's mere prettiness.

Picture taken
The Delphi Club (1st floor), Sudbury, Suffolk,
November 2015

> **I hate double standards. If I have sex with loads of women I get called a player, if a woman does it she shouldn't be called a slut, she should be called a lesbian.**

Jack Barry

I applied to Cambridge because I wanted to be in the Footlights, but when it turned out I wasn't clever enough I went to Leeds and joined the Tealights. I still do sketches with my friend Annie McGrath as the double act Twins.

I started doing stand-up when I graduated because it's easier to organise yourself. I speak fluent Mandarin, having spent a total of three years living in Shanghai throughout my life.

I was once on the German version of *Jim'll Fix It*. It was called *Hacky's Yellow Cab*. I've also been on TV as a criminal in a police line-up on *Panorama* and on *Eggheads*. My team lost spectacularly. In Germany I once spent a week doing work experience for the Augsburg Police Force. I was taken along on drugs raids and helped arrest a man carrying 30,000 euros worth of heroin on him.

Picture taken The Cavendish Arms, Stockwell, London, April 2016

> ❝ We're very safety-conscious parents. We have two stairgates, one at the top of the stairs, one at the bottom. It's absolutely fantastic, they play in there for hours. ❞

Rob Thomas

I started in 2010, did a course with the excellent Jack Milner in Stratford, East London. Usual story – stormed the showcase, died at the real gig.

I was run over by a bus when I was twelve.

I was a drummer for the London Olympic ceremonies.

I paused *Mission Impossible* on a shot of Tom Cruise's face in a private-jet lounge just as I knew he'd be walking in. He thought it was hilarious. I'm lying, it annoyed him.

I beatbox for an award-winning choir.

When I did hospital radio, I was asked to play a Rat Pack song for a chap in intensive care who had turned 95 that day. I didn't think it through and slapped on *My Way*.

In my twenties I could run 5K in 14:50. Now, I can't.

Picture taken Christchurch, Woking, December 2015

> **66** *I entered the Young Musician of The Year the other day. He was furious.* **99**

Matt Lucas

I started when I was eighteen years old. I used to go to the National Youth Theatre. I saw David Walliams and Jason Bradley do a double act. I did some open spots at the Comedy Cafe. Officially my first gig was at Punchlines, West Hampstead on October 3rd 1992. Five weeks later Bob Mortimer spotted me.

I get really upset when Arsenal lose.

I eat crisps in bed.

I think Lloyd Webber is Britain's greatest living melodist.

I don't know if melodist is a word.

Picture taken Hen and Chickens, Highbury and Islington, London, December 2015

Adam Buxton

I started making silly videos with Joe Cornish around 1984 when I was fifteen. We did our first TV show in 1995. I started doing live comedy 'properly' in 2004. My first paid gig was at the Amused Moose in Soho (£5). I did a character; a pretentious East European poet/animator called Pavel or maybe my character Ken Korda.

I have a first class honours degree in Sculpture.

One of my nipples is inverted but pops out when there's trouble.

I once stood in a corridor with David Bowie but he was talking to Ricky Gervais so I didn't say hello.

I once went on holiday to the Maldives with my wife and I think about it nearly every day.

Picture taken Koko, Camden, London, November 2015

" Sometimes it's hard being Chinese. Because I'm Japanese. "

Rick Kiesewetter

I took a stand-up class at the City Lit in 2003 and
have been trying to become the world's 20th
best Asian comedian since then.
I was a sergeant in US Military Intelligence.
I was a UK Gladiator contender 1993
and had a fight with Wolf.
I was adopted in Japan.
I was raised in New Jersey.

Picture taken Camden, London, November 2015

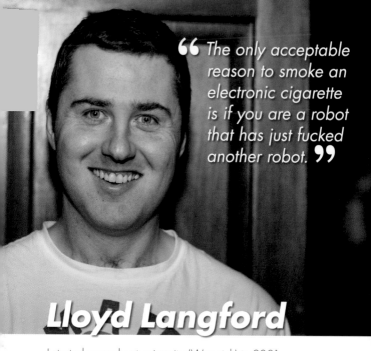

> **The only acceptable reason to smoke an electronic cigarette is if you are a robot that has just fucked another robot.**

Lloyd Langford

I started comedy at university (Warwick) in 2001.
I won Baglan Cub Scouts Shiniest Shoes Award in 1994.
I met Little Richard and he told me to follow the path of Jesus Christ.
I went on holiday with someone for our second date.
I once did jury duty with a man who said the most preposterous things. A couple of days in he said that in his opinion, golf was the easiest game in the world. One of the other jurors was a professional golfer. That was a long week.
I think the grapefruit is the most underrated of all the fruit.

Picture taken Koko, Camden, London, November 2015

> **I often wonder, when two fairgrounds meet is that fete?** 99

Frank Sanazi Peter Cunningham

I started performing comedy about twenty-five years ago running and hosting a Comedy Cabaret Bingo night at The Studio in Beckenham. I ran the shows successfully for a few years so decided to concentrate on character comedy, creating different singing comedy personas for my shows, culminating in the popular Frank Sanazi (A Crooning Sinatra/Hitler hybrid parody).

I used to be a cocktail barman and was out working in San Francisco in 1989 when the earthquake hit... I was fixing a customer a cocktail and as the rumbling finished I said, 'Is that shaken enough for you?'

I have a treasured Blue Peter badge which I got for appearing on the programme with a number of chosen Elvis impersonators after setting the world record (along with over 150 others) for largest number of Elvises singing 'Viva Las Vegas' in Selfridges, London 2005.

I can play the instrumental tune 'Popcorn' by Hot Butter on my teeth.

Picture taken Edinburgh, August 2015

412

> **66** *I phoned my electric company demanding a smaller bill, so now they send it to me on A5.* **99**

Chris Tavner

I did the gong show at the Manchester Comedy Store about ten years ago, because I didn't know there was anywhere else you could do it. Although a long standing member of the Socialist Workers Party as an adult,

I once performed 'Land of Hope and Glory' with a youth orchestra at the closing of the Tory Party conference. When my dad worked as a hotel porter, Tommy Cooper hassled and hassled him until he agreed to give him a lift to his gig that night. As soon as they got around the corner from the hotel he got him to pull over and said, 'It's all right, I'll walk from here.'
My girlfriend waited until it was a leap year and proposed to me on 29th February. She also managed to arrange a card congratulating us from Bournemouth manager Eddie Howe.
I've seen Cliff Richard perform live more times than any other musician.

Picture taken
The Rawhide, Liverpool,
October 2009

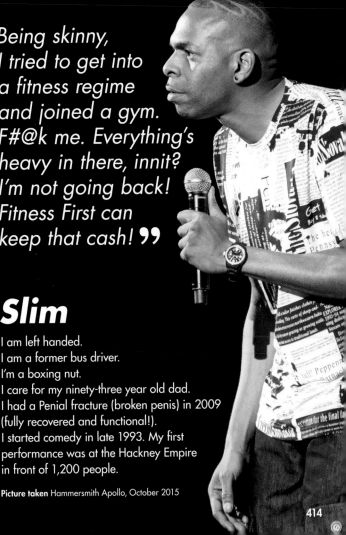

> **" Being skinny,
> I tried to get into
> a fitness regime
> and joined a gym.
> F#@k me. Everything's
> heavy in there, innit?
> I'm not going back!
> Fitness First can
> keep that cash! "**

Slim

I am left handed.
I am a former bus driver.
I'm a boxing nut.
I care for my ninety-three year old dad.
I had a Penial fracture (broken penis) in 2009
(fully recovered and functional!).
I started comedy in late 1993. My first
performance was at the Hackney Empire
in front of 1,200 people.

Picture taken Hammersmith Apollo, October 2015

> " *The greatest moment of my life? Four years ago I had a Pizza Hut buffet and they undercharged me.* "

Sean McLoughlin

Did a few gigs at university in Newcastle (2007–09), but started more regularly after I graduated.
I hate honey.
I saw Barack Obama whilst working as a waiter at the QE2 Centre.
I lost my virginity in a tent.
I have never bought anything on eBay.

Picture taken Ferneham Hall, Fareham, December 2015

415

> **My freezer is seriously chilled. You might say it's because of liquid evaporation... I say it's because of all the inner peas.** "

Jenny Lockyer

My first official gig was in 2003 in Hammersmith at Upstairs at the Rutland, a comedy/poetry night hosted by Jude Simpson.
I love custard.
I know all the places that sell custard or that might have custard within a half mile radius of my house.
I run an arts company called Funsense.
I host house gigs.
I have a poem published next to one by Spike Milligan! Pretty happy with that.

Picture taken
Christchurch, Woking,
December 2015

> **66** *St. Patrick's Day is how Ireland lets alcoholics know that Xmas is over.* **99**

Eleanor Tiernan

First gig was a heat of a comedy competition in Dublin in 2004.
Roast anything is my favourite dinner.
I love jigsaws and I hate jet lag.
I've been friends with people for years and not realised that they were baked off their heads the whole time.
I don't have a belief system but I think there might be some substance to Feng Shui.

Picture taken Winter gardens, Eastbourne, January 2016

417

> **66** *This is mind reading just like Derren Brown, and if you go in the West End he can cost you upwards of £50 or £60 per ticket... but then again he is a lot better than me so it is worth it.* **99**

Alan Hudson

My first magic show was at the age of eight on the mean streets of Long Riston (a leafy village in East Yorkshire) where I would charge passers by two pence to watch a trick. This was all after having a keen interest in Paul Daniels (it was the 80s!) and getting a magician to perform for my fifth birthday.

As a kid I had a job stocking chocolate bars in a shop.

I used to steal chocolate bars.

I once won £5,000 on online roulette. I then went on to lose £5,000 on online roulette.

If I wake up too early I balk.

Picture taken Southbank, London, September 2015

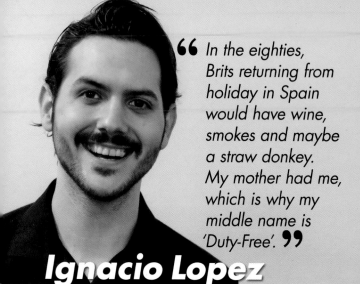

> **66** *In the eighties, Brits returning from holiday in Spain would have wine, smokes and maybe a straw donkey. My mother had me, which is why my middle name is 'Duty-Free'.* **99**

Ignacio Lopez

My first comedy gig was at a music venue in Swansea called The Garage, December 2009.

I'm a mix of Spanish, Welsh, Irish and Moroccan and I have a German sister.

I used to dress completely in black, some say goth but I'm actually a Lapsed Industrialist.

I've modelled live for Toni & Guy, the make-up artist pencilled on a moustache because I'd shaved mine off the night before. They made my hair orange.

I was once detained in Newark Airport, New York, as I'd taken a connecting flight in Trinidad and Tobago and they thought I was smuggling drugs in the cast for my broken foot. I wasn't.

Picture taken RAF Henlow, November 2014

> **"** *I wish I was white for a day – I'd do loads of shit. I'd buy a quiche.* **"**

Jamali Maddix

I started in a basement in Bond Street London in 2013.
I'm dyslexic.
I have a cat.
I was rated in high school most likely to go to prison.
I've watch *Warriors* over thirty times.
I'm 50/50 about the existence of aliens.

Picture taken The Old Town Hall Arts Centre, Hemel Hempstead, October 2015

Fascists – don't they just kill you?

Ray 'Buddy Hell' Campbell

I started while studying Creative Performing Arts in Newcastle Polytechnic as a student in December 1986. A year after that I set up Cabaret Agogo with two other people from the course.
I used to be a DJ on a pirate radio station.
Before stand-up I was a ranting punk poet in 1978/79, largely influenced by John Copper Clarke.
I'm an accredited cycling instructor.
I am doing a Ph.D. in Cultural Studies.
I came within one vote of winning Class President at high school. It was a boarding school. Not a posh one.

Picture taken Russell Square, London, February 2016

Alistair Green

I started eight years ago. First gig was The King's
Head, London.
I used to play table tennis for the county and now
play London league.
I used to work at the National Maritime Museum
giving talks on the Cornish artist Alfred Wallis.
I am a member of the National Trust.
I can do an excellent impression of weird
eighties children's TV puppet 'Pob'.

Picture taken Benicassim, July 2011

Daniel Simonson

I fully got into stand-up when I moved to London in 2007.
I grew up in Bergen in Norway.
My mum is Norwegian and my dad is Chilean.
When I was a kid my favourite comics were Hale and Pace.
I used to watch them over and over and re-enact their
routines to my friends to stunned silence.
As a teenager I was massively into skateboarding.
My favourite skateboarder is Tom Penny.

Picture taken Reigate, March 2013

423

I got asked if **I**'m good at performing massages... **I** said I'm a bit touch and go. "

Marlon Davis

I started stand-up February 2005 in an open mic
night in Soho and died on my ass!
I can hold my breath for sixty seconds
I can't tie my shoelaces.
I have never seen *Star Wars*.
I have a degree in Fine Art.

Picture taken Koko, Camden Town, London, November 2015

Kiri Pritchard-McLean

I think my first proper gig was Beat The Frog in Manchester, a gong show, January 2010. I was introduced to the stage as a man because evidentially 'Kiri' is quite a gender neutral name.

I am a Welsh person, a proud one too. Is there another kind? I grew up on a farm in Wales which means that I can loosely identify most native sheep breeds and I knew what a prolapse was by eight, and how to fix it with bailing twine.

I once saw someone get shot in the eye, pretty ghetto you might be thinking? Not really, it was at Pony Club.

I now live in Manchester, two streets away from Bernard Manning's World Famous Embassy Club. I have never been inside.

Picture taken The Harrison, King's Cross, London, June 2016

> **I really want to see a sequel to What Women Want where Mel Gibson learns to stop calling women bitches and whores.**

James Meehan

I started at Salford University Open Mic. 2009.
There was a free bar if you performed so I gave
it a go and I remember nothing.
I was in a punk band called Slow Motion Apartment Hunting.
We wrote three albums but never played live once.
My favourite actor is Chris Klein.
I once copied the lyrics to Sum 41's 'Fat Lip' and submitted it
for GCSE English creative writing. It contained the line 'the
doctor said my mum should've had an abortion'. I got a B.
I'm an avid supporter of the Friday night chippy tea.
Must have gravy or it doesn't count.

Picture taken The Harrison, King's Cross, London, June 2016

426

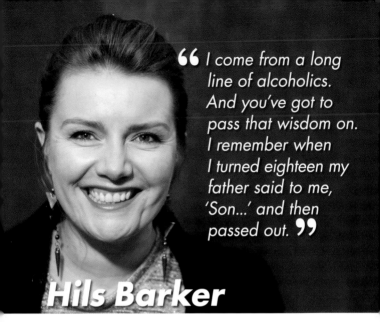

66 *I come from a long line of alcoholics. And you've got to pass that wisdom on. I remember when I turned eighteen my father said to me, 'Son...' and then passed out.* 99

Hils Barker

My first gig was at The Purple Turtle in Islington, a biker's bar, in 1999.

I nearly got expelled from school for accidentally setting fire to a plastics factory. I threw a fag end over the railings at the end of the school field. Three fire engines were involved.

My dad claims to have written the lyrics to the Foundations' song, 'Build me Up Buttercup'. He claims to have sold it to them for £40.

I had a mid life crisis two years ago and moved to Cambridge to become a recruitment consultant. I lasted three months.

I think I'd be better off living in the 18th century.

Picture taken King's Cross, London, February 2016

> **❝ Why do you never get a nipple in a breast of chicken? ❞**

Des Clarke

It all started in my home town of Glasgow. Blackfriars Comedy Club, April 2000. A proper old school basement gig. I still remember the smell of stale booze and fresh fear!

I used to be an altar boy.

I know the tune to the Finnish National Anthem.

I was the first boy in my class to get facial hair. Not the first person though. A girl called Fiona had a moustache years before me.

I share a birthday with Bill Bailey, Orlando Bloom and Suggs. What a gig that would be!

Picture taken Edinburgh Festival, August 2015

> **I tend to be quite lazy about saying I'm bi. I just say I'm gay because that way women know I'm interested and men... try harder.**

Catherine Bohart

I started comedy in April 2015 and my very first gig was at the Comedy Virgins' night at the Cavendish Arms in Stockwell.
I was obsessed with debating at university.

I'm the world's worst vegan (I really try though).
My parents are my best friends although they probably don't know that.
My real surname is as Irish as my face.

Picture taken Laughing Chili, Sunbury-on-Thames, February 2017

> **"** *People always say to me, 'You don't look gay', and I'll say, 'That's a good point... maybe I'm not.'* **"**

Sarah Keyworth

My first gig was in 2011 and it was at my sixth form college. I didn't start gigging regularly until 2014.

I am Jewish. I have a lucky dreidel.

I make a really good paella. Not a humblebrag.

I have never seen the end of the first *Harry Potter* film because I got scared in the cinema. I don't mind this because I know that he's OK.

My two best friends and I have matching tattoos – a result of a holiday during which we played board games and ate biscuits.

I can't write a joke without a hat on. It keeps my brain in.

Picture taken Leicester Square Theatre, London, February 2016

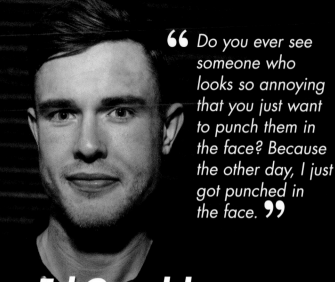

> **"** *Do you ever see someone who looks so annoying that you just want to punch them in the face? Because the other day, I just got punched in the face.* **"**

Ed Gamble

I started at Durham University, 2005. I was in a sketch group and I think my first appearance onstage was dressed as a rabbit. In many ways I have never topped that.

I auditioned to be the Milky Bar Kid.

I am type 1 diabetic (diagnosed many years after the Milky Bar Kid audition).

I had a wee next to Jamie Foxx once (it was a toilet and he was also weeing).

I am allergic to horses but it never really comes up.

Picture taken We Are Funny Project, Putney, London, April 2016

431

> **Hans Solo Centre for Masturbation Excellence.**
>
> A favourite tic of mine

Jess Thom
Touretteshero

I co-founded Touretteshero in 2010, and so began my mission to reclaim the laughter surrounding Tourettes. Having Tourettes means I say biscuit over 16,000 times a day... but I don't really like biscuits.
I may or may not lead a secret life as a part-time superhero, complete with mask, cape and a Lycra onesie.
As a freelance continuity announcer listen out for me introducing shows on Channel 4 and E4.
My tics love giving away secrets, which means I-spy, hide and seek, and poker aren't games I excel at.

Picture taken Edinburgh, August 2015

> *My family bought me a hamster to teach me leadership and responsibility, and I was completely responsible... for its tragic and untimely death.* 99

Jack Carroll

My first gig was at my parents' silver wedding anniversary party when I was eleven years old.

Rolf Harris sang to me in a lift.

I have a B grade in Art at GCSE.

I have a Pride of Britain Award (I don't know how either!).

I began learning to drive aged sixteen.

Picture taken Hammersmith Apollo, January 2016

> **" A little bit about myself... I used to be a child. "**

Joe Wilkinson

I started at The Bedford Arms in Balham at the new act night in 2004.

I share a birthday with Burt Reynolds and Goldie the dog.

I have wide hips. Too wide.

At school in Physics they did this experiment about speed versus weight to work out strength. And I had the weakest legs in my school.

I eat Oxo cubes.

I used to be double jointed.

Picture taken Chiswick, London, March 2016.

434

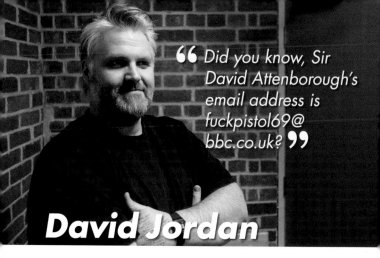

> 66 *Did you know, Sir David Attenborough's email address is fuckpistol69@bbc.co.uk?* 99

David Jordan

I started comedy three years ago in Brighton.

I once broke my arm on the first day of the school summer holiday and had the cast off the day before I went back to school and nobody believed me when I told them why I had a slightly thinner white arm.

I was in the front row of Live Aid.

I played the voice of HAL from 2001 in a Toshiba Advert when I was eighteen.

I can perform the whole of LL Cool J's 'Mama Said Knock You Out' as Gregory Peck.

My dad once changed the electricity meter in Sir Laurence Olivier's house and Larry was so pleased at my dad's courteousness and swift and tidy job that he insisted he stay while he made him a batch of fairy cakes and gave him a £5 tip when he left. Laurence Olivier definitely fancied my dad.

Picture taken Sutton and Cheam Rugby Club, Cheam, February 2016

> **66** *I'm an inventor –
> I've nearly built
> the perfect jet
> pack. But I've
> been so busy,
> that's gone on
> the back-burner.* **99**

Neil Cole

Initially started comedy in 1997 in double-act Hitchcock's Half Hour. Then solo stand-up in 2008. My first solo open-spot was booked at the Comedy Store, LA but it got pulled – so it happened in Peckham a week later.

I fractured my skull aged nine in a skateboarding accident.

I am officially a G-Monster having withstood sustained 6G in the human centrifuge without losing consciousness.

My inside leg, waist and hip measurement are all exactly the same.

I have two current UK passports.

I stood on the roof of the World Trade Center in New York in August 2001, two weeks before 9/11.

Picture taken We Are Funny Project, Putney, London, April 2016

> **The Germans are re-printing the Euro on a new kind of paper. This time it will be Greece proof.**

Neville Raven

I started comedy in the early 90s. First gig was in the East Dulwich Tavern, south London. Malcolm Hardee gave me an early break then vomited champagne over me at a party. In 2003 I moved to Amsterdam where I lived and worked for ten years.

I lived in Singapore until I was five.

I accidentally walked off a cliff on the Isle of Arran when I was sixteen. It was dark and I bounced.

I've never seen or read anything by JK Rowling and have no idea who Neville Longbottom is.

Hells Angels in Amsterdam let me work as portrait artist in their bar – 'You make some money for yourself and our customers are happy, yes?'

In 2000 I went to Cuba; hired a guide, a driver with a 50s car, and travelled across the country for a month.

At college I DJed on tour with Fatboy Slim who was called Norman back then and in a band called the Housemartins.

Picture taken King's Cross, February 2016

> *I used to live in Macarena, which was a little village just outside of Seville. Best place in the world. Actually it wasn't that nice. No need to make a song and dance about it.* **99**

Alex Horne

I started doing open spots at Cambridge University.
My first real gig was at The Purple Turtle in 2000.
My first job was on a potato farm. I used to work on the conveyor belt removing mouldy potatoes and toads (there were a lot of toads). I wasn't allowed to handle the good potatoes. I loved the job.
My granddad handled some of the first moon rocks that came from the first moon landing.
I've got a tattoo of a lizard on my left arm. I don't like lizards or tattoos.
I've got a giant African land snail. Got it on my son's first day at school from the school. It was half a centimetre long. I found out that they can grow to be a foot long.
It's currently nine inches.
I can fit a pound coin through my front teeth, end on not flat on.

Picture taken Hammersmith, London, February 2016

> "Some people think men are funnier than women. I know why... it's because men have a penis... and that's hilarious."

Ingrid Dahle

I started comedy in Brighton 2011.
I won a talent competition with my friend in Norway when we were thirteen singing and playing 'Tears in Heaven' on guitar.
I once touched a whale.

Picture taken Sutton and Cheam Rugby Club, Cheam, February 2016

> *My wife doesn't like anal sex but I make her do it to me anyway.*

Jason Cook

My first gig was at The Hyena
in Newcastle in 2000.
I'm a convicted pirate.
I've got a permanently
broken metatarsal.
I have a phobia of balloons.
My great great grandfather was the
first Geordie comedian on radio.
I used to be in the merchant navy.
I was on three ships that nearly sank.
I've got a tattoo of the devil as Eric
Morecambe climbing up my leg.
At the time I asked the tattooist what
was the stupidest tattoo he'd ever done
and he didn't even look up
and said 'this one'.

Picture taken The Comedy Store, London, March 2016

> **"** *I'm mainly Irish and New Zealand Maori. My wife is from the UK. I guess there's just something in my DNA that makes me want to get fucked by the English.* **"**

Ben Hurley

My first gig was in Wellington, New Zealand in 2001.
I've never shot a gun.
I was a 100m sprint champion at school. Comedy put an end to my athletic career.
I can name all 195 sovereign states in the world.
The first car I owned was a black Fiat Uno with golden mag wheels.

Picture taken (on a very old camera phone) Headliners, Chiswick, December 2006

66 *My parents told me not to talk to strangers. I married one.* **99**

Benjamin Bello
President Obonjo

My comedy career began in 2011 after being inspired by the election of President Obama. I have always dreamt of being President of a great nation since it did not happen with a real country like Nigeria and with time running out for me, I formed my own nation, Lafta Republic, and my ambition was realised.

I am afraid of dogs. A dog went for my mojo when I was young. I ran.

I play the harmonica.

I see funny people in my sleep.

I am an artist – abstract art.

Picture taken Leicester Square Theatre, London, January 2016

442

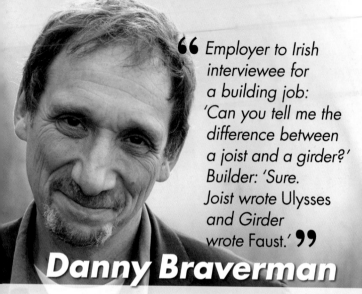

> 66 *Employer to Irish interviewee for a building job: 'Can you tell me the difference between a joist and a girder?' Builder: 'Sure. Joist wrote Ulysses and Girder wrote Faust.'* 99

Danny Braverman

I started at The Bedlam Theatre Edinburgh as part of Birmingham University cabaret 1981 with Jenny LeCoat (early feminist stand-up) and Steve Nallon (best known for Margaret Thatcher on *Spitting Image*). I was second reserve for Woodford and District Liberal Synagogue Under-elevens Football Team.

My mother wouldn't let me have a bike because of the dangers of getting run over in a quiet suburban cul-de-sac. I had forty great aunts and great uncles, before any of them got married. They're all dead now and two were called Celia Solomons. I met my partner by selling her a car on Facebook. I don't have a large intestine.

Picture taken The Festival Hall, London, February 2016

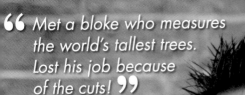

> 66 Met a bloke who measures the world's tallest trees. Lost his job because of the cuts! 99

Jools Constant

I started comedy in 2007 in Langtons Bar, Newport, South Wales telling jokes straight out of *100 Jokes For All The Family*.
I used to be a vicar.
I'm a builder, inventor, furniture maker, writer and classic car enthusiast.
I was a grandfather at forty-four.
In 2002 I got chatted up by Britt Ekland.
I once ran a music festival for 35,000 people and Goldie Looking Chain were the headliners.
I lost my virginity on my wedding night.

Picture taken
King's Cross, London,
March 2016

> **66** *I once stole so much money that the banks gave me a criminal nickname: Employee Of The Month.* **99**

Adam Drake
of Goose

Goose is made up of Adam Drake (writer-performer, pictured) and Ben Rowse (writer, thinks he's above photo shoots). We studied at uni together and started in 2012.

My dad is South African, and my mum is Irish. Quite the cocktail.

At school, a person's popularity was in direct proportion to the quality of their impression of David Brent. Yeah?

I'll show my kids the episode of *The Simpsons* where Homer goes to Clown College rather than taking them to church.

I live in a cottage in Deptford. The landlord left their rocking horse in the house. My flatmate and I named it Shakira.

I really want a pug but one that's low maintenance so, like, a cat-version of a pug.

Picture taken The Harrison, King's Cross, London, June 2016

> **First thing this guy said to me on a blind date was: 'That dress makes you look fat'. I replied: 'It's not the dress, love. I was fat before I got in it, twat!'**

Maureen Younger

I started in 2005.
I speak five languages – English, German (Austrian German to be precise), French, Spanish and Russian.
I'm the only comic to work regularly on the mainstream, urban and gay circuits as well as gig in German.
I got a Christmas present from Tom Hanks, thanks to playing an angry German woman in episode nine of *Band of Brothers*.
My father is convinced I'm called Mavis.

Picture taken King's Cross, London, March 2016

> 66 *I went to have botox the other day. £650! I couldn't even look shocked.* 99

Shazia Mirza

I started in Brixton in 2002. There was no seating, no microphone and no lighting. The audience was standing. Someone was being arrested outside as I was trying to perform.

I am learning to wake board, and it has taken me two weeks to just get up and be able to stand on the board. I collect fridge magnets of all the places I have been to in the world.

Every so often I go and sit in the desert for a week by myself, and not talk to anyone. I only wear knickers when I have to. I am scared of cats.

Picture taken King's Cross, London, March 2016

447

> **I wondered why that yo-yo was getting bigger... then it hit me!**

Maynard Flip Flap

Rick Allan

I first performed on Fargate in Sheffield, busking in January of 1990. I made £5.30 with dreadful fire juggling and a terrible magic trick.
My doctor's records list a perforated ear drum caused by a custard pie fight... Careless.
My driving license was revoked for confessing to the DVLA I smoked dope... DOH!

The first single I bought was 'Hit Me With Your Rhythm Stick' by Ian Dury... Cool?
I captain a friendly cricket team named The Sheffield Hitters... Howzat?
My highest snooker break is 33... Pathetic.
I am a Quaker...
Keep it quiet.

Picture taken Cabaret Heaven, Leeds, March 2010

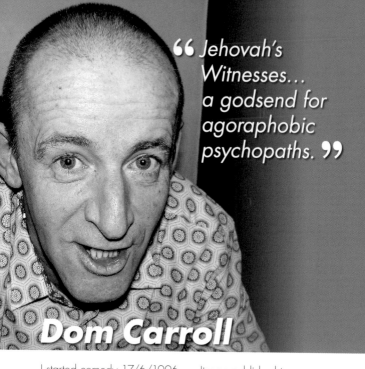

> **" Jehovah's Witnesses... a godsend for agoraphobic psychopaths. "**

Dom Carroll

I started comedy 17/6/1996.
First performance at the Frog
and Bucket. I know the date
because it was two days
after the IRA bomb
redesigned Manchester.
I once gave an interview to
the Soviet newspaper *Pravda*.

It was published too.
I hate all cheese.
I hate places in the North
West that begin with the
letter B.
I'm addicted to Lurchers
and running dogs.

Picture taken Jongleurs, Cardiff, October 2008

449

> **I want to start up a chickpea delivery service for dead people. It's called Post Hummus.**

Danny Ward

My first gig was November 22nd 2008,
The Bedford in Balham. New material night.

I suffer from negative buoyancy (I don't float). Fellow
sufferers include Paul Daniels and my friend George's dad.

I have the best badminton smash shot of any comedian
on the circuit. Happy to prove it.

I once burned a house down with a Pop Tart. I did,
in all honesty, leave it unattended.

In 1998 I went to Bernard Manning's Comedy Club in
Harpurhey, Manchester. His pink Rolls Royce took up four
spaces in the carpark.

I came second in my Year 11 Talent Show doing a striptease.
This was a full three years before *The Full Monty* was released.

Picture taken Norwich City Football Club, Norwich, December 2015

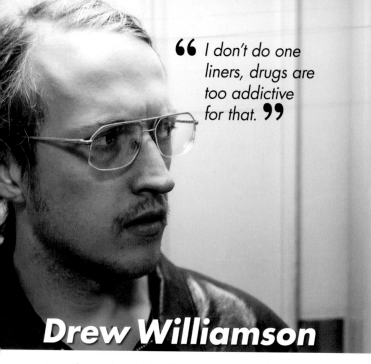

66 *I don't do one liners, drugs are too addictive for that.* **99**

Drew Williamson

I started comedy at Nolias 11 south London in autumn, 2012.
I invent things.
I am a qualified Laughter Yoga Instructor.
I signed my first autograph at eighteen after playing in a friend's band.

I ran a comedy night.
My favourite food is Lucky Charms.
I have written everyday most of my life.
I have had over 100 jobs and lived in over 100 places.
I sew hats.

Picture taken The Comedy Pub, London, October 2014

> 66 *My wife is not a housewife. I'm pretty sure she thinks that limescale is just a sophisticated system for assessing limes.* 99

Alex Smith

I had a fairly weird start in stand-up in that I actually studied it for my master's degree. I think most people start in the back room of a pub doing jokes about sex. I started in a classroom doing jokes about sex but I was being marked for it.
Got a first – not bragging – but also bragging.
I was born dead.
I did a module at university in circus skills and know how to do that thing where you climb up a bit of fabric and spin around a lot. Think it's called silk.
I almost lost my testicles as a result of a jellyfish sting.
I hate Ben Fogle intensely for no reason at all.
I was head boy and head chorister of my junior school, so naturally swamped by girls, at my all boys Catholic school.

Picture taken The Cavendish Arms, Stockwell, London, April 2016

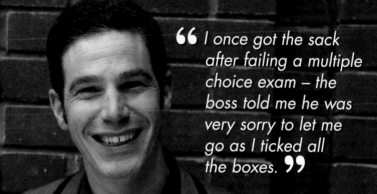

> 66 I once got the sack after failing a multiple choice exam – the boss told me he was very sorry to let me go as I ticked all the boxes. 99

Rod Woodward

I started doing comedy in 1997 with a few competitions and open spots. I then took a job as a warm-up man for HTV Wales.

My father, Karl Woodward, was an eminent sports journalist for the national newspaper of Wales, the *Western Mail*.

I arranged a scholarship to a private school specialising in music for a then unknown Charlotte Church after hearing her sing in a talent show.

I was very seriously injured falling off a banana boat ride in Benidorm and clashing heads with the man in front. I have since been told I was the reason behind the introduction of the helmet law!

I am a Cardiff City season ticket holder and did a song to celebrate them reaching the FA Cup Final in 2008 called 'Do The Ayatollah'.

I am a distant relative of Sir Tom Jones whose real name is Tom Woodward.

Picture taken Reigate Grammar School, March 2016

> **Basically I've got a party trick and I thought, yeah, this is a job.**

Luke Kempner

I started comedy at drama school, doing impressions of the teachers at the cabaret nights. To be honest I first got up and did impressions when I was thirteen at secondary school. I did footballers that no-one had heard of. I then started creating YouTube videos in 2012 and that's when I decided to do it professionally.

I understudied Gareth Gates in *Les Misérables*.

My cat was in *Aliens*.

I used to do police line-ups for extra cash.

My Austrian granddad saw Hitler speak.

I commentate on my own Fifa games, give players backstories. Yep.

Picture taken Reigate Grammar School, March 2016

66 *There's no good euphemism for lesbian sex, muff diving doesn't come close; what we were doing was more like... Have you ever seen a Jack Russell trying to get a tennis ball out from under a couch.* 99

Bethany Black

I started comedy in 2003 in Preston. I was an MC for a rock night and started telling jokes between the acts.
I have a single palmar crease, also known as a simian crease, on both hands, this is very rare.
I was the first openly transgender person to star as a transgender character on UK television and on US broadcast TV.
I have a copy of Marvel comics improbably named *Giant-Sized Man-Thing #1*.
I'm naturally blonde.
My cats are named after serial killers.

Picture taken The Rawhide, Liverpool, April 2009

> *It's the little things that get me down: my own phone autocorrects my name to the word 'Shit'.*

Ahir Shah

I did my first gig in May 2006 in the basement of a building run by the English Folk Dance & Song Society. I was fifteen, which is too young.

My main hobby at the moment is drunkenly bemoaning the state of the British left.

I support the Indian national cricket team, Queens Park Rangers Football Club, and the Labour Party. On all three counts, I'm not really sure why.

I've put on a stone over the last year, but am still doggedly insistent that all my clothes fit me. This does not fill me with confidence about how I'll cope with middle-age.

I had never used a dishwasher prior to the 2nd April 2016. Why did none of you tell me about dishwashers?

Picture taken The Cavendish Arms, Stockwell, London, April 2016

> " I once lasted with a girl for an hour and three minutes. I was cheating a little bit, it was the night the clocks went forward. "

Lee Nelson
Simon Brodkin

Started at school. Constantly getting kicked out of class for acting like the class bell-end.
I'm completely colour blind.
I love sweet potatoes.
I don't play the piano.
I have no foreskin.

Picture taken Epsom Playhouse, March 2016

> **I've been smoking for about five years, and recently I've realised it's become a problem for me, because I've started to enjoy it.**

Freddie Bencard

I did my first gig at the Duke's Head in Putney, with the We Are Funny Project (Alex Martini was the MC), on 8th October 2014.
I used to be a model, until I lost my looks at the age of one. (Highlight – played Tommy Cooper in a pushchair advert.)
I work for an accountant in Chalk Farm.
My favourite sitcoms are *Whatever Happened To The Likely Lads* and *Minder*.
The UK number 1 when I was born was 'The Only Way Is Up', by Yazoo; in the context of my life, not appropriate.
I'm a quarter Danish, but frequently exaggerate this to half-Danish to seem edgy and attractive to women.

Picture taken We Are Funny Project, Putney, London, April 2016

458

> ❝ *There's one thing I've found to be a very touchy subject... and that's Braille.* ❞

Mark Felgate

I first started performing at eleven years old doing kids' parties doing magic and ventriloquism.

I started stand-up in late 1996.

I once appeared in a short film with the porn star Linsey Dawn McKenzie.

Hank Marvin graded my electric guitar exam.

I used to play and teach guitar professionally.

For five years I was a kids' TV presenter on Nickelodeon.

I once turned down a kiss from Hollywood star Sandra Bullock.

Picture taken London, June 2015

> *Life lesson number one: Don't get too attached to your nana.*

Phil Ellis

I started in 2006 at the Stour Bridge Town Hall.
I worked in an air bag factory for four years.
I'm flat footed.
I had a mortgage at the age of twenty-two and lost it at the age of twenty-five.
I lost the use of my right hand for three months in early 2015.
It was a condition called Saturday Night Palsy, which sounds like a really shit sequel.
I've never tried any sauces. I only eat dry food.
I've also never had a curry.

Picture taken King's Cross, London, April 2016

> **"** I didn't know how to end it with my boyfriend, I would text him but he can't read. So I just poured a load of stain remover in his tea and went out, when I got back he'd vanished. **"**

Adrienne Coles

I have been going for eighteen months now.
I live in Bournemouth.
If I receive unwanted attention from the opposite sex I say
my name is Floribunda and develop a squint in my left eye.
I have overly large feet for my height.
I used a winning lottery ticket to block a draft in my
window frame for six months and one day.

Picture taken Durrington Working Men's Club, Worthing, November 2013.

> **Kind of kills it when my mattress sounds like it's enjoying itself a load more than I am.**

Jo Dexter

First gig on 19th May 2015, The Lion's Den Comedy Club, Bar Rumba, off Piccadilly Circus.

I once found two four-leaved clovers at the same time. I think the luck got cancelled out.

Often when I think of something very random I'll call my mum and she will have had the same thought.

I have a phobia of a specific sound. If I hear it I have to lift my feet off the ground.

In 2001 my eyes fell out. Not literally. They just don't work together any more.

I'm somewhere in the 2005 *Pride and Prejudice* movie. If you find me, you need a life.

Picture taken We Are Funny Project, Putney, London, April 2016

David Mulholland

> **" I'm so boring in bed, my safe word is 'stop'. "**

I started doing sketch and improv in Washington, USA, in 1993. Before that I had been a musician and a mime artist.
I'm a star in Eritrea. I did a topical, satirical comedy weekly show for four years, filmed in London and broadcast globally. No one watched anywhere except for East Africa.
I was a reporter in New York, Washington and London. My main topic was military technology. My last two years as a journalist I won the Defence Anorak of the Year award.
I used to be an economic analyst for the US government covering Eastern Europe.
I used to be in several bands playing lead guitar. My last band was called Lust Puppy. Our music was disco, punk rock, polka fusion with a country swing flair.

Picture taken
King's Cross, London,
March 2016

> **I've been diagnosed with anorexia, bulimia, compulsive overeating disorder, bipolar, anxiety, depression, agoraphobia, psychotic hallucinations... I have more labels than TK Maxx.**

Juliette Burton

I started comedy acting in Cambridge for writing workshops, then films, then started writing my own stuff in 2011 as one half of Mace and Burton and then solo career writing and performing started in 2012. Of course, it really all began when I was cast as The Star of Bethlehem aged eight in the school nativity play.
I was born in Cambridge.
I am hyperflexible (double-jointed) in all my joints.
My favourite fruit is cherries.
I used to work for the BBC.
I grew up on a farm.
I am in love with Gonzo.

Picture taken Edinburgh Festival Fringe, August 2016

464

> **"** Speed cameras catch you by calculating your average speed. They use mean average, obviously. **"**

Tom Wrigglesworth

I used to watch new acts and think I could easily be as bad as that. I finally conquered my nerves to try it in 2002.

I hum incessantly for about forty-five minutes before a gig. It both helps warm up my voice and annoys everyone surrounding me.

For a brief period as a student, I read tarot cards for a job. I was and still am utterly unqualified to do this.

Due to having an uncannily similar face, I have met one of the greatest American football players alive, Mr Aaron Rodgers. I am now officially a Green Bay Packers' fan.

Without question, I make the greatest hummus in the world.

> **UKIP had that poster saying '26 million people in Europe are out of work. Guess whose job they're after'. There must be at least one person going, 'Well it isn't mine, I'm Rolf Harris's defence lawyer'.**

Matt Forde

I did my first gig when I was sixteen at Mad Dog Comedy Club in Nottingham.
I was a mascot for Nottingham Forest when we played Crystal Palace in 1993. Brian Clough called me 'an ugly bugger'.
I often eat curry in bed. My Union Jack bedspread is covered in madras stains.
There's a piano in my bedroom and I play it every day.
I was at Tony Blair's resignation in the Trimdon Labour Club.
I'm highly regular and put this down to a chaotic diet and fast metabolism.

Picture taken Theatre Royal, Windsor, June 2016

> **"** *How long does it take to walk a dog in Mexico? Chihuahuas.* **"**

Rachel Fairburn

I started comedy in 2007 in Manchester. First gig at
the infamous King Gong at the Comedy Store.
I do a surprisingly popular podcast about serial killers.
I am a massive Oasis fan and have lots of memorabilia…
including three boxes of newspaper clippings.
I once tripped over a bloke's suitcase on a train.
I told him it was blocking the aisle. He apologised.
Turned out to be Sir Ian McKellen.

Picture taken English Comedian of the Year, The Udderbelly, London, July 2016

" I only ever go on holiday to one Greek island. Just Kos. "

Peter Halpin

I started in March 2013 in BBC's Comic Relief 'Stand Up If You Dare' competition. Although there was no official winner, I headlined the finalists.

My A-Level grades spelled out the University I went to – UCE (University of Central England).

My son has ginger hair but there's no history of ginger hair in either side of the family for as long as is known.

I've got osteoarthritis.

I was once (incorrectly) labelled a porn star by the *Daily Star*.

My middle name is William, after my mum's father.

Picture taken The Strand, London, June 2016

> **"** I'm a hypochondriac, or so my gynaecologist tells me. **"**

Barry Cryer

I started at Leeds University in a student show in 1955.
My first professional job was at the City Varieties in Leeds
in 1956, my home town. I appeared there last week
after sixty years.
I'm a 'BA English Lit failed' and an honorary Doctor of Arts.
I was number one in Finland in 1958 with 'The Purple
People Eater'.
I once spoke to Marilyn Monroe on the phone.
The radio show I'm in, 'I'm Sorry I Haven't A Clue...',
has been running for forty-four years.
I met my wife the very same day I met Ronnie Corbett –
I tossed a coin and married her.

Picture taken Ealing Comedy Festival, July 2016

> *Heard about the Eskimo lottery? You have to be Inuit to win it.*

Rory **Bremner**

I started on the London circuit in 1983 – Finborough Arms, Donmar Warehouse, Jongleurs.

I have a degree in French and German and a Fellowship from King's College London.

I translate operas and plays, including *Carmen, Orpheus in the Underworld* and *Seven Deadly Sins*.

I once bowled Brian Lara in a charity cricket match. (Big mistake.)

I turned down an OBE from the Blair government in 2007.

I won the Scottish Open Pro-am Golf Tournament in 2015.

Picture taken Bafta, London, June 2016

> **"** I rang the IT help desk about my Outlook. Apparently my outlook is quite bleak. **"**

Tom Curran

I started this solo clown business at a night called Lost Cabaret in Stockwell about three years ago. I finally got the courage to go up and perform after doing some clown workshops with Aitor Basauri from Spymonkey and Mick Barnfather from Complicite, really incredible teachers.

I sat next to Terence Stamp at a wedding once. All I could manage was a limp handshake.

I discovered when playing Widow Twanky that I look frighteningly like my mother in drag.

My mother's mother tongue is Gaelic. She comes from Connemara.

I may be obsessed by my mother and Terence Stamp.

Picture taken We Are Funny Project, Dalston, London, October 2016

> **I moved from Straightzvill to Lesboland, and if you don't know where that is look it up in the dyketionary.**

Victoria Howden

I lived in Israel for twenty-eight years and served in the army.
I am a musical theatre fan and have a show tune for every occasion.
I love *The Golden Girls* and consider myself a Dorothy.
I do a wicked Louis Armstrong impression.

Picture taken
We Are Funny Project, Dalston, London,
October 2016

Acts Chapter 9 Verse 18

'And Saul said to Peter after walking the road to Damascus, 'Have you ever noticed how all personalised number plates spell the same name... Wanker?' Peter laughed and they bonded not only with mirth but also truth.'

Kai Motta

I first started performing when I was eighteen as a musician. My first gig as The High Priest was 2006 at the Windmill Pub in Brixton right next to the prison.

I was once hired to be a chef after I put 'ticklish and good-looking women' as my weaknesses for part of the job entry process.

I am a complete obsessive compulsive, to the point where I read every book about it, watched every programme I could find about it and in turn became absolutely completely obsessed with it.

For a period in 2012/2013 gigs got so dangerous I had to learn how to box.

Picture taken King's Cross, London, July 2016

> **"** *What sort of a country sends people to prison for not having a television licence?! In prison, they'd be able to watch it for nothing.* **"**
>
> As Magnus

Richard Rycroft

I did my first gig at Downstairs at the King's Head, Crouch End in August 2007. I now work as the character Magnus Turner MP, whose first 'public speaking engagement' was at La Torretta wine bar in Rochester, Kent in April 2014. When I was sixteen, I saw Bo Diddley eating beans on toast in Bournemouth (and have a photo to prove it). A doctor once told me I have unusually big bones. It was the happiest day of my life.

I've appeared in *Game of Thrones* as Maester Wolkan. In the early 90s, I once spent a happy evening with a friendly Frenchman I'd just met in a bar in Brussels. We bought each other drinks, we made each other laugh, we sang songs in each other's language – he was a big fan of *The Lambeth Walk*. I left early, when someone told me I was having a lovely time with Jean-Marie Le Pen. (This was before he nearly became President – not so well known back then, honest.)

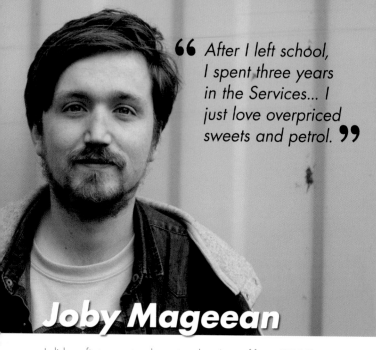

> After I left school, I spent three years in the Services... I just love overpriced sweets and petrol.

Joby Mageean

I did my first ever stand-up gig when I was fifteen (2006) above a pub in Newcastle called the Chillingham.
Although I didn't start properly until 2012.
I once pogo-sticked a mile.
I was nearly cast as Billy Elliot in the West End.
I have an irrational fear of ketchup.
My dad took Enya to court.
I once drank a bottle of hot sauce (tabasco) to impress my Film Studies teacher.

Picture taken English Comedian of the Year, The Udderbelly, London, July 2016

> **" Hello, my name is Mo. No relation. "**

Mo Omá

My first ever gig was on 18th May 2016 in Swansea which I coached to so I wouldn't back out last minute. I could speak and now have forgotten Arabic but still mention it on my CV.
I despise honey and will not eat something if I know I get the slightest whiff.
Sometimes I'll make up a cultural fact to avoid an awkward situation.
I can't swim. I can swim to get out but no more.
I don't like heights, because who likes heights?

Picture taken We Are Funny Project, Dalston, London, September 2016

> **66** What do we want?
> A cure for ADHD!
> When do we want it?
> Let's play swingball! **99**

Joe Lycett

I started comedy in Manchester
in 2007ish. My first gig was a
university charity show at the
Manchester Comedy Store
and I went on after a storming
set by Jack Whitehall.
I'm a trained swimming instructor.
I have a deep love for fonts
and typefaces.
I like violent video games.
On a trip to Tanzania I watched
a goat being slaughtered and
was eating it within the hour.
It was DELICIOUS.
I'm a vegetarian but I eat meat.

Picture taken BBC, London, July 2016

Faye Treacy

I started comedy three years ago. I won Best Newcomer at the Musical Comedy Awards in 2015 and came runner up in the Bath New Act Competition 2016.

My dad was a punk, so I rebelled by studying classical music. I'm now a professional trombonist, a graduate of the Brit School of Performing Arts and The Royal Academy of Music. I've enjoyed a busy freelance career so far, highlights including playing for Kiko Bun, The Maccabees, The Selector, The Chrissy Lee Bigband and I was the resident trombonist in the house band for *Chris Moyles Quiz Night* on Channel 4!

Picture taken We Are Funny Project, Dalston, London, September 2016

Darrell Martin

I started running a comedy club called Just the Tonic in Nottingham in 1994. I had no idea how to become a comedian or what to do, so I organised it instead. It took two years to get the bottle to do it.

First gig was a little club in south London, which went really well. I got cocky, called a promoter I knew in Manchester who ran the Buzz Club, told him I was really good. Went up there, and totally died for about seven minutes.

I won a race-tuned Lambretta in 1986 at the Isle of Wight Scooter rally.

I used to teach English in Barcelona.

I appeared on *Blue Peter* dressed as a pantomime horse after winning the first and only Sprint Print Sprint Cup (still the holder of the title).

I can blow bubbles on my tongue.

Picture taken English Comedian of the Year, The Udderbelly, London, July 2016

> **I see Channel 4 are filming a sequel to Queer As Folk in Newcastle. It's called Queer Like Fuck Mate.**

Alan Anderson

I started at Murphy's Malarkey, Manchester. January 1998. It is all Toby Hadoke's fault. Student days I was a regular drunk heckler. Lee Martin was also a regular punter. One week I was too drunk and too loud and Toby told me from stage, 'Next week you get up here and do five minutes or never come back.'

I hold the record for the fastest cycle down The String Hill on Arran. 61 mph.

My dad invented the machine that wraps netting round joints of meat.

When I was four he made me a Spiderman costume complete with exploding webbing.

Aged fifteen or sixteen I got the chance to race head to head against World and Olympic Ski Champion Franz Klammer at a dry ski slope in Glasgow. I was leading until the last gate which I clipped and crashed.

As well as doing the commentary for the Cycling and Triathlons, I announced the first and last medal ceremonies at the Glasgow Commonwealth Games.

Picture taken English Comedian of the Year, The Udderbelly, London, July 2016

480

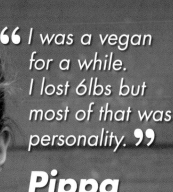

> **❝** *I was a vegan for a while. I lost 6lbs but most of that was personality.* **❞**

Pippa Evans

My first gig was at the Tut and Shive, Highbury in 2001 with Andy Fox. But then I didn't gig again really until 2006 'cause I had nothing to say!

I am the co-founder of Sunday Assembly – a network of secular congregations.

My 2nd toe is bigger than my big toe, making it my actual big toe.

I am an avid collector of *Postman Pat* memorabilia.

I have an undercut.

I make a mean buffet spread.

Picture taken
Conway Hall, London,
July 2016

Nathan
Cassidy

I started at The Bedford in Balham around the millennium. I then had an eight year break from stand-up.
I have played the xylophone on television.
I helped to create Real New York Tours, a tour business in New York which became New York's best rated tourist attraction.
I have travelled the world writing novels.
I spent a year giving money away at random for a documentary *I am Orig*.
I'm obsessed with eighties gameshow *Bullseye*.

Picture taken We Are Funny Project, Dalston, London, September 2016

> 66 *I married a Japanese girl and my mum had a big problem with that because she's a bit old and racist. I said, 'Mum, it's completely up to me if I want to marry an old Japanese racist.'* 99

Damian Kingsley

My first gig was in Tokyo in 2007.
I did my first comedy competition in Japanese. I died on my arse.
I've been booed onto stage at a gong show.
I've had several arguments with Paul McCartney and a hand-towel fight with him on his private jet. I was fourteen and it was my first time on a plane.
I once gatecrashed the BBC greenroom, told them I was the warm up comedian for *Children in Need*, and then got taken backstage with Terry Wogan and Ferne Cotton.

Picture taken Whyteleafe Tavern, Whyteleafe September 2015

Mark Steel

My first gig was aged eight at a talent contest in a holiday camp somewhere in Devon.
For my In Town radio show I've read the dullest books in the world, including *A History of Engine Sheds in Walsall*.
I wanted to be a cricketer, and would have been, if it wasn't for the unfair system that discriminated against me for being fucking useless.
Once, at the exact moment I was going on stage, I saw my daughter hit my son square in the eye by chucking a lemon.
Prince Andrew wanted to go on a date with my half-sister.

Picture taken Balham Banana, July 2014

> **"** The media say
> we are the worst
> binge drinkers in
> Europe, why is
> that a bad thing?
> Nice to see us
> winning something
> out there, isn't it? **"**

Ed Pownall

I started comedy 27th
October 2013.
I was a betting expert for
The Daily Politics (BBC2)
for five years.
I have a physical reaction
to Phil Collins music.
I went bald at twenty-two.
I have two knees.

Picture taken
We Are Funny Project, Dalston, London,
September 2016

> **When I tell people my name's Kai Samra, they always ask me where my grandparents are originally from. I was born here, but my grandparents migrated here in the 50s, unable to speak basic English, from a poverty stricken part of the world… called Birmingham.**

Kai Samra

My first ever stand-up gig was at a place called Jolly Rogers in February 2016.

I'm the lead singer and guitarist in a band called Paris Pickpockets. Recently did gigs with The Libertines, Bloc Party and Primal Scream.

My kickboxing teacher is Alex Reid, a *Celebrity Big Brother* contestant, who was recently married to Katie Price and also likes to cross-dress.

I have had essentially the same haircut since the day of birth.

Picture taken We Are Funny Project, Dalston, London, September 2016

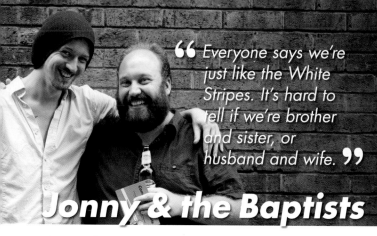

> *Everyone says we're just like the White Stripes. It's hard to tell if we're brother and sister, or husband and wife.*

Jonny & the Baptists

We started our career in 2011 in the back garden of our friend Will, sat together with two guitars and a list of grievances against the new Conservative-led government. Before we'd even really worked out any of the songs, we got booked to play at a weird festival in Croatia with Colin Hoult and Dr. Brown. It's been downhill ever since.

Jonny I am allergic to raspberries.

I once sang for the Queen as a child.

I'm surprisingly good at table football.

I once had dinner with Steve Punt.

Paddy I was once crushed by a cabinet of toolboxes.

I now have a biosynthetic metal arm.

I was once shot with a crossbow.

I was hospitalised on day two of my first ever Edinburgh Fringe run.

I once had dinner with Steve Punt.

Picture taken Conway Hall, London, July 2016

> ❝ The good thing about lending someone your time machine is that you basically get it back immediately. ❞

Chris Coltrane

I started in 2007 at an open mic above a goth pub that is now a chain burger restaurant. My punchlines were so powerful they had to close the place down.

I'm a tax justice activist with direct-action protesters UK Uncut, who occupy and shut down shops like Vodafone for tax-dodging.

I'm chemically addicted to chocolate.

I'm the official UK Nintendo Champion, 1992 (I got to meet Mario and Pat Sharp).

I have been online over sixteen times in my life, visiting such esteemed websites as Google, Ask Jeeves and Geocities.

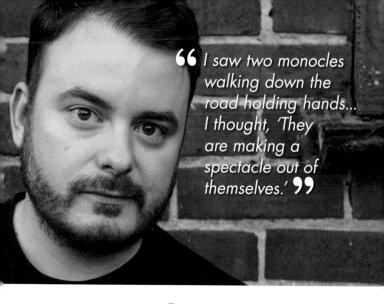

> 66 *I saw two monocles walking down the road holding hands... I thought, 'They are making a spectacle out of themselves.'* 99

Tom Holmes

I started comedy in 2011 when my other half got sick of me saying I might give stand-up a go, and just booked me an open spot in Stockwell.

I co-host the world's biggest Fantasy Premier League Podcast *The Gaffer Tapes*.

I once made former Manchester United footballer Lee Sharpe laugh out loud.

I was part of Enid Blyton's *Secret Seven* (the voice of Colin in a series of dramatised audio-books in the late 90s).

I have never eaten a Nandos.

Picture taken The Stoke Pub, Guildford, September 2016

> **" *I used to live above a candy shop. It was on-sweet.* "**

Dave Chawner

I started stand-up in Southampton eight years ago. There was an open mic night at the student bar. I signed up to do it. At the time I didn't realise it was just for music. When I began some people thought it was avant-garde rap! However, I'd brought along all of my flat mates and it was really good fun. I got the deluded idea I could keep doing it, and I've been deluding myself ever since.

I have licked an RAF helicopter.

I share my birthday with Nicholas Cage.

I am related to the poet Rupert Brooke.

My favourite film is *Mrs Doubtfire*.

Picture taken
Soho Theatre, London,
September 2016

490

> **My dad's American and my mum's Iranian. People used to ask me, 'Are you worried about the Americans invading the Iranians?' I'd say, 'No – that's how I got made.'**

Ariane Sherine

I gigged for six months in 2003, got to the final of the Laughing Horse New Act of the Year, and was then an idiot and quit for thirteen years. I restarted in February 2016 and fell in love with musical comedy and stand-up all over again.
I have a lump on my neck which the doctors call a gill. I like to sing a Temptations song about it: 'My Gill'.
When I was nineteen, Duran Duran asked me to sing and play piano on two tracks on their tenth album, *Pop Trash*. My five-year-old daughter is white and I'm brown, so I call her my Secret Asian.
I appeared on *Countdown* but, despite my comedy often being rude, failed to spot the word PUBIC.
I have been introduced on stage as Arlene, Aryan Shrine and Ariel Sharon.

Picture taken The Stoke Pub, Guildford, September 2016

> **Being 6ft 7 I find it difficult to fit in and blend into the background. I am the human equivalent of an erection in an OAPs home.**

Ryan Dalton

I first ever attempted stand-up at the ripe age of nineteen whilst travelling (and intoxicated) in Australia in a small underground comedy club.

I once got bitten by a spider monkey whilst I was working in a zoo and spent two days in hospital.

I don't like olives, despise them. Like seriously, why? They are like slimy Play-Doh balls.

I am terrified of dark water.

I've been head butted by a sea lion – also whilst working in a zoo.

Picture taken
The Stoke Pub, Guildford,
September 2016

> **66** *Before we had our child, myself and my wife decided we wanted a natural birth so we didn't post anything on Facebook or Twitter.* **99**

Keith Farnan

Started in Dublin, 2006. I could navigate at sea before I could drive a car. I'm the only person I know who ever loved the coffee flavoured sweets in a Roses box.

I was the kid who told all the other kids there was no Santa Claus.

The first girl I ever asked out ran away screaming.

The last girl I ever asked out ended up marrying me and probably wishes she had run away screaming.

I love games, computer, board, field, you name it, and like to wind other players up. I once invented a transaction in Monopoly where I paid a player not to sell property to another player for at least two goes.

Picture taken Conway Hall, London, July 2016

> *What's a crocodile's favourite card game? None. They haven't got time for such inane activities as they're too busy eating people's heads.*

Harriet Dyer

Comedy was a module at my uni so I acquired interest then but first started actual gigging in 2010 at a gig I put on myself (because I didn't know where to find gigs) in a little pub in Birmingham. A memory that stands out was one day the chef of the pub died halfway through cooking someone's dinner.

My dad left my mum for another man and moved to Greece with him to set up a legal highs shop.

I once missed the train I was waiting for because I got distracted watching an insect.

I went to school with a girl whose brother was her dad.

When I was seventeen I died twice.

Picture taken Screaming Blue Murder, Derogate Theatre, Northampton, September 2016

> **Apparently one in three Europeans are conceived on an IKEA bed, which is mad because those stores are really well lit.**

Mark Smith

My first gig was for the Chortle Student competition at Leeds University in 2008. It went absolutely 'fine'.

I've never been to France.

I have a scar on my eye from when I was a five-year-old Michael Jackson fan and I tried to replicate his spin move only to land on the sharp corner of a coffee table.

I once met Russ Abbott and lost my mind.

Once while sleepwalking I tried to climb off a fourth floor hotel balcony.

Picture taken Outside the Box, The Fighting Cocks, Kingston, September 2016

495

> **I just want a relationship like my parents because they have been together FOREVER... because they're brother and sister.**

Stephen Bailey

I did a comedy writing class in 2010, then I got a social life and then I officially did my first gig in February 2011 when the boy I fancied didn't fancy me back.

I have a black belt in Tae Kwon Do. People find this shocking because I am so glamorous.

I am fluent in French. I lived in France for year and it got me into rugby.

I used to have a head brace and a lisp and I had to sing to get rid of it.

I once had a girlfriend called Joanne because I grew up on a council estate and it was a pre-requisite.

I was never ever picked last in PE for the football team – which I think is a nice surprise to us all. My classmates were forward thinkers.

Picture taken The Stoke Pub, Guildford, September 2016

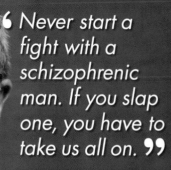

> 66 *Never start a fight with a schizophrenic man. If you slap one, you have to take us all on.* 99

Steve Rawlings

I got into performing when I went to work as a life guard/red coat at Butlins Bognor Regis at the age of twenty. I was a very keen snooker player until I started juggling with a top break of 56. I have no sense of danger when it comes to animal experiences and would happily hug a tiger if someone told me it was safe. I was very into punk as a kid and followed bands such as the Ruts, the Members, the Damned and Stiff Little Fingers. Very keen on gardening but only manage to keep the front garden flowering nicely, and always try and grow some vegetables but they usually die of neglect as I'm always abroad working. Biggest ambition is to watch the sun coming up in Machu Picchu.

Picture taken Ealing Comedy Festival, July 2016

> **I sponsored an African child, I couldn't believe how much it cost me... £100. I mean, how many miles is he going to run?**

Adam Montgomery

I started stand-up in 2000 after a few years of promoting a comedy club. (The first gig I ever promoted starred Ross Noble and Ed Byrne.) It took me a long time to pluck up the courage to get up on stage. Finally after attending an evening class in writing and performing comedy, I gave it a go, and I realised that I was funnier than everyone else in the class and the tutor. I haven't done a gig for three years.

I once worked as a private investigator – don't worry it was before phone hacking.

I once managed a poet for a living. 15 per cent of fuck all is not much!

I once helped to burgle my neighbours' house by accident (it's a long story). Thankfully I was then able to help catch the culprits.

Picture taken The Marr's Bar, Worcester, September 2009
Author's note Out of all the comedians in the book Adam has taken the longest to answer the questions – some three and a half years! 😊

498

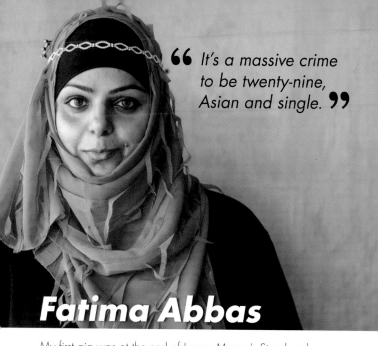

> **It's a massive crime to be twenty-nine, Asian and single.**

Fatima Abbas

My first gig was at the end of Logan Murray's Stand and Deliver course in Clerkenwell, London, Easter weekend 2015.
I like murder mysteries – books and TV.
I nearly died when I was a kid. I had a wobbly tooth and my older brother punched me and knocked my tooth into my throat. As I was choking the ambulance people were on the phone giving my brother advice on how to help.
When I was eight years old and on holiday in Pakistan I gave a pair of someone's shoes to a poor woman in the street.
For my thirtieth birthday I plan to do a sky dive.

Picture taken The Southbank, London, October 2016

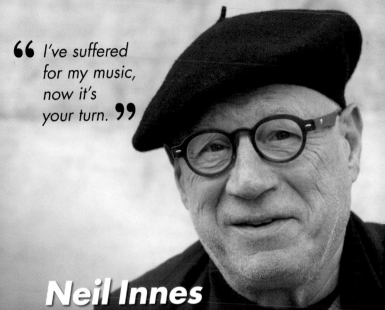

> **I've suffered for my music, now it's your turn.** "

Neil Innes

I started in 1964 – in the Royal College of Art canteen, with the Bonzo Dog Doo Dah Band. Born in 1944 – mother startled into action by exploding V1 'Doodlebug'. Started piano lessons aged seven – in Germany – father was in the Royal Artillery. 1956 – appeared on BBC TV Children's Caravan playing Russ Conway's 'Side Saddle'. Urged by grotesque Floor Manager to smile – could not understand why… Experienced 'success' with the 1968 hit 'I'm The Urban Spaceman' – won an Ivor Novello Award. 2014 – invented the word 'Surrealisation' – which means anything you want it to mean…

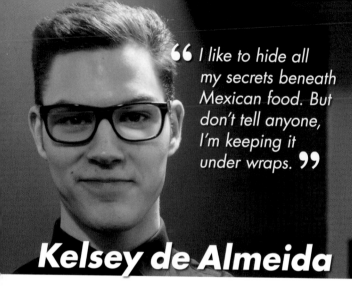

> **" I like to hide all my secrets beneath Mexican food. But don't tell anyone, I'm keeping it under wraps. "**

Kelsey de Almeida

I did my first gig in a function room of a theatre in Croydon in 2014. They were a lovely audience and even forgave me for going up with notes because my memory was so bad... at least that's what I think happened. I can't quite...

As a child I could only sleep if I had three torches in my bed with me. (No idea why.)

At a school disco I won a HUGE jar of jelly beans because I correctly guessed the amount inside. Everyone else was busy kissing girls but I knew what was really important.

I can easily walk past people I know without them noticing if I just take my glasses off. But unfortunately, no, I can't fly.

I won a *Mock the Week* competition for 'Best Joke' that month for a really filthy joke when I was fourteen/fifteen years old.

Picture taken Gag House Comedy, Bagshot, October 2016

> ❝ Facebook have copyrighted the letter 'F', that little 'f' that's their logo so it belongs to Facebook now. And all I say to that is, 'Uck you, Mark Zuckerberg, 'uck you'. ❞

Gerry Carroll

My first gig was with We Are Funny in November 2013. I used to be an internal auditor, a job for people who find accountancy too exciting.
I lived for nearly thirty years in Bournemouth, where people retire to, and then I retired to London.

I followed my two grown-up kids to London, and now they've both moved on, and I'm still here.
I come from Dublin, and I lived in Nigeria for two years many years ago.
I share a house with my landlord, a ninety-year-old Nigerian man.

Picture taken We Are Funny Project, Dalston, London, October 2016

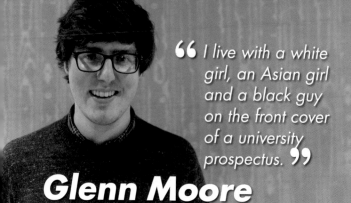

> 66 I live with a white girl, an Asian girl and a black guy on the front cover of a university prospectus. 99

Glenn Moore

My first gig was as a student in 2011. A friend of mine was running a gig and the compere dropped out – there was no one to fill in. So with an hour's notice, I desperately wrote some jokes backstage. I still do some of them in my set, which either says good things about that gig, or some very bad things about my writing not improving in the last few years.

Ronald Regan is my fourth cousin. It's had absolutely no bearing on my political beliefs, which I'm awfully keen to stress.

I was once in a Bollywood movie. It admittedly hadn't been a key ambition of mine to delve into Indian cinema, but I'd be lying if I said my role as News Reporter #4 in *Someday* hasn't paid dividends, career-wise.

My full name is, unfortunately, Glenn Roger Moore.

My dad's full name is, unfortunately, Roger Moore.

I can turn off my taste buds at will. If someone makes me a horrible meal, I can politely eat it and not taste it. Such a useful superpower.

Picture taken Hadlow Manor Hotel, Kent, November 2016

> **The early bird catches the worm, but the second mouse gets the cheese.**

Clive Anderson

I appeared in lots of comedy shows and revues at school and at university, but I suppose my first stand-up gig was at the opening night of the Comedy Store in London in 1979.
Like David Baddiel, I am left-footed and right-handed, but I have had less success than he has in keeping my hair.
I have been arrested twice in Nigeria and once in China.
I have pulled the communication cord on a train.
I am President of the Woodland Trust.

Picture taken The Comedy Store, London, November 2016

> **❝** I can't count past seven in French. I have a huit allergy. **❞**

Aidan Goatley

My first gig was 4th August 2009 in Brighton.
I was born with three thumbs.
Harrison Ford once wished me a happy birthday.
I have ten tattoos.
My wife writes my second best jokes. My daughter writes the best ones.

Picture taken
King's Cross, London,
November 2016

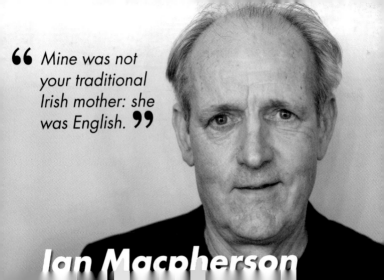

" Mine was not your traditional Irish mother: she was English. **"**

Ian Macpherson

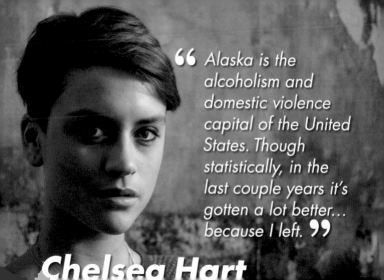

" Alaska is the alcoholism and domestic violence capital of the United States. Though statistically, in the last couple years it's gotten a lot better... because I left. "

Chelsea Hart

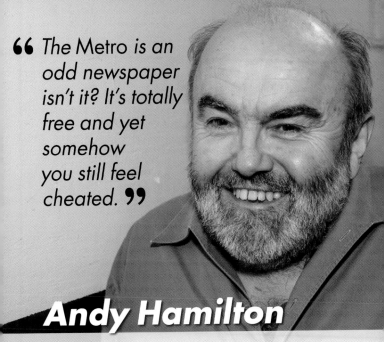

> **"** The Metro is an odd newspaper isn't it? It's totally free and yet somehow you still feel cheated. **"**

Andy Hamilton

I started writing and performing in 1976 at Cambridge. Not the Footlights but CULES (Cambridge University Light Entertainment Society).
I write with my left hand but my brain is right-handed.
I learnt to write with my left hand because I had my right thumb amputated.
I once co-presented *Woman's Hour*.
My mother-in-law is a world-class swimming champion many times over.
I got a dart in my head when I was four.

Picture taken The Union Chapel, Islington, February 2017

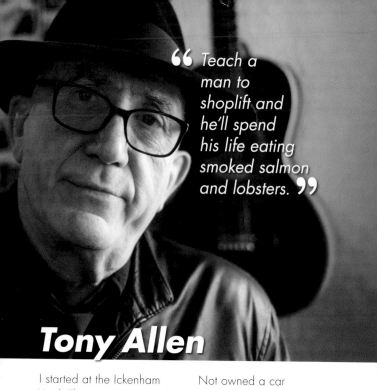

> 66 *Teach a man to shoplift and he'll spend his life eating smoked salmon and lobsters.* 99

Tony Allen

I started at the Ickenham Youth Theatre Variety Night in 1967. I did a tight seven, all nicked from Max Miller and Frankie Howerd.
I got to the last sixteen in the 1961 World Amateur Youth Snooker Championship.

Not owned a car since 1973.
Haven't eaten meat since 1978.
Not smoked tobacco or taken any other drugs since 2002.

Picture taken The Comedy Store, London, November 2016

> **"** As a kid, I was so used to being blamed if things went missing. When boys in my class talked about losing their virginity, I apologised and promised to retrace my steps. **"**

Dan Cardwell

I've been on and off with stand-up since nine years ago, when I did my first gig at Pear Shaped Comedy in Turnmills.
I can sing but only in one key.
I once headbutted an Oscar-winning actress (accidentally!).
I have watched all seven seasons of *The West Wing* fifteen times.
I had a recurring dream when I was young that I would die at fifty-eight. I don't believe in premonitions but it still scares me.

Picture taken Folkestone, December 2016

> **Me:** *Thanks for lending me the disposable BBQ.*
> **Dad:** *It wasn't a disposable one.*
> **Me:** *...Well I suppose all BBQs are disposable in a way, it's family that's important.*

Josh Pugh

I started comedy in 2014 at the Wettmore Whistle Pub in Burton upon Trent.
I once played in an under-fifteens rugby match aged twenty-four.
I once failed to register a score on a punching machine with three consecutive attempts.
I have NEVER had a nickname.
I am suspicious of anyone with a first name as a surname.

Picture taken English Comedian of the Year, The Udderbelly, London, July 2016 (winner)

> **Unlike European mustards that bring out the subtle flavours of food, English mustard makes your nose bleed.** "

Jack Dee

I started at the Comedy Store,
22nd September 1986.
I cook. I quite like doing BBQs.
I go around on a motorbike.
I own dogs.
I recently went on a narrowboat holiday.

Picture taken Outside the Box, The Fighting Cocks, Kingston, September 2016

One way of helping to fund the making of this book

Rebecca Yang

Picture taken Fitzrovia, London, February 2015

513

was to have a selfie with the author Steve Best

Amy Sayer

Picture taken The Southbank, London, February 2015

Acknowledgements

Where the hell do I start?

I remember Bob Mills and a few other comedians on the circuit mentioning to me, as I was roaming the comedy clubs as an act with a little point and shoot (not a euphemism), what a good idea it would be to have a record of the comedy circuit. And so it began. I published my first book, *Comedy Snapshot* a very similar book, with 527 comedians, 528 counting me, on 1st April 2014. An apt date. This was done with the immense help from one damn fine comedian/graphic designer, Drew Barr/Drew de Soto (one and the same). He was the true catalyst. If it hadn't been for Drew Barr/Drew de Soto then none of this would have ever come to fruition and you would not be looking at this page and thinking, 'What a fantastic book this is.' Much of Drew's great design of the first book has been emulated for this second book, **Joker Face**. And here enters Catherine French, delightful, dazzling designer of this book. She has set down these pictures and words you are indulging in with her own stylistic panache. Look at how well she crafts and kerns.

While finishing my first book I had aspirations for the second book but wanted to up my game on the photography front. I would enter Parks Cameras and browse the vast array of photo apparatus. I kept coming back to the Fujifilm range and eventually bought a Fujifilm X-Pro1 body and a 18mm and 35mm lens. Wow! I was now a comedian and a photographer.

and thanks

A meet with Johnny Murph (page 103) some months later, who worked at a very prestigious camera shop by day, upped my game further. He understood straight away where I was coming from, what I wanted to do, and where I was going. He put me in touch with the bearded, trendy hat-wearing, vintage-car enthusiast, Fujifilm worker/expert Nathan Wake. This man understood me too. Through our numerous coffee drinking, occasional hat browsing sessions, and one delicious Indian cuisine looooong lunch at the fabulous Dishoom (you've got to go, but prepare to queue… the cat is out the bag) with Andreas Georghiades, the shaker and mover at Fujifilm, we organised a gentlemen's long-term lending agreement of Fujifilm kit. I am so grateful. Their cameras and lenses are truly sublime.

Along this comedic photographic journey there has been many a person I want to thank. My next door neighbour of some years back, Javier Garcia, a tip top professional sports photographer. He looked at the first few of my images, slapped me across the chops, brushed up my skills, and sent me on my way.

A huge thank you goes out to Andy Coles and David Bostock, both publishing gurus of the highest order, both amazingly altruistic by nature. They have been invaluable and unbelievably helpful and genially generous of their time in guiding me through the pitfalls and pratfalls of the publishing industry. I thank Sue Odell for introducing these men to me, and for introducing another man, her son, Billy Boyd Cape, who filmed my promo video. He's a director, editor, film maker extraordinaire. Watch out for this whipper snapper. I thank Scott Pack from Unbound, my publisher and knower of all things books. Well, firstly, John Lenehan (comedian/magician/all round good bloke) for introducing me to Scott Pack at a rather feisty gig in Windsor (who'd have thought?). Scott and Unbound have been wonderful in making it possible to get this book published without bank loans, remortgages and the selling of at least one kidney.

Which brings me on to Carl Day (page 370), comedian and comedy club organiser of Big Cheese Comedy by night, comedy fan and logistics operator by day. I did a gig for him a year or so back and I mentioned the idea of this book, and the need for some sizeable dosh to get the project off the ground. He asked me how much? I mentioned a sum. He didn't bat an eyelid and said he could help. No one else has been as financially generous. Here's to the next twenty books ☺!

Which brings me on to all the pledgers, givers, and pre-orderers who went to the Unbound funding page... With your generosity we reached the 100 per cent mark pretty damn quick. Thank you, your names are duly noted in the back of this book.

I thank my fabulous frenetic family for putting up with me; Aleksandra, Anastasia, and Luka.

The comedy circuit is a rather closed establishment. I would like to think that my many years, and dare I say, standing on the circuit, gave me access to a place and people that very few non-comedians are allowed to go. I thank the comedians for being up for the project, and for answering the questions, some on the night, and others taking bloody ages, email after email, Facebook nudge after tweet, text, carrier pigeon... we got there in the end (mostly!).

I thank all you other people for forgiving me for forgetting to thank you in this edition. Remind me, and hopefully when it comes to the reprint I will duly amend. Samantha Terry, remembered just in time!

And lastly I thank you, dear punter, dear reader, dear art lover for getting this book. I really hope you enjoy the gems within these pages.

Steve Best July 2017

www.stevebest.com

🐦 @SteveBestComic

📷 @stevebestpics

Huge thanks to

Unbound is a new kind of publishing house. Our books are funded directly by readers. This was a very popular idea during the late eighteenth and early nineteenth centuries. Now we have revived it for the internet age. It allows authors to write the books they really want to write and readers to support the books they would most like to see published. The names listed below are of readers who have pledged their support and made this book happen. If you'd like to join them, visit **www.unbound.com**.

Fatima Abbas
Rachel Abel
Sue Adamson
Geoff Alderman
Steve Alexander
Karen Allan-Jones
Karen and Stuart Allen
Kay Allen-Palmer
Richard Allum
Gavin Arnold
Richard Bald
Currer Ball
Graham Ball
Wayne Bamforth
Michael Banahan
Paco Banos
Daphna Baram
Barnstormers Comedy
Sam Beale
Sarah Beamish
Alasdair Beckett-King
Pete Beckley
Sanjay Bhandari
Mark Billingham
Andrew Bird
Don Biswas
Ashley Boroda
Ruth Bourne
Rex Boyd
Rory Bremner
Eddy Brimson
Noel Britten
Christopher Brochon
Toby Brown
Adele Browne

Rousha Browning
Penny Bryant
Mike Butcher
Andy Caldwell
Sarah Campbell
Joy Carter
Nathan Cassidy
Lynn Chambers
David Chapple
Jarred Christmas
Predrag Ciric
Damian Clark
Helen Clark
Laurence Clark
Andrew Clover
Fiona Collier
Adam Connell
Les Connelly
Jools Constant
Clive Copeman
Christelle Couchoux
Mark Cram
John Crawford
Matt Crockett
Dorian Crook
Matthew Crosby
Dawn Cruttenden
Jake Cuddihy
Luca Cupani
Tom Curran
Darius Davies
Sian Robinson Davies
Carl Day
Spring Day
Kelsey de Almeida

Drew de Soto
Wayne Deakin
Stephen Delaney
John Dexter
Stephen DiPlacito
Barry Dodds
Justin Doran
Oliver Double
Tiernan Douieb
Keith Dover
Dawn Downes
Jonny Drewek
Sarah Eckert
Nick Edwards
George Egg
Nick Elleray
Martin & Pam Erving
Simon Evans
Olaf Falafel
Theresa Farlow
Noel Faulkner
Mark Fenlon
Richard Fitch
Richard Fletcher
John Flockton
Louis French
Phil Friend
Dominic Frisby
Max Fulham
Katy Funnell
Paul Gallagher
Mark Gamble
Chris Gilbert
Jennifer & Rosie Goatley
Graham Goddard

Richard Gomm
David Goodge
Lucien Green
Nino Grillo
Viv Groskop
Mike Gunn
James Hall
Pete Harris
Philip Harris
David Harry
Cheryl Hayes
Spencer Hayes
Ana Paula Hey
David Hicks
Sarah Higgins
Craig Hill
Paul Hill
Peter Buckley Hill
Pierre Hollins
Sally Holloway
Hot Water
   Comedy Club
Col Howarth
Jim Howarth
Peter Howarth-Lees
Robyn Howell
Alan Hudson
Derry Hunter
Roland Ibbett
Elizabeth Jaedicke
Mark James
Sion James
Steve Jameson
Javier Jarquin
Laura Jellicoe

Jonathan Jester
Alfie Joey
Amy Jones
Milton Jones
Simon Jones
Spencer Jones
Trevor Jones –
   House of Stand Up
Nobby Kash
Warren Kaye
Nik Kealy
Noah Kelly
Sarah Kelly
Declan Kennedy
John Dempsey
Sajeela Kershi
Dan Kieran
Rick Kiesewetter
Anthony King
Nathan King
Kelly Kingham
Simon Kitt
Athena Kugblenu
Gerry Kyei
Josephine Lacey
Stephanie Laing
Paul Lamb
Lloyd Langford
Tori Johanne Lau
Kate Lawrence
Marie Lawrence
Haiminh Le
Tracy Lee
Wendy Lee
Joff Lelliott
Jamie Lemon
Paddy Lennox
George Lewis
Matthew Lewis
Judith Liddell-King
Tamasin Little
Rene Llowarch
Jenny Lockyer
Sharon Lockyer
Lateef Lovejoy
James Loveridge
Sonya Lukić

Dagfinn Lyngbø
Colin MacKenzie
Mariola Magovcevic
Mark Maier
John Mann
Dea & Gian Marco
Dawn Marshall-Fannon
Darrell Martin
Alex Martini
Darren Maskell
Elliot Mason
Neil Masters
Kate Mawby
Simon Mayhew
Tom Mayhew
Peter Maynard
Martha McBrier
Mick Mcgrane
Nathaniel Metcalfe
Peter Milburn
Chris Miller
Simon Minty
John Mitchinson
Killian Monson
Ian Moore
Jane Morris
Richard Morton
Hannah Moulder
Jeanette Muff
Tom Mullen
Deborah Munday
Duncan Munday
Johnny Murph
Logan Murray
Alexandra &
   Daniel Myers
Carlo Navato
Max Newton
Øystein Nilsen
Josiah Norris
Jeremy O'Donnell
Scott Pack
Sanja Paic
John Pendal
Andrew Pepper
Ian Phipps
Justin Pollard

Ricky Powell
Lawrence Pretty
David Prew
Chris Purchase
Visnja Randall
Lisa Redpath
Jonny Rex
Elizabeth Ann Rice
Gareth Richards
Laura Richards
Rachel Riley
Andrew Risner
John Robertson
Paul Rogan
Paul Rogers
Wee Roo
James Ross
Joe Rowntree
Kris Rutherford
Karen Saich
Vicki Salmi
Paul Savage
Ian Saville
Amy Sayer
Neil Sayer
Christian Schulte-Loh
Reuben Scott
Matt Shaw
Mike Sheldon
Derek Shephard
Ariane Sherine
Lenny Sherman
Julian Viti Siebert
Mark Silcox
Jason Simmons
Lee Simpson
Ricky Skinner
Keith Sleight
Andy Smart
Mathew Smith
Will Smith
Nat Snell
Claire Snodgrass
   & Ross McTavish
Penelope Solomon
Arielle Soumahoro
Andy Stedman

Jean Stevenson
Adnan Sulejmanpasic
Kit Sullivan
Atelier Tammam
Sarah Tennant
Alastair Thomas
Huw Thomas
Nelly Thomas
Rob Thomas
Paul Thorne
Mark Tidmarsh
Justyn Trenner
Karen Trethewey
Stu Turner
Kate van Beek
Sindhu Vee
Brett Vincent
Richard Vranch
Steve Walker
Adam Walsh
Phil Wang
David Alfie Ward
Felicity Ward
Keith Ward
Henning Wehn
Don Weir
Mal Wharton
Matt Whitby
Katie Whitehouse
Marc Whiteley
Suzy Wilde
Nicky Wilkinson
Gerry Williams
Zoë-Elise Williamson
Gareth Wilson
Chris Winsor
Tim "woody" Woodfield
Debbie Wythe
Rebecca Yang
Andy Zapp
Mina Zardkoohi
Sameena Zehra

*Their kind
donations
made this
book possible.*

520

Index